ACKNOWLEDGEMENTS

To the following with heartfelt gratitude, and without whom I would not have completed this book:

To Margi Lewis for her hours of patient editing and encouragement
To Bill Visick, whose positive words gave me the courage to continue
To Annette Lockamyeir (Counselor) for suggesting I write Jim's story
To Marie (Savard) Kraft, Sonny and Mary (LaPlante) Savard,
Dick and Don Savard for background material
To Rick Watkins, Jr. for his cover design
To Jim's friends: Ron Miller, Dick Honeck, Jim Bolthouse,
Sal Sciremammano, Bill Fitzgerald, Jim Weinkauf,
Luke LaClair, Ray Bardol, Phil Johnson, and the Gourmet Club for their constancy of friendship

Copyright 2013 © by Sue Savard
First Print Edition, March 2013
ISBN: 13-978-1482725469
ISBN: 10:1482725460

Edited by Margi Lewis
Book Cover Design by Rick Watkins, Jr.

No part of this publication may be reproduced or distributed in print or electronic form without prior permsision of the author. Please respect the hard work of the author and do not participate in or encourage the piracy of copyrighted materials.

TABLE OF CONTENTS

ACKNOWLEDGEMENTS	ii
THROUGH THE LOOKING GLASS OF TIME	1
CHAPTER 1 - THE UPHOLSTERY SHOP	2
CHAPTER 2 - CHILD NUMBER FOUR	5
CHAPTER 3 - THE WOODSMEN'S FIELD DAY	13
CHAPTER 4 - WE'RE ALMOST COUSINS	18
CHAPTER 5 - SEMPER FI AND COLLEGE LIFE	29
CHAPTER 6 - MOVIN ON	59
CHAPTER 7 - LIVING ON LOVE	71
CHAPTER 8 - THE GREEN BEANIE	85
CHAPTER 9 - BIRDS ON A WIRE	99
CHAPTER 10 - SALVAGED SNIPPETS	126
CHAPTER 11 - FAMILY ALBUM	156
CHAPTER 12 - SHATTERED DREAMS	168
CHAPTER 13 - I WAS LOST AND NOW I'M FOUND	188
CHAPTER 14 - HE CHOSE LIFE	191
CHAPTER 15 - CAT WITH TEN LIVES	204
CHAPTER 16 - CONFLICT AND TURMOIL	223
CHAPTER 17 - THE TIME IS RIGHT	226
CHAPTER 18 - THE BIRTHDAY GIFT	231
CHAPTER 19 - ALONE	235
CHAPTER 20 - LEGACY	237
CHAPTER 21 - HEALING	248
CHAPTER 22 - THE INTERVIEWS	258
CHAPTER 23 - PARENT'S BACKGROUND	275

April, 2010

My darling Jim,

This is my final letter to you. I have loved you for so long, I can barely remember my life before we met. I've been rereading the letters we sent one another while we were dating. They bring me closer to you and remind me once again of the young, insecure boy I fell in love with so many years ago. When did you change so much?

The more I read our letters, the more determined I am to write your story. I believe if I could just get it down in black and white, you would still be with me. Maybe you would want me to lock your narrative away, but I consider it worth telling.

We both know so little of our ancestors. When we lost our parents and grandparents, we lost part of ourselves. They didn't write journals or letters and left few photographs. I can't interview them to get a deeper understanding of who they were and how they lived.

I don't want that to happen to you. I want to be a witness to your life so you continue to live in the hearts of our children and grandchildren. With this memoir, our descendents will have a sense of their history and know who came before them. From depths I never knew I possessed, I feel an overwhelming urge bubbling up inside me to tell everyone about you.

The story I am leaving is a gift to our family and to myself. I want them to have a window into our lives before and after we married. In telling your tale, I cannot ignore your parents, your home, and your siblings.

Sometimes as I write, I feel your presence—as if you are watching over me. If so, I hope I weave the tale to your approval.

Always,

Sue

CHAPTER 1 - THE UPHOLSTERY SHOP

When I picture Jim's family life, I think of a play, and I can visualize the scenes. The curtain rises on a scene set in an upholstery shop—the setting for most of the family dynamics. The time period is the Great Depression, the lights are dim, and the air thick with tension. Scattered around the room are a sewing machine, half-finished furniture, a few chairs, bolts of fabric, and a cutting table. Leon, short and powerfully built, commands the stage and plays the benevolent father, but as the play unfolds he reveals his sinister nature. Jim's mother, Gladys, feels trapped in her marriage and weeps helplessly on the sidelines. Other cast members are reluctant participants. They have no choice. All eight children play themselves—afraid, hungry, insecure, wanting, but resilient.

Gladys moves about the room like a rough current. She stomps to the sewing machine and begins to sew cushions, Sonny and Dick are covering a chair, Marie is sweeping the floor, Jim is climbing into the room through a back window, Evelyn is whispering on the phone, Ed and Don are huddling under the cutting table and munching a stale piece of bread stolen from the kitchen, Roy is nursing his bruises from Leon's beating.

In the play, Marie tells her siblings their father has a girlfriend. She whispers that she followed her father and his date the previous night. "His girlfriend placed a pink bow in my hair and warned me not to tell our mother."

By the end of the act one, Leon begins to show his true colors. He drinks heavily and rarely works. When he does work, he blows his money on booze and women, leaving his wife and eight children to starve and survive on welfare. Gladys doesn't react to his philandering ways. Like the children, she's afraid. He doesn't hesitate to beat her when his black moods occur. In one scene, Gladys musters up enough courage to place laxatives in his coffee just before he leaves on a date. He cancels his date.

The audience finds sympathy for Gladys and disgust at other times. She has no escape from her domineering husband; she's consumed with her aches and pains; she cares little what she says to others. Her life appears to be one of self-preservation. She's large boned, heavy, and crude like her parents, but she demonstrates a kinder side when she shows her children the only love they receive.

Why an upholsterer? After Leon's leg is injured while working on a road crew for the town, gangrene sets in. Part of his leg is amputated. The municipality sends him for training so he can support his family and get off welfare. Once trained as an upholsterer, he opens his business in a garage. He's a good craftsman, and his trade grows. In order to get money for a bigger place, he allegedly lights the garage on fire, falsifies the insurance papers, collects the money, and builds a new shop. Marie suspects the truth and fears her father will be sent to jail.

Until very late in the play, onlookers are unaware of what's happening behind the scenes. Relatives, neighbors, teachers, and friends turn a blind eye to the children's fear. Leon uses his charm on outsiders and customers, especially those important in the community. He's a chameleon. He screams at Sonny and Dick for making a mistake on a chair and swats Jim for reading a book. The phone rings. He answers in a velvet voice.

"We'd love to give you an estimate, Dr. Bury."

The children exchange disgusted looks.

Towards the end of act one, the sound of crying can be heard. It's evening and Roy and young Don enter from stage right. Tension increases. The front and legs of Don's pants are wet. He's sniffling. Leon glares.

"You've wet your pants. Why are you crying?"

"Rah-rah-Roy made me walk ahead of everyone along the tracks. It was so dark in the woods, I couldn't see, and I bumped into a cow. I got scared. I thought it was a bear."

"You little fool. I'll teach you not to be afraid."

Leon, furious, grabs Don, lays him prone on the cutting table, and tacks his clothes to it.

"You'll be in more trouble in the morning if you rip your clothes trying to get away."

Leon leaves Don in the dark room all night. The curtain closes on the wet, shivering, and frightened boy.

Why am I writing this way? Similar to the audience, I am wondering. How did the absence of a nurturing environment affect Jim's life? What scars did he carry with him, and what did it take to change the way he felt about himself?

****

Reflection: Jim's parents wrote, directed and produced this narrative. Like a Broadway show, it runs for years in the minds of the young cast members. They spend their lifetimes trying to forget.

Dedication: The scenes are based on a true story, and every story has a hero. In this real life drama, I nominate Sonny and Mary for sacrificing their own dreams in order to support Gladys, Leon and Ed (for which they never receive a Tony award); Marie for guiding her siblings on the right path of life.

PART I

CHAPTER 2 - CHILD NUMBER FOUR

Reflection: Understanding Jim's early life was like untangling the plot of a mystery. I wanted to find out what he was like as a young child to help me understand how he morphed into the man he became. His lifelong habit of hiding his feelings about his upbringing meant that I needed to do some research. Learning about Jim's home life and portraying him accurately filled my days. The fact of his birth on September 29, 1934, as the fourth of nine children was a given. From there on, I was like a detective interviewing his siblings, relatives, and friends and fitting the clues together. I followed the threads wherever they led. Just when I thought I knew all about Jim, I discovered a new layer of information.

******

The smell of bread toasting on top of the black wood stove made two-year old Jim's empty stomach gurgle. His two older brothers and his sister gulped down their meager breakfast before hurrying out of the door to avoid their father. Jim rocked back and forth, sucking his thumb for comfort and rubbing his left ear so much it became deformed. His cherub-like appearance with blond curly hair, rosy cheeks, and sleepy blue eyes belied the tension he sensed from the chaos around him and the strident tone of his parents' voices. The rag used for his diaper was wet, and he whimpered for his mother to nurse and change him. Frustrated by her husband's womanizing, Gladys had little patience to give Jim the attention he craved.

"Stop your crying. I'll get to you as soon as I can," she scolded.

He jammed his thumb back into his mouth and waited. The kitchen reeked from the dirty laundry piled on the floor. He watched his mother struggle to roll the wringer washer from the closet into the room and hook the rubber hose over the edge of the sink. She filled the washer with buckets of cold water from the tap and began to stuff whites and colored things in together. After adding a small cup of laundry detergent, Gladys turned on the washer. She scooped Jim into her arms, removed his wet diaper, threw it onto the pile of dirty clothes, and cradled him as he nursed. Once fed and changed, Jim drifted to sleep listening to her heavy breathing, the beat of her heart, and the purr of the washer. The current practice of using nursing to prevent pregnancy failed her. One and a half years later, Evelyn was born, and Jim looked to his older siblings for attention.

By age four, he followed Marie, Sonny, and Dick everywhere and wanted to do what they were doing, as long as he was away from his parents' bickering.

"I wanna go to school," he repeatedly cried to his mother.

"Shoo, shoo, don't bother me. I don't have time to listen to your whining. Jesus, Mary, and Joseph go to school with your brothers and sister if you like."

"I wanna go with you," he shrieked in September to his siblings. Taking long steps with his spindly legs, Jim trailed behind on the short walk to the nearby school.

"You're too young. Go home," they coaxed in unison.

He continued to follow. Jim was ashamed of his school clothing. He and his brothers wore hand-me-downs from neighbors and relatives who donated adult-sized pants and shirts to Gladys for her boys. They never knew the pleasure of new clothing—only used.

"Stand still," their mother admonished while rolling the pant legs up to mid-calf and pulling in the waist with a rope. When Jim discovered a real belt in a drawer, he punched extra holes in the belt to fit his narrow waist and then began to cut off the dangling end. His father grabbed his arm and barked, "Don't cut that belt. Someday, you'll grow into it."

The children often went barefoot or slipped their sockless feet into black rubber boots held closed by cross clips. Sometimes welfare provided new shoes with metal cleats on the toes and heels to prevent them from wearing. As Jim walked up the steel steps of school, the cleats made a click, click, clicking sound. He heard the snickers of wealthier children and saw them pointing at him, branding him a welfare brat from the wrong side of the tracks.

Yet, each day he followed his siblings to the two-story, wood framed elementary school and managed to find his way to a first grade classroom. Rules were lax in the 1930s. Nothing stated a child had to be five by a certain date to attend school. Kindergarten or preschools weren't available, and school personnel didn't question Jim's age or send him home—just let him stay.

Climbing into a wooden seat, his feet dangling above the floor, elbows on the desk, Jim sat quietly through the entire school year, ears alert as the teacher read stories in a soothing, song-bird voice. He watched her pick up white chalk from the dusty tray and make strange marks on the blackboard. Too young for school, he repeated first, then second grade. After four years, Jim's age and placement finally synchronized.

The family lived in rented apartments in The Junction, and when Jim was six, they rented a house on Webb Row. Carelessly, the previous tenants had turned off the heat but left the water running. Six or seven inches of ice covered the kitchen floor and had collected on the cellar stairs. Their father turned on the heat before moving, and he and his boys chipped the ice away with a hammer.

Their unpainted two-story house had a kitchen, dining room, and living room on the first floor. On the second floor, radiating off an octagon-shaped hallway, were three bedrooms and a bathroom with a pull-chain flush toilet and a bathtub. Behind the tub, holes in the walls were stuffed with paper bags and newspapers to keep out the cold and make warm nests for the ever-present mice. By the time the last two children were born, eleven people were crowded into the house.

Cleanliness was a constant issue for the Savard family. During cold weather, when they took baths, the children soaked in a large galvanized container in the kitchen, the only warm room in the house. They pushed the old tub close to the sink and filled it with water heated on the wood stove, then took turns from the cleanest to the dirtiest in the same water. With only one thin worn towel to share, the last bather drip-dried.

Rooms were filled with an assortment of mismatched, well-worn furniture given to the family by relatives or friends. Wide cracks in the uninsulated siding and in the windows allowed snow and wind to blow into the house. For blankets, Gladys sewed large squares of upholstery fabric into heavy, warm quilts. But, by morning, a dusting of snow covered the top of the quilts. Jim, Sonny, and Dick slept together in a double bed with Jim in the center. As Dick and Sonny rolled to the outside of the bed, the blanket became taut above Jim, allowing cold air to flow down on him. He snuggled closer to his brothers to borrow body heat and tucked the heavy quilt under his chin.

The warmest place to dress for school was near the kitchen stove. The children gathered around it until they heard their father coming down the hall, then grabbed their clothing and dressed outside in the cold rather than face him. Jim dawdled, not wanting to brave the bone-chilling elements but finally had to leave the house. On their way to school, Marie stepped through the deep snow with her feet clad in thin socks and shoes. Her toes were nearly frostbitten from the cold. A red bruise on her cheek from her father's slap glistened in the morning brightness.

"Yesterday a woman came to the shop and asked why I didn't have overshoes," she told her brothers. "I didn't know who she was or where she came from, but I begged her not to talk to Dad. He'd be so angry with me."

Condensation sprayed from their mouths as they talked. "I'm freezin," Jim said. "I don't got any hat or mittens."

"Here, walk ahead of me," Marie said and cupped her hands over Jim's ears. "Put your hands in your pockets, and we'll hurry."

Cold-to-the-bone temperatures in the Adirondacks sometimes reached forty below. It was almost impossible to keep their home warm. Leon was unemployed and proud—too proud to have neighbors know he couldn't afford to heat his drafty house. When the winter darkness fell over the town, he forced the oldest four children to steal coal from the trains parked at the nearby station. Stealing went against their sense of right and wrong. Each week they recited the commandment "Thou Shalt Not Steal" in catechism class. They didn't know which was worse, offending God or defying their father. But, they needed the warmth and reluctantly headed to the train station pulling a sled with a box strapped on top.

"Look along the tracks and pick up as much as you can," thirteen year-old Sonny said. "I'll get on top of the coal car and throw some down to you."

The children worked quickly, their stomachs tight with tension, listening for the railroad detective's pounding steps and watching for his swinging lantern.

They heard Sonny whisper. "He's coming. Get into that open boxcar and squat down until he passes."

After the detective had walked by, the children filled their box with coal and turned towards home. Their small bodies strained against the cold wind as they pulled and tugged the rusted sled, their efforts made more difficult by the sand spread on top of the snow-covered roads. When they got home, their father demanded, "That's not enough to last the night. Go get another load." They were too exhausted and frozen to go into the night again, but they knew better than to refuse. His strap was always near at hand.

Warm housing wasn't the Savards' only problem. After the town had closed the public dump, sewer rats moved into the neighborhood. Jim entered the house late one night, turned on the light, and rodents scurried in every direction. He saw a rat in the crib biting his baby brother on the foot. Jim yelled and clapped his hands, and the rodent scuttled away, but not before Jim shuddered at the thought of being bitten.

As a solution, their father suggested, "I'll give you a penny for each one you catch," and handed out traps with the children's names scratched on the bottom. The boys scrambled to be first to ambush the scoundrels in the potato bin, certain they'd catch the most and earn the pennies.

Marie's job was to keep track of her younger siblings while her mother sewed in the shop. Jim was eight and playing in a puddle in front of his house when a stray dog approached. Unsuspecting and anxious for a pet, Jim reached out to stroke the animal's back. The mongrel growled, bent forward on his forelegs, and lifted his hindquarters. The stray bared its teeth and lunged, burying them in Jim's left arm. It shook its head side-to-side, further tearing flesh. Jim cried for help, but no one came. Finally, with one swift kick into the dog's ribs, he freed himself. He ran screaming to his mother. She hurried from her sewing machine, grabbed a few cinders from the road, and pitched them at the mongrel. "Get out of here you devil," she screamed.

Unable to afford a doctor, Gladys poured iodine on his arm and ripped an old pillowcase into strips to cover his injury. The wound left two puncture scars on his left arm.

Undercurrents of anxiety were always present. The children spent their days waiting for the next argument, the next beating. One day, Leon sat drinking his morning coffee when Gladys heard a knock at the door.

"The owner's son is here to collect his rent," she called.

Leon reached into an old coffee tin on the shelf and pulled out the rent money. His wooden leg aggravated him as he limped through the front room, opened the squeaky screen door, and stepped onto the porch. Gladys strained to hear but couldn't catch their conversation. Unexpectedly, Leon went down the steps, got into the man's car, and they sped away. Then, Gladys knew. He and the owner's son would drink the rent money away. She wouldn't see her husband until later that day.

When Leon staggered in singing a jingle, a knockdown fight ensued. "You're no good," she yelled. "You're chasing other women and drinking instead of supporting your children."

"Shut up," he warned, pounding his fist on the table, but she continued.

"Shut up, I said."

Exasperated, Leon began to beat Gladys, knocking her backwards against the stairs. Still, she wouldn't stop. All but Marie ran out of the house and hid behind the garage, covering their ears to drown out the thunderous ruckus.

"Dad. Dad. STOP IT," Marie begged and pulled at his sleeve. "You're going to kill her."

He turned and looked at Marie with a strange expression, as if he had just come back from a dream, and abruptly left the room.

The next morning was Sunday—a day reserved for church. Their mother insisted they attend mass. The Catholic religion's teachings had been instilled in Gladys by her mother who had been brought up in a convent.

"Why do we have to go to church and Dad doesn't?" the boys asked.

"Never mind about your father. You have to go, and that's that. Go get cleaned up for church."

Once ready, Marie held protectively onto Jim's hand, and they hurried out the door. Sonny and Dick skipped along the few blocks to church. In Marie's haste to get cleaned up and dressed, she hadn't checked Jim's appearance. An oval of scrubbed skin in the center of his face was the only clean spot. The remainder of his body was gray with grime. It was too late to do anything about his condition, so she prayed no one in the church would notice.

Many years later, Marie told Jim the story of their father's refusal to attend church. "During the depression, the priest was always exhorting parishioners to bring food for the rectory and convent, as well as give a weekly offering on Sunday. When Dad went to do some work in the rectory basement, he saw shelves laden with cans of vegetables, fruits, coffee, pasta, and every food stuff imaginable. He became angry because he and other members of the church had been depriving their own families in order to donate to the priest and nuns. After that, he wouldn't attend services. Making us attend mass was just one more way for Dad to keep up appearances. He thought neighbors would be impressed to see his wife and children going to church and not notice his absence. He had standards for us but not himself."

If Jim and his brothers weren't in church or school, they were left to their own devices for entertainment. They didn't have televisions, video games, computers, bikes, or toys. But, when it came to having fun, they were inventive. The empty garage behind their house was an irresistible lure. The rafters became their jungle gym and trapeze. Sonny and Dick would climb on a wooden box, reach as far as they could to grab an overhead beam and then swing their bodies until they gained enough force to fly to the next one. Jim was jealous and determined to copy his brothers.

"I can do that. Help me up," he begged.

"No. Go in the house. You're too little. You're gonna get hurt."

"Am not. I can do it," he argued, determined to convince his brothers.

Dick and Sonny at last lifted him by his skinny legs until his small hands gripped tightly to the first beam.

"Now, swing your legs out as hard as you can, Jim."

He smiled at his brothers and kicked the way he did on the swings at school. Back and forth, back and forth he went, feeling like a trapeze artist ready to soar to the next rafter. He flew with his arms stretched straight above his head but missed and crashed into the wall with a thud.

A large protruding nail punctured Jim's arm and tore a long gash as he slid down the wall and fell in a heap to the ground.

"Now what?" Sonny asked. "Dad's gonna to kill us for sure."

Blood ran down Jim's arm onto his legs, his pants, and into the dirt. It wouldn't stop. They hurried into the house. Their mother wrapped his arm in rags and rushed Jim to Dr. Bury. A few weeks went by, and the injury was almost healed when Jim decided to show off to a friend.

"I know how to run the wringer washer." He grabbed a wet shirt from the tub, turned on the washer, and began to feed the shirt through the rolling bars. The rollers caught onto a piece of hanging skin from the previous accident and peeled it back like a banana all the way to his elbow. Back to the doctor he was rushed.

"That's a bad tear," Dr. Bury said, shaking his head. "I'll close it with catgut. It'll leave a nasty scar, but it's the best I can do."

Forever after, Jim was leery of strange dogs, wringer washers, and trapezes.

By 1944, Jim's family was still struggling financially. Once Leon completed an apprenticeship, and before beginning work, he wanted a vacation to visit relatives, fish, ride horses, and relax. He called the children together.

"Your mother and I are taking Donny and going away for awhile. You kids listen to your sister. She's in charge now," Leon warned.

When told she'd be responsible for six siblings, Marie's nerves tightened as though someone had screeched chalk across a blackboard. *I'm only seventeen for God's sake. What are they thinking, leaving for Canada for a month? I'm without money. All I have is a small chunk of ice in the icebox and no food except what the Welfare Department gives us. How will I ever take care of them?*

On the day of departure, Marie and her charges lined up on the platform at the train station and watched their parents and baby brother climb the stairs to the coach. Tears trickled down Jim's cheeks when the train slowly chugged away.

Two weeks passed, and a wooden box arrived in the mail. Excitement was high as all seven gathered around.

"I wonder what's in it. Hurry up, hurry up, Marie, and open it."

The package held three large salmon wrapped in canvas and dry ice. Her only place to store the fish was in the oak icebox. Its lower section had a zinc-lined interior and shelves; the upper section contained a tray intended to hold a block of ice. When Leon had money, he'd place a cardboard sign in the front window. Written on one side - 25 and, on the other - 50, indicating how many pounds of ice the deliveryman should leave. But, Marie was left without money so their icebox was warm.

With no way to preserve the fish, Marie cooked it. Every day they ate it and ate it.

"I'm sick of salmon," Jim groaned. "I hate fish."

"It's better than going hungry," Sonny reminded him.

A few neighbors offered to buy some of the fish, but Marie was afraid of her father's wrath if he found out.

While their parents were away, Marie and the boys cleaned the entire house, organized all the dresser drawers and kitchen cupboards, and rearranged the furniture. They wallpapered one room using supplies donated by their grandmother, and painted another. For the first time in their young lives, they weren't ashamed of their home. It was organized and clean. During the day, they went swimming at Coney Beach and participated in games with neighborhood friends. In the evenings, they played cards.

For Jim, cleaning his room nearly meant disaster. He had a habit of running upstairs, grabbing the doorjamb, swinging back and forth for momentum, and leaping onto his bed. In her frenzy to organize the house, Marie had switched his bed and dresser around. Jim was midair before he realized his mistake and crashed into the dresser. He landed on the floor in a heap and laughed at his own stupidity.

For that month, the Savard children didn't have to be afraid or pretend. With their time of fun and freedom, they could be kids and laugh until their sides hurt. When their parents returned, life resumed its normal pattern of dread and the children's *us against them* philosophy. Their upbringing left all of them with scars, but they proved to be resilient, coping in their own ways, determined not to repeat their parents' mistakes.

CHAPTER 3 - THE WOODSMEN'S FIELD DAY

Reflection: In the close-knit Adirondack community of Tupper Lake, neighbors sat on front porches and chatted while children played kick the can or hide and seek. Jim's family lived in a rented house in a poor section of town nicknamed The Junction where the Hurd and Webb railroad spurs connected. The advent of train service to the village generated a surge of construction of outbuildings to handle the fast-growing lumbering industry. The Junction's streets bubbled with commerce from the frequent arrival of freight and passenger trains. Summer tourists flocked to the area to escape the heat of the cities and to spend their vacations enjoying the lakes, rivers, and wildlife.

******

From their bedroom window, the three oldest Savard boys heard the clickety clack of the train's wheels and the *all aboard* of the conductor.

The brothers awakened early to the sound of dishes rattling and the rich aroma of freshly brewed coffee. It was their third Saturday of summer vacation in 1949. Today the village would be alive with commotion—the Woodsmen's Field Day was coming to town. Tossing down a scant breakfast of sliced potatoes cooked on top of an old wood stove, they slurped a cup of strong coffee and dressed hurriedly in cut-off pants and ripped shirts. They hoped to leave the house before their father woke up and turned his anger on everyone in his path.

Slipping slices of stale bread in their pockets, the boys scampered out of the house being careful to close the door quietly. After breakfast, their father would work a few hours at his gas station, close early, and then join his drinking companions. Their neighbor, a train engineer spotted the brothers as they headed down the street. He tossed them an orange from his lunchbox and chuckled at their excited response.

"Wow, can we really have this?" Dick asked and began to peel the orange with his fingers.

"Sure. What're ya boys doin'?"

"We're gonna see the parade this afternoon," they all responded at once.

"Great. Everythin'll be rollin inta town shortly. Have fun today."

The orange's pungent odor and the smell of dew-dappled grass reached their nostrils as they skipped along the mile-long boulevard that connected The Junction to Uptown, the affluent area of Tupper Lake. They neared the Oval Wood Dish Veneer factory just when the morning shift headed into work.

A station wagon with a speaker on top blared, "Don't miss the parade at two o'clock. Gates at the park open at six p.m. G-e-e-t your tickets for the drawing at the ticket booth. Watch the powerful lumberjacks compete in a log-splitting contest. Stay for the spectacular fireworks starting at 9:30. Ticket booth opens at five-thirty tonight. G-e-e-t your tickets."

Excitement buzzed as the three boys ran down the dirt roads of Sissonville—a group of homes built by the OWD for their employees. They passed men in firemen's uniforms heading for the parade's starting point.

"Let's go Uptown and see if we can do a few jobs for the cook at the Altamont Hotel," Sonny suggested. "Maybe he'll give us some money."

The sweet smell of fresh sawdust from the nearby sawmill wafted through the air, as they got closer to Uptown. Looking up, they noticed the fog over Mt. Morris lifting, exposing the majestic mountain. Park Street was already lined with parked cars, and all the stores' colorful striped awnings were down giving the street a festive look. A farmer's hay wagon, decorated with crepe paper and pulled by a team of workhorses, clattered down the street. In it, able-bodied vets from the Veteran's Hospital smiled and waved to passers-by. The driver slapped the reigns, clucked a few times, and guided the horses towards the parade's gathering point.

The brothers ran the short distance to the three-story Altamont Hotel and knocked on the back door. The odor of stale beer mixed with tobacco smoke escaped from the backroom when the cook yanked open the door. Dark circles around his eyes and his unshaven face made him appear tired and surly. He hollered at Marcelle, the bus boy who was scurrying around the kitchen. For a split second, Jim thought better of Sonny's idea. He finally choked out, "Got any chores for us?"

"Are you kiddin? I can use the help. I'm full up this weekend. I'll give ya ten cents to take out the garbage."

They struggled to pull two large bags of garbage to the backyard bin. With their earnings, they hurried to Newberry's Five and Dime store and purchased a chocolate bar. Their eyes searched back and forth for their father and spotted him leaving a saloon across the street. Jim felt a cold dread and grabbed Sonny's arm. "There's Dad. Let's get out of here before he sees us and boxes our ears. They darted behind a store, sat cross-legged on the ground, and divided the candy bar. The brothers savored the sweet taste of bits of chocolate melting in their mouths.

In the early afternoon, Dick suggested that they stand on the hitchhiking corner. "Maybe we can get a ride back to The Junction before the parade starts." Only local residents understood why the boys were waiting on that particular corner. Within minutes a neighbor stopped, and the boys climbed into his car.

Crowds lined the parade route along The Junction's main street. People who lived in bungalows that hugged the roadsides on the outskirts of the village or in rough-hewn log cabins nestled deep in the woods arrived in town. Hordes of lumberjacks streamed into the village to catch the excitement after their month's long stint in the woods. Dressed in plaid flannel shirts, suspendered trousers, woolen porkpie hats, and heavy leather work boots, the men's pockets jingled with wages earned from bone-grinding work. The three boys shoved and pushed their way through the crowd and watched the caravan wind its way towards the municipal park. They thrilled at the sight of the long parade passing before their eyes: logging trucks filled with fresh-cut timber rumbling along the street, a jeep pulling a float carrying young girls vying for the title of Woodsmen's Queen, clowns dancing and throwing candy at the on-lookers, the school band marching briskly behind the Veterans' Honor Guard, firemen pulling an old pumper truck, two horses outfitted with large purple plumes cantering by to the cheers of the excited crowd.

The brothers listened to the cacophony of familiar speech—the lumberjacks who spoke a twangy French Canadian and the Lebanese who still purchased their wives from the old country. They heard an occasional strong New York City accent from the few Jewish families who came to Tupper Lake to open establishments like Ginsberg's Department Store.

Following the caravan to the field, the three watched all afternoon the firemen, lumberjacks, and volunteers bend their backs to the task of unloading the logs for the debarking contest. Laughter and banter grew louder and sweat poured down the men's faces as they grunted and strained. Slowly, the logs were in place. It seemed like magic. The boys didn't want to leave but were hungry and hoped there would be food on the table for dinner. They ran home past the jumble of rundown clapboard houses. A steam whistle blew and black smoke puffed from the smokestack of the five p.m. train chuffing into town. They waved to the engineer and watched the well-dressed travelers descend the stairs.

That evening, Sonny, Dick, and Jim sneaked into the park, being careful to watch for their father. Hundreds of people filled the bleachers. They crawled on their bellies to the edge of the fence. With muscles tight with fear, they lifted the wire and snaked their bodies underneath. A guard's large hands suddenly clamped on the boys' ankles and pulled them back, scrapping their stomachs against the dirt.

"Get out of here you ragamuffins before I call the police."

Disappointed they'd miss the fireworks, they headed home and climbed through their bedroom window, not realizing their father and his drinking partner were at one of the more welcoming bars at the edge of town. Owned by a widow and her granddaughter, the tavern was a favorite hangout for the rough and ignorant lumberjacks. During the weekend, the men boarded at one of the cheaper hotels and spent their evenings drinking, smoking, cussing, and challenging one another to arm wrestling and boxing. At the bar, laughter was growing louder when a hulking Frenchman burst through the door. He slapped a few dollar bills on the bar, raised his hunting knife, and jammed the point through his money into the bar's surface. He scowled, daring those near him to take his money.

The owner estimated her establishment would be extra busy, and she calculated in her head the take for the night. Stories have been told over the years of how she ran her bar. It's said she made everyone welcome with a friendly back slap and a quick refill of strong whiskey. Keeping a sharp eye on consumption, she noticed whenever a patron was almost ready to faint. Then she'd prepare his final drink of the night—half whiskey, half ether. When the man passed out, she stole his money.

As the story goes, the bar owner made a bad mistake when she slipped the boys' father half and half on his very first drink. Shortly after Leon left the bar, he fainted. His buddy was startled and called Dr. Bury, whose evening was already hectic. When the doctor arrived and smelled Leon's breath, he asked, "Where's he been? He's been drinking ether. As soon as he can walk, get him home."

In their darkened house, the brothers were snuggled into bed listening to the crackle of fireworks in the distance. Jim had trouble sleeping and felt a clammy fear when he heard his mother's sobs. He tiptoed into the kitchen. A cigarette dangled in Gladys's right hand and smoke billowed above her head.

"What's wrong, Ma?"

"Nothin. Off to bed with you."

He returned to his room and climbed into bed. Tiredness overtook him, and he drifted into a peaceful sleep. Later, the boys were awakened by the unmistakable sound of angry voices. Leon had finally stumbled home, and Gladys confronted him about squandering his wages on booze. As the boys slowly fell asleep, they wondered how miserable their father would be in the morning and knew their bellies would be empty once again.

The next morning, Dr. Bury reported the widow to the police. She was charged and fined. Soon word spread and patrons stopped frequenting the tavern. Her reputation was ruined, and the establishment closed.

*****

Reflection: Ultimately, our family shapes us. The lives of the nine Savard children born to Leon and Gladys Savard were forever affected by their humble and abusive beginnings.

CHAPTER 4 - WE'RE ALMOST COUSINS

Reflection: If you hold to a philosophy that everything in life is pre-ordained, then you would say our meeting and ultimate marriage were pre-determined by a higher power. I'm not certain how I feel about that philosophy, but I do know that Jim and I were meant to be a couple. Through his family and my family, we were destined to connect, even if only to become good friends. Grace LaVallee was sister to my mother, Bertha. Buck Savard was brother to Jim's father, Leon. When they married, Buck and Grace were Jim's aunt and uncle as well as my aunt and uncle. Likewise, their three girls were his first cousins and my first cousins.

The inter-relationships became more complicated when his brother, Sonny, married my sister, Mary, in 1953. Later, Jim's first cousin, Allen, married my first cousin, Joan. The partial family tree shows all the links.

Savard/LaPlante Inter-Relationships

```
Edmund Savard — Rose Savard (M. 1/9/1909)
    |
Fred (Buck) Savard, Leon Savard

Randolph Boucher — Agnes Boucher (M. 1903)
    |
Gladys Boucher

Duchere LaVallee — Alexina LaVallee (M. 6/11/1901)
    |
Romeo LaPlante — Bertha LaVallee (M. 7/13/1929), Grace LaVallee

Leon Savard — Gladys Boucher (M. 2/1926)
    |
Sonny Savard, Jim Savard

Romeo LaPlante — Bertha LaVallee
    |
Mary LaPlante, Sue LaPlante

Sonny Savard — Mary LaPlante (M. 9/12/1953)
Jim Savard — Sue LaPlante (M. 11/24/1957)
```

Because most of our relatives lived in Tupper Lake, NY, it was my family's vacation destination. My father, Romeo, could fish and hunt with his relatives, and my mother, Bertha, could visit her sisters and brothers.

******

For my siblings and me, Tupper Lake was a magical place of never-ending excitement.

One morning, my father announced, "We've rented a cottage on Little Wolf Lake starting tomorrow. Get packed. We'll leave early in the morning." I was twelve, and this was the first time we'd been able to rent a cottage instead of staying with relatives.

"Hurry up, hurry up," my mother said the next morning as all six of us crowded into our two-door black sedan. "Armand, you sit between your father and me. Otherwise, you'll have all three of your sisters in tears before we get out of the driveway." (He had that uncanny ability).

All three of us girls crowded in the back seat with our legs propped on boxes filled with clothing, linens, and food. Within an hour, the endless questions started.

"Are we there yet? How much farther? Can we stop for lunch?"

It took most of the day to make the grueling trip to Little Wolf Lake over rough two-lane roads. Once there, the arduous trip was forgotten. The sound of gravel and dirt crunching under the weight of the car's tires as Dad drove along the driveway toward the log cabin was like music to me. I looked around. "Good," I said, "an outhouse."

"Are you crazy?" Mary asked.

"Well, it's not really camping unless we have an outhouse."

Mary and Janet smirked and shook their heads.

I jumped out of the car, ran past my mother and sisters, opened the creaky screen door, and bounded into the log camp. The musty smell of old wood penetrated by years of fireplace smoke permeated the cottage. The small kitchen cupboards were spilling over with assorted chipped dishes, and black cast iron griddles hung on nails in the wall. A battered coffee pot sat on the gas stove; the sink held a porcelain dishpan; a hand pump was screwed onto the counter next to the sink.

The living room walls were decorated with paint-by-number pictures, a stuffed deer head, and a pair of snowshoes. A clutter of old magazines and books spilled from a makeshift bookshelf.

The large living room-dining room combination had a round, oil-clothed table surrounded by mismatched chairs. A brown velvet easy chair sat in front of the large window overlooking the lake. The springs had long since lost their tension, and the nap of the velvet was worn shiny from countless bodies snuggling deep into its sagging comfort. An old wooden rocker next to a smoking stand and a day bed were the only other furniture in the room. The cabin had everything I wanted: three bedrooms, a screened in front porch with a metal glider, a crumbling fire pit in the yard for roasting marshmallows, and freedom for a week.

When I rushed to claim a bedroom, my leg brushed against the soft floral covering on the day bed. Three sagging stuffed cushions rested along the back against the paneled wall.

"I claim this bed." I flopped backward onto the sagging stained mattress and heard the crack of metal coils beneath me. I rolled on my stomach, peeked under the bed, and spotted a chipped china thunder bucket painted with blue morning glories. *Great. If I need to go during the night, I won't have to walk to the outhouse in the dark.*

My days started by 6 a.m. I was restless and eager to be out in the early morning by myself. I tiptoed through the cabin and eased the screen door shut against my hand. When a cape fog covered the lake, I reveled in the aloneness and a chance to row around the lake in an old wooden boat. The gentle splash of oars hitting the water barely broke the quiet. I felt the boat rocking and watched the parallel lines behind the rowboat as it cut through the placid water. The mournful sound of loons echoed across the lake.

During the day, I swam, hiked, and played with my cousins. When the temperature rose, we sneaked into the nearby icehouse. It was filled with blocks of ice harvested in the winter months from the frozen lake and buried under a foot-thick layer of sawdust. The damp, crisp air was a welcome relief from the sweltering heat. At night, my siblings and I stayed up late listening to the adults' stories.

When the sky turned pitch black, fireflies filled the area with their magic. We gathered them in glass jars and marveled at their flickering lights. Soft voices of other campers floated across the water. We lay on the dock and gazed at the infinite spread of heaven—a sky like no other. A jeweled canopy—it seemed so close—as if we could reach out and scoop up a handful of stars.

That was the same summer I fell in love. I was twelve, and he was sixteen. Evelyn Savard and I were just hanging out on Pine Street. It was dusk, and the cool mountain air brought goose bumps to my arms. The smell of the surrounding pine trees and of wood fires burning in neighboring houses filled my nostrils.

Streetlights cast a warm glow on someone striding toward us. He was wearing a varsity sweater, canvas high-top sneakers, and jeans. I noticed how his hips moved with the smooth, graceful control of an athlete. A slow smile spread across his face.

"Who's that?" I whispered.

"That's my older brother, Jim."

My eyebrows arched upward when he stopped. My heart beat double time.

"What are you two up to?" There was a soothing quality to his voice.

"Not much. Just talking," Evelyn answered.

His good looks and friendly demeanor drew me to him.

He suddenly turned to head home.

"Don't stay out too late." The smack of his steps echoed in the night's stillness as he walked away. His voice trailed off. "Dad will be mad."

Darn. Why is he leaving already? I was annoyed and sensed he barely noticed me, as if he could brush me away like an annoying gnat. I wanted him to pay attention to me; say something. *He must think I'm just a giggly pain in the neck.*

"Holy cow," I said, "your brother's really cute."

"I guess so. I never thought about it, though."

"Does he have a girlfriend?"

"Oh, yes. He's in love with one of the cheerleaders."

I felt foolish for being so disappointed.

"Hey, why don't ya stay at my house tonight?" Evelyn asked.

It didn't take much to convince me. When we arrived at their Webb Row house, I met Gladys for the first time. Wearing a worn housedress and sitting in a kitchen chair with one leg crossed over the other like a man, she was gnawing on a chicken leg held in her greasy hand. She smacked her lips with immense satisfaction, and nodded her head in my direction. She was so different from my mother that I thought she was comical.

I turned at the sound of footsteps behind me. It was Jim. "What're you doin here?"

"Nah, nah, nah." I stuck out my tongue.

"Get out of here you pest." Then, he chased me around the house with a broom.

I was happy to have attention—even negative.

The next morning, Evelyn said, "I'm goin to watch Jim's football scrimmage ta'night. Da ya wanna come along?"

"Sure. But it'll be cool out, and I didn't bring a sweater."

"Here, you can wear Jim's." She handed me his varsity sweater.

I hugged it to me. *I'll be wearing something he touched.*

Later that evening, Evelyn said, "Boy, my brother told me his girlfriend was mad at him for letting you wear his sweater. He tried to explain that I was the one who gave it to you, but she was still angry."

I was baffled. *Why would she be upset? After all, I'm just an annoying girl who hangs around with his sister.*

A few days later, my cousins and I met for an afternoon of swimming at Little Wolf's public beach. I headed for the dilapidated changing booths built during WWI. The outside wood walls were cracked, and the doors hung askew. I was almost changed when I heard the door in the booth next to mine creak and its hook and eye closure give way to someone yanking it open.

"Wha da ya think you're doin?" Jim yelled as he pulled the Peeping Tom from the booth. "Get outta here before I knock ya on your butt." He sent the boy scuttling away.

I emerged dressed in a pale blue bathing suit and white rubber bathing hat. I was tall for my age and had long legs like a newborn foal. My breasts were just beginning to protrude, and my waist and hips were slender. My face took on a pink glow, and I felt awkward and embarrassed.

How did my hero know someone was peeking at me through a hole in the wall? I didn't ask. I just basked in warm feelings for my savior that day. Jim laughed at me and chased me across the blistering beach. Once again, I thrived in his attention.

"Help! Help!" I shrieked with joy, kicking gritty sand into the air as I ran away pretending to be afraid.

"I've got ya now." Swiftly he lifted me off my feet, carried me to the water, and threw me in. In my twelve-year old absurd mind, I was in love.

I came out of the water, sputtering, clearing my eyes, and swiveling my head around.

"Where's your brother?" I asked Evelyn.

"He's gone home."

"Why's he always in such a hurry?"

"He's gotta work in the shop. He's not allowed to hang out."

I was baffled. What's wrong with hanging out at the beach with friends? I didn't want my encounter with my newest heartthrob to end, but it ended that day. Soon, my vacation was over, and I returned home. With my immature self, I went forward in the business of growing up. I had small crushes along way. There was Don, John, Jack, Mike and Harlan, but tucked into a corner of my brain like a recurring song, there was always Jim.

He, on the other hand, continued to view school as an escape from his home life. Jim was well liked, busy with sports, and head over heels in love with the school's most popular girl. They dated throughout high school, and in his mind, she was the one he planned to marry.

By the time Jim was a sophomore, the Savard's financial situation had improved, and Leon, and his boys built a residence for the family at the back of their upholstery shop. It was small for the size of their family—five children still lived at home. The apartment had a small kitchen, living room, back porch, one bathroom, a laundry closet, and three bedrooms. Still, it was an improvement from Webb Row.

High school basketball, Jim's favorite sport and the one at which he excelled, provided a way for him to feel important. Townspeople packed the gym on game nights and went wild when the team won the Northern League Basketball Championship in 1952. People were so proud of the players that they collected money for team members to travel to Syracuse to attend a game between the New York Knicks and the Syracuse Nets.

On the weekend of the game, Coach Perry and other parents volunteered to drive the boys to Syracuse. When ready to leave, the coach handed over his car keys, "Here, Eagle Eye, you drive."

Jim drove without mishap to the outskirts of Syracuse. After stopping for lunch, the coach said, "We're getting in heavy traffic now, Eagle Eye, so you'd better let me drive."

Two blocks later, Coach Perry had an accident. When the rest of the team heard what had happened, they were so amused, they clapped. On the following day, the New York Knicks topped the weekend off by inviting the Tupper Lake players to pose in front of the Knick's private plane for a picture.

But, Jim's years as a high school basketball star were rapidly drawing to a close. He was a senior, and he and girlfriend were going to the biggest event of the school year—the prom.

He asked his dad, "Can I use the van to drive Pat to Lake Placid to buy a gown for the prom?"

"Okay, but be back by five. I've got a delivery."

Just as they were entering Lake Placid, Jim noticed the spinning lights of a trooper's car behind the van. He pulled over, not certain what was wrong.

The trooper arrested him for stealing the family vehicle.

Jim was embarrassed in front of his girlfriend and furious with his father.

How could Dad do such a thing? How low can a father get?

He had no choice but to drive back to Tupper Lake with the trooper following. When they arrived home, the trooper questioned Leon. After a short time, he said, "That's okay, son. I think we've got the true picture. Don't worry about it."

His father's eyes flashed with anger, and Jim knew he would extract a price. The trooper left, and Leon grabbed Jim by the neck and threw him so hard against the laundry room door that the door broke.

Don, his youngest brother, was afraid to move and cowered in the corner. Tears streamed down Don's face, but he dared not look at Jim.

"Leon, stop it," Gladys yelled. "Stop it. You're going to hurt him."

Jim was young and strong and wanted to strike out at his father, but instead walked away.

On the big night, Jim borrowed his Uncle Wilbert's car. The evening was made all the sweeter when he and Pat were chosen king and queen of the prom.

His girlfriend, sports, friends, school, and a camp at Gull Pond continued to be the center of Jim's world. For a number of years, Leon leased land on Gull Pond, a pristine lake 3 ½ miles from Tupper Lake, from the International Paper Company where he built a one-room hunting camp. There was no road into camp, just a path through the woods. The interior had double bunk beds, an old wooden table and chairs in front of windows that overlooked the lake, and a wood stove for heating and cooking. Candles, flashlights, and gaslights gave the campers soft light when the sun went down. It was a fisherman's dream for Leon, his friends, and his boys. The water teemed with great northern, whitefish, lake trout, and bass. In the summer, the boys skinny dipped at the pond's white sandy beach.

One day, Sonny found an old railroad pump cart in the woods. He and Dick repaired it, and on warm summer days, they loaded Leon and his gear on the cart and pumped it along the tracks to get their father as close to the camp as possible.

Sometimes, Leon invited just Jim to Gull Pond. Jim told Sonny, "Dad just wants me there to row the boat and clean his catch. I don't get to fish. Dad poaches fish. He hooks up a car light with batteries, shines it along the shore, and spears the whitefish and lake trout that spawn in shallow water. One night, Dad caught a 21-pound great northern and told everyone the fish was so big, he had to beat it to death to kill it. I can't stand the smell of the fish. When I clean and fillet them, the smell turns my stomach. If Dad serves fresh fish for supper, I refuse to eat it. I don't care if Dad beats me. I'd rather go hungry than eat fish."

The cabin often became a getaway for Jim and his school chums. One night, a bunch decided to hike in and spend the weekend fishing, playing cards, and swimming. When Sonny heard that Jim and his friends were in Gull Pond, he and a few of his buddies planned a prank to scare the younger boys. Sonny's group sneaked quietly through the woods being careful not to snap a twig or make noise. They got close to the camp undetected and dragged a tree branch along the outside wall of the cabin.

"Somethin's out there. Maybe it's a bear tryin to get in," one of the boys whispered.

Sonny let out a screech.

"Get the gun," yelled a camper.

"Don't shoot. It's us," Sonny hollered.

They all howled with laughter at the prank and settled in for a card game.

Fun times like these were coming to an end, and decision time was close at hand. Jim realized he didn't have plans for his life after high school graduation. There was no counseling going on at home, and he hated working for his father. He was recruited and accepted by Potsdam and Canton because of his basketball ability, but was so insecure, he made excuses and backed away from those opportunities.

In July 1953, Luke, Larry, Charlie, and Jim went to Roy's Restaurant. None of them had any money in their pockets.

Roy said, "Here. Take out the garbage and clean off those tables, and I'll get you boys some coffee and pie."

Luke was worried and confided, "I think I'm going to be drafted. I'm going to enlist. Let's all make an agreement right now to go to Albany and join the Marines."

The four friends shook hands, and the next day, they drove to Albany to enlist. That decision started the next phase of Eagle Eye's life, but not until after September when he was scheduled to usher at Sonny's wedding.

Mary was my first sibling to wed, and I was excited about being a bridesmaid. I was especially eager to see my old crush again. It had been three years since I'd seen Jim. Mary and Sonny's wedding on September 12, 1953, would give me an opportunity to reconnect with him.

Just three weeks before their wedding, a car hit Gladys when she crossed Main Street. It threw her over the hood, and she hit the pavement so hard that the candy in her pocket spilled onto the street. For a while, it seemed the wedding might be delayed. I was worried. If the wedding were postponed, I might miss seeing Jim—he was leaving for the Marines. I prayed Gladys was all right.

Disaster was averted. Gladys was bruised, but nothing was broken. Eventually, she received a $2,000 settlement. Once Sonny realized his mother was all right, he joked, "If you get hit one more time, Mom, we'll be able to pay off some bills."

I was giddy with anticipation for the wedding and for seeing Jim. *Will he notice me? What will he look like now? Will I still get goose bumps when I see him?*

As I dressed for the wedding, I looked at my reflection in the mirror and gave myself a critical assessment. *Yes, the mint green, cocktail length gown is pretty. It's not my favorite color, but okay.* I twirled around several times the way I did as a little girl and let the gown's full skirt swirl outward. I loved how the white baby doll heels made me appear taller and sophisticated. I wished Mom had let me wear more than just bright red lipstick. I situated the narrow green band in my hair and leaned in closer to the mirror. My hair was cut shorter than normal—maybe too short—but its shiny black color was a perfect contrast to my gown.

One last twirl and a final glimpse in the mirror assured me that I was ready. When I walked to my father's car, the morning sun warmed my back and crimson, purple, and gold leaves swirled around my feet. I stepped into Dad's car for the short ride to church. Glancing out the side window, I noticed how the brilliant fall colors of the trees electrified the mountainside.

With a jumpy stomach, I walked into the vestibule of Holy Name Church. Jim was there, fidgeting with his bow tie. He was even more handsome than I remembered. I imagined myself being held in his arms. When he gave a slight smile of recognition, my muscles tightened. *Did he notice how grown-up I looked?* The florist broke my concentration and handed me a bouquet. It was a wreath encircled with daisies and mums. When the organ music started, Margaret Larkin's exquisite voice filled the church. I felt a thrill when my dreamboat looped my arm through his.

"Ready?" he asked in a mellow voice.

My head was swimming with the glamour of the day and of romantic ideas I learned from movies like *Roman Holiday*. Maybe someday, it will be my turn—but who? Surely not Warren, the troubled young boy I was currently dating.

A short ceremony, a few pictures, and we headed to the Riverside Restaurant for an afternoon reception. The long, one-story white restaurant looked out over Tupper Lake. The interior's lower walls were covered in dark wood paneling and the upper in wallpaper. It had a large dance floor and corner bandstand. Adult guests smoked as they waited for the bridal party to arrive and the banquet to begin. My father—not given to generosity—bought a round of drinks for everyone. A drum roll echoed through the restaurant when the bride and groom filed into the room followed by their attendants.

"Ladies and gentlemen." Another drum roll. "Please welcome Mr. and Mrs. Sonny Savard." Clapping. "They'll start the party off with their first dance as a married couple."

A few catcalls and a *here, here* from the crowd. Mary's face glowed as she and Sonny glided around the floor.

What will it feel like if I get a chance to dance with HIM?

Introductions continued. First, the maid of honor and best man. Then, "Sue LaPlante escorted by Jim Savard." I was surprised, not knowing it was customary for the bridal party to begin the dancing. More clapping and cheering.

He reached for my hand and motioned to me with his head. I held back, feeling awkward. *What if I trip? What if I can't follow him?*

Then he cupped his hand over mine and led me to the floor. I could feel the pressure of his hand on the small of my back when he pulled me closer. My back was rigid, my muscles tight all the way to my neck. Jim was edgy and preoccupied. His eyes shifted back and forth.

Determined to get his attention and glancing directly into his eyes, I asked, "When are you leaving for the Marines?"

"Not for a few weeks yet."

"Are you excited?"

"More nervous than excited."

Now the big question—the one that had been nagging me—my fingers crossed.

"Where's your girlfriend?"

"She already left for college."

"Oh. It's too bad she had to miss the wedding," I said and nestled my head onto his shoulder. A smile quivered on my lips. I could feel the warmth of his body and smell a hint of Old Spice aftershave. *If this is a dream, don't let it end.* Slowly, my body relaxed, and I felt light in his arms as we moved around the floor to "No Other Love." It seemed so right, as if we had been dancing together forever. When the music ended, so did the glow I had been experiencing.

"Will the bridal party please take your places at the head table?" the bandleader announced.

Jim thanked me for the dance, pulled out my chair, and sat next to me. Then, he turned away and engaged his brother, Dick, in conversation. *I want him to notice how pretty I look and talk to me.* My shoulders sagged. I fiddled with my napkin and realized at ages 15 and 19, we were worlds apart.

I'm just the same annoying twerp he chased around the house with a broom, and he's the athlete who's still in love with someone else.

Although it was just one dance, I could still feel his touch and hear his voice for months afterwards. Two years would pass before I again lay eyes on him.

PART II

CHAPTER 5 - SEMPER FI & COLLEGE LIFE

Two weeks later, September 29, 1953, Jim moved to his new hell home—boot camp, Parris Island, South Carolina. The Marine's welcoming committee of one mean Corporal greeted the new recruits when the bus arrived at the base.

"You are now in the U.S. Marines, and you're the property of Uncle Sam. From now on you won't eat, sleep, or whistle until someone tells you to. Give your soul to God. The rest of your sorry ass is mine."

Jim sneaked a glance to Luke. *What have we gotten into?*

"How do they expect me to turn you maggots into Marines? You're not even human beings. Get off the bus you ugly scum. I'm taking you to the beautician to try and make you pretty. Follow me."

Jim and his friends grabbed their bags and followed like ducks in a row to the barbershop. Another recruit sat slouched in the barber chair, "How do you like your hair cut young man?"

"Don't mess with the sideburns," the unsuspecting recruit answered.

Zip. Zip. It was all gone—just like Yul Brynner.

Jim and Luke steeled themselves against the inevitable. After the barber finished, Jim's curls lay in a puddle around the chair. The two friends looked at each other and burst out laughing.

"We sure are an ugly pair," Jim said. His dark, wavy hair was gone at the hands of a sadist who loved to reduce all Marines to the same level.

Next the DI, *drill instructors,* began to work their magic. They stripped recruits of individuality by standing inches from their faces and screaming commands, confiscating personal items, and stepping on pictures of girlfriends.

Jim's hard-bitten, impatient DI shouted, "You are the most pathetic bunch of worthless individuals I've ever seen. What sewer did they drag you out of?"

Jim couldn't believe his ears. *This DI is a madman.*

"When I speak, you will say *yes sir* at the top of your lungs. Let me hear it."

"Yes sir," came the chorus of voices from the worried recruits.

"Louder."

"YES SIR."

"When I call chow time, you will run as fast as you can to the mess hall. I don't want to see anything but assholes and elbows. Is that understood?"

"YES SIR."

All of this activity was part of the Marine Corps strategy to build a team dedicated to following orders and fighting the enemy, even though their brains told them to run. Jim soon learned the jargon, too. Bunks are racks, a latrine is a head, a bar is a slop chute, and a cafeteria is a mess hall. He learned to make a bed so taut a quarter would bounce on it, to spit shine his shoes, and to iron a razor-sharp crease on his trousers. Adjusting to other things proved more difficult. After a few weeks of suffering from constipation, he became accustomed to the fifty toilets lined up back to back along the center of the bathroom.

The four friends remained close, and one day, Jim came to the rescue of Larry.

"Jim saved me from getting a severe beating," Larry said. "I kept saying *gangway* instead of the required *stand by* when the drill instructor entered our Quonset hut. I just couldn't remember the right words.

Jim yelled. 'Baldy. It's *stand by*.'

"The drill instructor left me alone and instead gave Jim a beating for interfering."

Jim had escaped abuse at the hands of his father only to receive the same kind of treatment at the hands of Uncle Sam. I would have been panicky for him had I known what he was going through.

While he adjusted to life as a Marine, I immersed myself in high school activities. Homework, dramatic club plays, part-time work as a soda jerk, boyfriends, and school friends became part of my everyday routine. The teen club was my favorite hangout. My fashion of choice consisted of blue jeans rolled up to mid calf, my father's white dress shirt hanging out over the jeans, a colored silk scarf tied rakishly at an angle on my neck, penny loafers, and white bobby socks.

For a year, I went steady with a high-school dropout named Warren—the type who rolled cigarettes into the sleeve of his T-shirt and had a pinup's picture in the spinner knob on his car's steering wheel. He was sullen, jealous, and angry at the world, but I couldn't garner the spunk to break up. One night as we left the movies, a young disabled boy from my class said hi to me.

"Hi Bobby. How are you?" I said.

Warren immediately bristled. "Hi Bobby," he mocked in a phony woman's voice.

Yanking my hand from his, I turned to look to him. The fog cleared from my eyes, and for the first time, I saw Warren for what he was. *I'm miserable being with him. I deserve better.*

"Get lost. I'll walk home," I said and turned to leave.

I felt lightness in my step, as if an oppressive presence had suddenly vanished. That put an end to Warren.

In 1954, at the beginning of my senior year of high school, Mary said, "Jim loves to get mail. He's lonesome. Why don't you write him?"

I thought back to my crush on Jim and sent him a short note.

(October 5, 1954) Hi, Jim. I just got back from Tupper Lake and heard you were anxious for letters so I'm dropping you a line. I broke up with my boyfriend Warren. I never want to go steady again. Do you miss home? . . . Mary and Sonny are so proud of their new little baby, Randy. Drop me a line when you have time. I'd like to hear from you. Sue

I wasn't certain Jim would reply. The memory of our dance at Mary's wedding sent a chill up my back, and I prayed he'd respond. When I received a letter from him a few weeks later, I was so delighted and touched that I read it to my two best friends.

I didn't respond right away. I was a busy high-school senior, and the year was speeding by. My friends, Joan, Diane and I did homework together, went to football games in the fall and ice skating in the winter. We stayed overnight at each other's homes and spent our evenings together knitting. I was attempting to knit a two-piece mauve dress with white angora trim and pearl buttons. We stayed up late and talked for endless hours about school and boys. I finally wrote Jim again.

(November 5) Hi Jim, Thanks for your letter. I was glad to hear from you. I'm sorry I didn't write sooner but I've been really busy in school. Mary told me about the Dear John letter. I'm sorry. I know you were crazy about Pat . . . How do you like the Marines? Sincerely, Sue

Jim replied more quickly than I expected.

(November 9) Hi Sue, So you didn't think I would write, huh? Well I guess you don't know me very well. I was happy to hear from you even though you were slow. My old girlfriend is just the past. It doesn't bother me anymore. Just about all girls are alike. When you are in service, they just can't wait. That's why the "Dear John" letters are plentiful around here. You asked if I like being in the Marines. I don't know why I signed up. I was on guard duty last night. When I looked at the sky, I wondered if it's the same moon that shines over Tupper Lake. I was asked if I wanted to ship over for six years by the 1ˢᵗ Sgt. If it wouldn't have been held against me, I would have told him what he could do with the Corps. I think college would have been a breeze compared to this. God Bless You, Jimmy

His letters got tucked into my wooden keepsake box. I admitted to myself that I still had a crush on him and imagined how handsome he would look in Marine Corps dress blues. Later, I learned he saved my letters in his Marine Corps locker and marked each on the back with the date on which he wrote me.

(January 7, 1955) Dear Sue, Today is Saturday so I only had to work half a day. I made a coffee run for the Lt. and made tags for our keys. Rough work, huh? This afternoon we went up to the slop chute and bowled six games. I'm going to the movies tonight. Love, Jimmy

Our correspondence stopped temporarily. I missed his letters but was active with high school. He occupied himself by corresponding with pen pals who noticed his request for letters in a military magazine.

In the winter of my senior year, Mr. Prior, the principal, gave a morning announcement over the PA system. "Any seniors wishing to tour Morrisville Junior College next week should sign up by this Friday."

"Why don't we go on the trip?" I asked Joan. "We'll get out of classes for the day, and I've never been on a college campus before."

College was a mystery to me. When I was growing up, my parents never mentioned the word college. None of our relatives went to college, and no one I knew had a college education except my teachers. All I saw on the visit fascinated me. For the first time, I thought maybe I should attend college.

I said to my mother in the afternoon, "I want to go to Morrisville in the fall and study gemology."

"College is for the wealth, not for us," she said.

She turned away and continued preparing supper.

Her comment hurt. *Just once, I'd like some encouragement.*

Discouraged but not defeated, I made an appointment with my guidance counselor, and in the next few weeks, he steered me through the application and testing process. Once accepted, I realized I'd have to work to earn my own money for college.

High school graduation arrived in June of 1955, shortly after I turned 17. I couldn't believe my ears when my name was called to the front for graduating with honors. For a while, my girlfriends and I were giddy with the ceremony, the speeches, and the anticipation of upcoming celebrations. Underlying our excitement was the unsettling reality that we were leaving the safe confines of school and our friends. Later, we dissolved into tears as we hugged fellow classmates.

"You'll be my friend forever and ever," we promised one another.

I scoured the audience during the ceremony and on the lawn afterwards looking for my parents. I was fuming that my mother and father didn't attend my graduation. *How could they not support me? This is a special event. Everyone else's parents are here.*

I walked home and slammed the front door when I entered the house. "Why weren't you there, Mom?"

"We were."

She was dressed in a housedress. Certain she was lying, I went to my room to get my emotions under control, and for the next few days, I avoided them.

The day after graduation, I began work as a secretary at Griffiss Air Force Base in Rome, NY.

When my first paycheck arrived, I handed my mother the required $15 for room and board. She said, "You don't have to pay room and board this summer as long as you're saving for school." Her comment came as a shocker. My siblings and I knew we were expected to pay room and board the minute we graduated and found work. I quickly added the fifteen dollars to my savings account.

Joan, Diane, and I went to Tupper Lake over the 4th of July weekend. We spent the early part of the day at the beach and returned to our motel to shower and change.

"Let's dress up in our graduation outfits and go uptown shopping," I suggested.

We dressed in matching sheath dresses overlaid with a sheer floral outer garment similar to a peignoir. My outfit was hot pink, Joan's soft pink, Diane's peach. With a little makeup and high heels, we felt grown up and sexy.

Jim was home on leave. He and his brother Sonny were making a furniture delivery with the van when they saw the three of us walking towards town. They stopped. Jim jumped out of the van, ran over, and encircled me in a bear hug. I was stunned, and I remember that hug as if it just happened today.

"Hi, Sue. Thanks for your letters. Where are you girls headed?" he asked. "We'll give you a ride."

Jim was 21, and I was 17. During the ride, I noticed he was smiling at me and looking directly into my eyes as we talked. He didn't turn away as he had at Sonny's wedding, and he seemed more interested in what I had to say. I wondered if the high heels, makeup, and tight skirt made him realize I was no longer the fifteen-year-old he remembered.

In the 1950s, Tupper Lake was a happening place. A number of hotels had large dance floors, and live bands entertained on Saturday evenings. Couples loved to dance, and the jitterbug was all the rage. My girlfriends and I didn't drink, but we loved to flirt and dance. That weekend, we went from place to place, finally ending up at the

Waukesha. When the Waukesha band played "Get Up Those Stairs Mademoiselle," everyone in the room crowded onto the dance floor. They stomped and twirled causing the floor itself to bounce up and down. Joan, Diane, and I danced until the wee hours of the morning with a number of young boys I'd met on my many trips to Tupper Lake. After all, we were all unattached to boyfriends, and we had jobs and spending money. Life was good.

Jim was there that evening, too. I sat on his lap, tussled his hair, teased him, and flirted. He acted as if I were nothing more than the twelve-year-old pest who once played with his sister, Evelyn. I left with my friends and a young boy named Gary, and we headed for the Miss Tupper Diner to top the evening off with a snack. When his leave was over, Jim returned to Camp Lajeune, North Carolina. Within a few days of returning, he posted a letter to me.

> *(July 11, 1955) Hi Sue. Just a note to see if my girl is all right. How was the trip back to Oneida? Joan must have kept everyone going. She wouldn't be so cute if she didn't talk so much. Of course, Sue, you are the sweetest. Lucky Gary. I wish I were handsome. Love, Jimmy*
> *P.S. Ans. soon*

"Golly," I said to my girlfriends, "he called me *my girl*. I'll have to write him more often."

I was back at work and hated my secretarial job more each day. My boss was an Air Force captain named Mike Shay, a recent law school graduate. He had brilliant blue eyes and the longest eyelashes I'd ever seen on a guy. He kept track of the comings and goings of my group of friends and made our days tolerable by taking us to the officer's club after work for parties and dancing.

> *(July 15) Dear Jim, Gosh, I could kick myself for going out with Gary. You're so much nicer. If I had only known you were interested. Do you remember the 4th of July weekend at the Waukesha? I even got to sit on your lap because it was so crowded there weren't any chairs left. Sue*

(July 20) Hi Sue, I do remember the 4th of July weekend. You sat on my lap. It was a big thrill for me and nothing for you. I wish you had stayed on my lap all evening. It's funny when I stop and think about it. I was a fool to let you go without a fight. I'm glad you started writing again. Love, Jimmy

(July 25) Dearest Jim, I received another letter from you today. I forgot to tell you how much I liked the poem you and your buddy wrote for me. I wish you had asked me out on the 4th of July weekend. You asked what I do with all my money. I save some. Three dancing lessons a week amounts to quite a bit, and I pay for a ride to work. Love, Sue
    P.S. Write soon

(July 30) Dear Sue, I wanted to be with you but I didn't think you cared. As for me being interested, I must face facts. I think I am. I didn't want to ask and be hurt if you turned me down. I messed up my chances. That would have been all of two more days to be with you. Sonny told me to try and prevent you from going out with Gary. I guess I should have taken big brother's advice but I'm kind of bull headed. Love, Jimmy

(August 25) Dear Jim, I was just thinking of the fun we used to have when I went around with Evelyn. I used to joke around with you. I'll never forget the "dog food" your Mom used to fix (just joking). I can't wait for the weekend. I'm so sick of work in Rome. The only thing I like is payday. I got one yesterday and I only have $2 left. Love, Sue

By late August 1955, I wasn't certain I wanted to go to college and cancelled my admission. Our letter writing became more frequent, and we both hoped for a chance to date.

(September 2) Dear Sue, Received your letter last night. Here's hoping I get a leave over Thanksgiving. I can't wait to see you. I just realized I shouldn't have stopped keeping in touch with you. I think I knew it was you who called my name that night at the Waukesha but I didn't respond. I guess I was mad at you for some reason. You can squeeze me to death when you see me and I won't complain. Love always, Jimmy
  P.S. M.M.R.L.H. means Marine Mail Rush Like Hell

(September 5) Dear Jim, Well, I've decided not to go to Morrisville after all. Everyone keeps telling me that I won't finish school and that makes me kind of mad. Golly, I shouldn't have let anyone talk me out of it. . . . Remember when you gave me a peck on the cheek at the Waukesha. You said you'd see me Thanksgiving. Was that a promise? I took some more pictures the other day. They were terrible. In one I'm even standing on my head. Write soon, Sue

(September 24) Dear Sue I've been busy lately. My squad rushed off to the woods for a three-day field problem. I found your letter when I came back. I hope nothing goes wrong before Thanksgiving weekend. It would break my heart. Don't say those things (if I don't want to see you to let you know). You know very well I want to see you. So you plan on getting married, huh? Who is going to be the lucky man, Sue? So am I, I guess, but not for some time. The girl hasn't shown up quite yet. I'm going to go to school when I get out. Love, Jimmy,

(October 1) Hi there Sweetie, Sue if you really want to go to college, don't let anyone talk you out of it. You said you think an awfully lot of me. Try to like me more than you do. I sure hope I get Thanksgiving weekend. I'll travel farther than that on a weekend just to see you. Don't plan on it too much. Right now I'm on the roster for rifle range in November. The service is known to ruin plans. So, you're making a special knit dress just for me, huh? What color is it? I can just see you in a knit dress. m-m-m Love, Jimmy

(October 10) Dearest Jim, Gosh, Jim. I hope you can make it for Thanksgiving. I won't make any plans until I hear definitely if you're coming or not. Joan and I are going to New York that weekend if you don't come up. It's a three-day weekend and I don't feel like staying home. Love and kisses, Sue
P.S. Answer soon. xxxxxxxxxxxx Your payment for writing back so soon.

(October 11) Hi Sweetheart - I received the pictures today. They are great. I'm crazy over you. I could look at you all day. Luke and I will be in Oneida if I get the weekend. The field problem starts the 19th of this month and ends on the 12th of Nov. I can't wait to see you again. I might squeeze you to death. As of right now, I love you. I always liked you very much, Sue, but I never thought I'd fall. When I saw you in July, that did it. Love, Jimmy

(October 12) Dearest Jim, I'm at Diane's house and they're playing "Autumn Leaves." I'm crazy for that song. I'm crazy period. I went to the ballet Monday night. It was wonderful. Do you like ballet Jim?... I don't have to try to like you—it comes natural. I wish Thanksgiving would hurry up. I think I'm wishing half my life away. Some day I'm going to wish I had some of this time back. I hope you get that leave in November so you can come to Oneida. Is that first kiss going to be something! If you can't come up, call me at Oneida 157-M. Love and kisses, Sue

(October 15) Dearest Sue, I may get New Year's leave. I can't miss the "Wash" and going out with you... I must close for now. Stay well and try to like me a little. Love, Jimmy

(October 16) Dear Jim, I don't have any news but I still owe you a letter. You know when you said for me to have a good time in TL and to think of you, I didn't think too much about it. Well I'm having a good time but I'm thinking of you. Gosh I wish you were home again. I hear the football team has lost every game. I remember when you played football and the team was pretty good. I miss you. Love and kisses, Sue

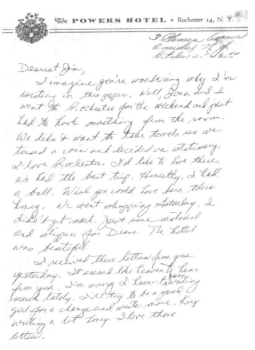

Jim was saving for his November trip to Oneida, but he needed civilian clothes and used part of his $35 bi-weekly income to splurge. After shopping at the PX, he placed his new duds in his footlocker. For the ragamuffin kid from Webb Row, buying new clothes was a significant event.

> *(October 29) Hi Sue honey, I bought two sweaters, one brown and one light blue, a blue suede jacket, and wool argyle socks. I still need to get some trousers. We have been on ship since Wednesday cruising up and down the coast from Virginia to Florida. One of these days we're going to have a practice landing and invade Va. Beach. Then, we'll invade Jacksonville, N. C. and Onslow Beach. These war games are crazy, just like playing cowboys and Indians. There is some skinny being passed that they may give us a weekend from Thurs. to Mon. If we get it, I'll be hauling to the Empire State. Say a prayer. Love always, Jimmy*

While aboard ship on maneuvers, someone broke in and stole all of his new clothing. He was furious. He didn't have any more money and couldn't prove who was the crook.

One of the songs Jim liked to sing was from the "Hee Haw" show. "Gloom despair and agony on me. Deep, dark depression and utter misery. If I didn't have bad luck, I'd have no luck at all." Having his new duds stolen was definitely a case of bad luck.

In November, I applied to SUNY Albany to major in business education. Where did I get the courage to pursue college? I don't know the answer. My family didn't encourage me, support me financially, or help with the application process. I walked to the high school to take my entrance exams, arranged my own travel to Albany by train for an interview, and saved most of my paycheck for college.

> *(October 30) Dearest Jim, Have you thought any more about college? My application is in and I take my test December 3. I got a part-time job at the drugstore. I'm going to pick up an extra 22 hours. I need money for school. Dad won't help me and I do like to eat. I went to the doctors today*

for a physical. Next week I'll probably get a bill for $3. I hope I don't change my mind this time. I feel as though I'm wasting my time on this job. I'll try to get New Years off. You'd better send me some pictures pretty soon. If I close my eyes, I can almost feel your arms around me. Mushy, huh? Love and kisses, Sue

Jim and Luke headed to Oneida, New York, on November 3, 1955. They had a 72-hour pass, and I couldn't wait to be with Jim. I paced the floor for hours waiting for their arrival. At one a.m., after driving straight through from North Carolina, Jim said, "I can't drive another mile. I'm not exactly sure where her house is. Let's find a spot to pull over, sleep for a while, and find it in the morning."

"Fine with me," agreed Luke.

Fate was with us that night because they pulled into the parking lot right next to our house. It was a comforting sight to see a car pull in. I ran out.

"I just knew it had to be you. I've been watching out the window all night and worrying about your driving so far."

His arms encircled me, and he pulled me into a hug. I was hooked.

We talked for a short while, but they were both exhausted from the long drive and soon Jim and Luke were sound asleep.

The next morning, I hoped to impress my honey with my cooking ability.

"Your breakfast is ready," I called.

I didn't know that when a man is called to breakfast, he first has to shower, shave, put on after shave, comb his hair, and look like a million bucks before he's prepared to eat. By the time he came down, the food had lost all resemblance to breakfast. On his plate sat hard dry eggs, burned bacon sitting in congealed grease, and dry toast. He was polite, ate the disgusting breakfast, and drank the cold coffee.

That morning, he hugged me again and said, "I love you." Although elated, I couldn't believe he was sincere. *This is our first date, and we barely know each other. How can he love me?*

The 72-hour leave was soon over, and they returned to Camp Lejeune. Their time in boot camp was finished. For the first time in his life, Jim's surroundings were organized and his days structured. He and his three Tupper Lake friends received different assignments but kept close tabs on one another. When the brass found out Luke was a four-letter man, he was placed in Special Services, in charge of all sports equipment. Jim was put in a supply outfit where he handed out and kept track of military gear. In their spare time, they went bowling, played basketball, and went to base movies. Jim remained especially close to Luke, often spending hours talking with him late into the night. As much as they talked, Jim kept his own counsel and pretended his childhood didn't exist.

(November 10) Dear Jim, Here I am again. You didn't know what you were getting in to when you wrote me. I'm so glad you called. I was really surprised. In fact, I thought you'd be so sick of my crazy chatter you wouldn't want to come up again for a long while. I nearly died of boredom yesterday. I went to church and then over to Diane's. Then we went to the movies. Boy, was it dull. I thought the stinkin picture would never end. I didn't leave because I knew I'd be even more lonesome for you after the show. Do I ever miss you! I didn't think you'd be lonesome for me. After your call tonight, I realized you care for me. All my love, God Bless You, Sue

(November 17) Hi sweetheart, I made Sgt. That means a little extra in my paycheck. I knew what I was getting into when I wrote you. I was trying to make a friend but you proved to be more than a friend. Every chance I get from now on, I'll be at your door. It makes me feel good to know that you miss me Hon. My leave is going to start the 30th of Dec. until the 12th of Jan. When I get home on leave, we'll have to dance our feet off to "Autumn Leaves." I love that song. Love and kisses, Jimmy

(November 22) My dearest Jim, I love getting your letters. I could read them a hundred times. I was so scared of your driving all the way to Oneida. I'm always a worrier about driving. What a relief to see you. When you come home in January, let's go to the high school and look over some college *pamphlets. Maybe that will help you decide. All my love and kisses, Sue*

In hopes he'd have a long leave over the Christmas holidays, Jim and I planned details through letter writing.

(December 6) My dearest darling, Yesterday the supply officer of the 10th Mar. Regiment called down to the 3rd Bn. for a Brick Sgt. with a 3011 m.o.s. for transfer. I'm the only Sgt. who qualifies. I'm leaving for Vieques, P.R. I can't say if I'll get any leave before we disembark. New Year's leave will have to take more than praying. I was shocked when I was told. I'm glad you liked the watch I sent you. I also got you a red and black garter with U.S. Marines on it. I only have nine months to do and you can bet I won't ship over. Love me always, Jimmy

(December 6) My Dearest Darling, I'm still counting the days until you get home. Golly I miss you. Every time I get feeling bad, I remember what you said about keep smiling. It's easier said than done. But if you want me to keep smiling then that's what Ill do even if I have to tape a smile on. Please write soon. Love and kisses, Sue

(December 8) My darling Sue, Well, honey, I got transferred today. I'm now by myself in an old broken down condemned trailer. It's filthy dirty. I got lonesome for the guys in one day. As it stands now we are supposed to get only 7 days leave. We aren't scheduled to leave for P.R. until Feb. Pray

*that I get New Year's leave. All my love and kisses,
Jim*

(December 15) My Honey, I'm convinced that you'll be home New Years. I don't know why. I just have that feeling. At least it gives me something to look forward to. Just let me know and I'll be in Tupper fast. Love always, Sue

(December 19) My darling Sue, I got the straight skinny on my leave. I'll be leaving on the 27th of Dec. I got my name on a flight list. I leave here 9 a.m. on the 27th. I get in NYC by noon and have to thumb it the rest of the way. It's going to be hard to get out of Brooklyn. Be ready to pack and be there on the 27th or 28th. Love and God bless you, Jimmy

(December 25) My darling Jim, It's Christmas day and I'm working. I won't get through until 6 p.m. I went to midnight mass and then over to Diane's and didn't get home until 3:30 a.m. Boy was I tired. I'm planning on going to Tupper for a week. I'll keep my fingers crossed that you still want to see me. I leave Utica at 1:55 Saturday and get in at 5:30. I want to have you waiting for me when I get off the train. I can't wait to see you, Sue

    I traveled by train from Utica to Tupper Lake on a chilly winter day. Snowflakes melted on the train's warm window as I watched the scenery glide by. When the conductor announced, "there are no services on this train," I was glad I'd eaten lunch. The background of houses and Christmas lights came into view when the train neared the Tupper Lake station at dusk. Jim was on the platform watching it rumble to a stop. My brown eyes sparkled when I descended the train stairs and spotted him. His big welcoming smile was like a Christmas present wrapped in exquisite paper. In my mind's eye, when I think of that day, time seems suspended. I can see his warm breath crystallizing in the cold mountain air. He's wearing a red plaid shirt, jeans, boots, and a red toque on his head. The silent snowflakes are falling and gathering around his feet. That picture is engraved in my mind.

Someone once said, "When Jim entered a room or smiled, he lit up the place."

He lit up my world that day.

We both loved to dance and just fit together as a couple. He was my Fred Astaire—smooth and easy to follow. During his Christmas leave, we stopped at the Waukesha in the middle of the afternoon. He put a few coins in the jukebox and selected what was to become our song, "Autumn Leaves." The restaurant was deserted, and we had the large dance floor to ourselves. We used the entire floor while, in our own circle of love, we spun and twirled to the music for several hours. Jim dipped me low as each song ended. His touch was like a soft caress, and I felt light in his arms.

What a beautiful memory.

I stayed at his home during that visit. The kitchen had a banquette seat built around a long red Formica table. At lunchtime, Jim sat at the outside of the far end of the booth with a clear shot to the back door. He sat forward with his legs crossed and with one butt cheek on the seat.

"Why do you always sit like that instead of sitting back on the seat?"

"That's so I can get a running start if the old man goes into a tirade."

His statement mystified me. In the few times I'd been around Leon, he seemed quiet and unthreatening and was so ill, he needed an afternoon nap and everyone had to be quiet. Gladys's idea of being quiet was to stomp down the hall and shout, "Be quiet. Your father's sleeping."

After Leon's nap, Gladys begrudgingly fixed her husband supper, and then he worked a few hours in the upholstery shop.

On my previous visit to Jim's home, Leon was gracious and considerate, even offering me a sandwich and coffee. On this visit, he showed his true personality.

"May I have a cup of coffee?" I asked Jim.

Leon's eyes flashed in annoyance, and he later told Jim, "She thinks she can come in here and make herself at home."

Jim kept his comments about his father's behavior close to his chest but was obviously annoyed. It was then I realized Leon had a changeable side. I never stayed there again.

We celebrated New Year's Eve with Mary and Sonny and an evening of dancing at the Waukesha. I wore a red taffeta strapless dress I'd sewn especially for the occasion. Jim looked dashing in his new sport coat and trousers. At the stroke of midnight, the band played "Auld Lang Syne," everyone kissed, cheered, and blew noisemakers. One of the tipsy revelers was a bit too arduous when he landed a giant, wet kiss on my lips. Jim's eyebrows knit together; he cupped his hand under my elbow and pulled me to him. His arm went around my waist. "Happy New Year, Honey," he said and gave the man a *get lost* look. After the midnight hoopla died down, we all headed for Sonny's car. The freshly fallen snow was slippery, and Jim decided to be Sir Galahad. He swept me off my feet into his arms, promptly slipped on the snow, and landed on his back so hard with me on top of him that the tube of lip balm in his back pocket flattened.

Later that week, we spent a picture-perfect day in Lake Placid. The air was brisk and the sky a vivid blue. Neither of us noticed the cold. We skated on Mirror Lake, raced each other, and grabbing hands, spun around in a circle. Arm in arm, we walked around the village, window shopped, and peeked at diamond rings in the jewelry store window. Snow swirled around our feet and gathered in mounds against the curbs. We giggled and looked lovingly into each other's eyes and walked for blocks before we stopped at a small cafe for lunch. People came and went, and we paid no attention to their stares or comments. It was as if the rest of the world didn't exist. The day was magical.

Jim's leave was coming to an end, and I had to return to Oneida, turn in my notice of resignation at Griffiss, and prepare mentally for becoming a college student. Jim's hug goodbye at the train station was too brief; I wanted to cling to him for courage.

(January 1, 1956) Dearest Sue, I got back to the trailer at 4:45 a.m. I slept until 7:30 in my clothes. That was the worst trip I ever had. I couldn't stand a long goodbye at the station. I always make like I don't mind saying goodbye, but when I leave I break inside. I've been singing "He" and "Woman in Love" all day. Boy we really played "Autumn Leaves" quite a bit. I love to dance with you. Love always, Jimmy

(January 5) My dearest Jim, The picture of us New Year's Eve was swell. When I saw the one of Mary, I could have sworn Mary was me. She looks more like me than I do. I love to dance with you although we didn't dance that much. We just stood on the dance floor smooching. When I look at the picture, I can just see those pretty blue eyes smiling at me.

Golly, even though we didn't skate that much in Lake Placid, I had a swell time. I think I caught a cold sitting in the snow outside the Waukesha. Love always, Sue

(January 9) My dearest honey, If you remember, you weren't sitting in the snow. You were on top of me. My poor pants got wet. It's a wonder neither of us was hurt. I know it won't be 3 1/2 years before we marry. I'm all mixed up about college. I don't know if I can do it, but I'll try my best. I guess my big trouble is getting up the nerve to go. If we were together, we could be a great team. I miss you. Write often, Jim

I was headed into the unknown without a safety net of support from my parents. Once home, I decided to try one more time to get financial help from my father. "Please, Dad. Can't you give me at least $5 a week? I know you can afford it, and that would help me so much."

Dad took a few bills out of his wallet and threw them at my feet. I watched the bills flutter to the floor. I wanted to throw them back in my father's face, but I didn't dare. A tear trickled down my cheek when I leaned over to pick up the money. I felt ashamed for my father that money was more important to him than I was.

"Sue, if you insist on going to college, why don't you become a doctor or lawyer? You can't even make a living as a teacher."

Exasperated and angry, my lips puckered. "It's too late for that advice, Dad. I haven't taken the math or chemistry required to become a doctor or lawyer."

He glared at me, turned away, and clomped down the hall. *He just can't understand why I'm not happy as a secretary. I'm only seventeen and I'm not yet ready to be surrounded by adults who sit at metal desks all day long smoking and typing endless documents that I don't understand. I don't know what I'm typing or why I'm typing it. Where does it go? What purpose does it serve? I'm too young. There must be more to life than this.*

The next day after dinner, I was drying dishes with my mother. "You'll last two months and be back home," she said.

I was taken aback, but it may have been the push I needed. *I will prove you wrong.*

(January 18) Dear Sue, Boy you were in a tough mood last night when we spoke. Don't ever say your Mom and Dad don't want you around. They hate to see you go. They think they're losing their little girl. They love you. Don't worry about being away from home. You'll make it. I have faith in you. Have faith and trust in me. I'll square away some day. Love and kisses, Jimmy

With the money Dad had thrown on the floor and what I had saved, I could last one semester. I purchased a set of blue Samsonite luggage with my final paycheck and started to unload my closet and drawers. It seemed strange to be leaving home, and I felt so unsure of myself. *What will college by like? Will I pass college courses? Will I like my roommate? Will I have enough money?*

In his next few letters, Jim expressed an understanding of my new situation.

(January 23) My dearest Sue, I'm not worried about your going out with other guys. I expect you to. Have a good time, but remember you belong to me. Don't worry about Pat anymore. I'll admit I still loved her until the day we gave you a ride in the van. You hit me at that moment. The night Gary took you home, I knew I wanted you more than I imagined. Keep writing. I get all fouled up inside when I don't hear from you. Love always, Jim

I was certain I was in love with Jim, but his lack of goals was a concern. I continued to push him towards college and, from his letters, I sensed my persistence was beginning to pay off.

My father seemed angry that he'd lose a day's work driving me to Albany. A deadly silence pervaded the car on the three-hour drive. At Newman Hall, a small Catholic dorm on Madison Avenue, the housemother, Mrs. Langley, greeted us and escorted us to my room. Dad and I carried my belongings to a third-floor bedroom, a large private room down the hall from the bathroom. It was sparsely furnished with a desk and chair placed below a dormer window, a single bed, a small dresser, and a rocking chair. Dad left my luggage on the floor, barely said goodbye, and hurried from the room. For a few minutes, I felt grown up. But, lonesomeness for familiar faces and the strangeness of my new surroundings made me question my decision. It was the first time I'd been entirely on my own.

A knock on the door startled me. "Hi and welcome to Newman." The greeting came from a group of fellow students.

"I'm Palma, and this is Gretchen, JoAnne, and Patty. Let us know if you need any help. Dinner's at 5:30, and we have to dress for dinner. No pants are allowed."

We talked for a few minutes, and my jittery stomach began to settle. When they turned to leave, Palma said, "We'll see you at dinner. You can sit with us."

After organizing my clothes, I made my bed. The last thing I unpacked was a beige stuffed dog given to me by a high school girlfriend at my going-away party. I held the dog up and wondered, *What am I supposed to do with this? It's the strangest gift I've ever received. I've never had a stuffed animal before.* I shrugged, leaned it against my pillow, and sat at the desk to write Jim.

(February 1) My darling Jim, The roads were terrible today. We finally got here at 3:30. I had to laugh at Romeo on the trip. He kept saying I was going to be lonesome here. I think he hated to see me go. I went downtown last night & bought a green bedspread, red and white checked curtains and a red pillow. Write soon to my new address. Love & kisses, Sue

That evening as I was preparing to turn in, I heard singing from male voices. It seemed to be coming from outside. I ran to the window, pushed it open, and stuck my head into the frosty air. A group of fraternity brothers had gathered in the snow below my room and were serenading me. I couldn't stifle my smile as I listened.

Maybe this was the right decision after all.

I waved, thanked them for their welcome, closed the window, and laid my exhausted head down. I knew the next day would be filled with surprises as I learned the ropes of navigating my way around campus and adjusted to college life.

Within days, I heard stories of panty raids—the current form of college prank whereby large numbers of male students would sneak into girls' dorm rooms and steal panties. The craze started in 1948 and spread to college campuses across the country. Often girls hung out their windows and threw their panties at the boys. Newman Hall was such a small dorm (only 55 girls) that a panty raid was hardly worth the effort.

> *(February 2) Dearest Sue, You give me confidence I never would have. You've helped in squaring me away. I wish I had the confidence you have. You have something that conquered me. I wish I had realized that long ago when you had that crush on me. I think I'll talk Ted into the idea of going to school. Two heads are better than one. I always liked school. I used to enjoy the idea of turning in one of the best. Love and kisses, Jim*

While I was adjusting to college and homework assignments, Jim was handling other assignments—like the night he met Chesty Puller. Lieutenant General Chesty Puller was a BIG DEAL at the time. He was the most decorated U.S. Marine in history, but Jim had never met him. There was a huge event at Camp Legeune, and Jim was posted at the entrance with instructions from his commanding officer. "Don't let anyone in unless they have the necessary pass."

"Yes, sir." Jim saluted.

Shortly, a man in civilian clothes approached.

"Excuse me, sir. Your pass?"

"I don't have a pass, Sergeant," the civilian said.

"I have strict orders. No one without a pass will be allowed into the event."

The man was irate and proceeded to give Jim a tongue-lashing. Jim had his orders. He wasn't going to be pushed around.

An officer inside heard the fracas. "Sergeant Savard. You may allow him entry even without a pass. The man is Chesty Puller."

At the end of the evening, Chesty apologized. "I congratulate you, Sergeant. You did exactly as you should have done. You followed orders."

Following orders and regulations while in the Corps kept Jim out of trouble except on one occasion when he narrowly escaped a tour in the Camp Lejeune brig. He couldn't account for one rifle.

"It's simply missing, and I don't know what happened to it, sir," he told his commanding officer.

A military judge questioned him at length, and then sent Jim out of the room. He smoked and paced in the hallway until the judge ruled.

"You're relieved from all charges, Sergeant Savard. After questioning you, we realize you have neither stolen nor sold the rifle. Someone else got into the supply area and took the rifle. Case dismissed."

In spite of Jim's grumbling about the Corps, it was a time for him to grow up. It gave him a home, a job. a paycheck, structure, and the building blocks for his life. More importantly, the Corps helped Jim develop his NEVER QUIT MINDSET that he desperately needed in his later years.

Although I had a sense that Jim struggled with low self-esteem, I never realized the depths of his inferiority complex.

> *(February 7) My darling Sue, I can't remember the sound of your voice. When I get out of here, I'm never going to let you out of my sight. Maybe you've already noticed, I don't have the guts to face facts, the world and life. I have a complex, an inferior one to be truthful. The doctor told me that. I run myself down. I think everyone is better than myself in every way. You make me feel good when you say I am the only one you want. There is no doubt in my mind as to what I would want to do. Be an athletic director but that may be out for sure. I hope we can manage things together. I love you, Jim*

> *(February 10) Honey. I don't know why on earth you feel inferior. To me you're perfect. Please don't keep feeling that way. It makes me sad when I think you're not happy. I miss you so much. All my love and kisses, Sue*

A more immediate worry was my diminishing money supply.

> *(February 15) Dear Jim, I'm tired of knocking myself out to get money to come to school. In the first place, I know Dad can afford it. He's just a little miserly though. It nearly killed him to give me enough money to eat for the next month. Write soon, Sue*

Because we had so little contact, we agreed that while I was in college and he was in the Marines, we could date others. Even though he professed to be okay with that arrangement, he was concerned he'd be receiving another *Dear John* letter. I thought of Jim night and day. He didn't believe my sincerity. I rarely missed a day of writing, but mail arrived sporadically at the base. Sometimes he didn't receive letters for several days and then four or five would arrive at once. At other times, I was swamped trying to stay ahead of homework, term papers, tests, and my part-time secretarial job.

> *(March 1) My darling Jim, I didn't think we were going steady. . you never asked me. . .all you have to say is you don't want me to go out with anyone else and that's the way it will be. I don't want to lose you. I love you, Sue*

> *(March 5) Dearest Sue, I'm sorry for being doubtful Sue, but it's hard to keep my thoughts straight. . . I believe you when you say your dates are just friendly . . but I'm afraid to lose you. I know I never asked you to go steady. I just assumed we were. It's up to you if you go out or not. If we love each other, we should go steady. I love you very, very, very much, Jim*

Making a phone call in 1956 was another challenge. To place a call, Jim first had to reserve a pay phone days in advance. Then, he wrote to inform me of the time and date of his call. For my part, I had to sit near the dorm's pay phone waiting for his call and pray no other student wanted the phone. One twenty-minute call cost Jim $9.28—a large portion of his $35 bi-weekly paycheck.

Periodically, Jim was transferred for maneuvers to Vieques Island, Puerto Rico.

> *(March 8) Dear Sue, I haven't written because my mood is so bad. We are driven nuts all day for some foolish_____ . . . Then, after that, I stand duty in the tent every other night plus standing duty NCO once a week. The chow is rotten and the lines are long. There are water hours here. You*

don't drink during the day and the water is usually off before we have time to get a shower. Then we have to take a G.I bath out of our helmet. There's no beer in the slop chute. We only get five nights off the whole while we are here. To make matters worse, the mail hasn't arrived in 4 days. Have I a good reason to be mad? Love, Jim

As Jim's next leave and his discharge date approached, we were both counting the days on calendars. He applied for a weekend pass in May.

(March 8) My darling Jim, If my calculations are right, it's only 203 more days until discharge. That makes 4,872 hours without you. If you come home on May 5, that's 56 days and 9 hours before I'm with you. That's 1,353 more hours. If you don't get that leave, I'll have to start calculating all over again. Love and kisses, Sue

Although I remembered that he seemed interested when he gave us a ride in the van, it came as a big surprise that I had hooked Jim's heart on that day in July.

(March 10) My darling Sue, I had ideas in my head the first day I saw you when we picked you and the girls up on the boulevard. I really thought to myself, Boy, Sonny is right. She is some gear. . .but the night you went with that LaPorte yo yo really did the trick. I found myself mad and hurt. It wasn't your fault because I didn't have enough sense to ask you out but I decided I would try to get you by letter. Slowly but surely it worked. I love you. Love and kisses, Jim

(March 21) Dear Sue, I filled out my application for Canton and forwarded it to the high school principal for a reference. It cost me $5. That's a lot. If I decide to go, I'm sure I can manage the expenses. The studies will give me trouble. To this

day I can't figure out how I received a state diploma. I must be smart and don't know it. Love forever, Jim

Days were long and tedious in the supply building until Jim found a radio.

(March 26) Dearest Sue, Today we scrounged a broken down radio and repaired it. You don't know how nice it is to hear music again. So many songs remind me of you. Do you like "He" or "Standing on the Corner?" . . . I just saw the name Desiree in a book. The name fascinates me. Our daughter should be named Desiree. Do you like it? Do you still want 7 kids. I hope not. Love always, Jim

From Vieques, phone calls were even more difficult, so he tried to arrange a call through a ham radio operator.

(March 27) Dearest Sue, I'm trying to make arrangements with a ham radio operator to put a call through to you. If I get the call through it will be at noon or 5 p.m. If the radio operator can't get New York, he will connect through North Carolina. The charges will have to be reversed. Only one of us can speak at one time. I'll speak. You'll have to wait till I say over then click the button and speak. Everyone in the states may hear us, but it's the best I can do. Love me as I love you, Jim

Besides counting the days and hours before Jim's discharge, I was also counting calories. I had done the typical *first-year-in-college* stunt of gaining fifteen pounds. I frequently wrote about my struggles with dieting, but he didn't believe me.

(April 4) My honey, I'm on a good diet now. I've really got to lose around 15 lbs. Today I had fruit (65) coffee (40) eggs (200) bread (60) coffee (40)

bread (60) peanut butter (100). Not bad. Boy, I'll really be ashamed to have you see me like I am now. I'll lose it though. Love and kisses, Sue

(April 9) Dear Sue, Gosh Sue. From the sounds of your letters you are making me think you're fat. I'll bet you don't weigh over 120 pounds. I really miss dancing with you, but when we went to the Wash you made me feel like Murray himself. Love always, Jim

When he pulled in front of the dorm, I ran down the sidewalk to greet him and noticed the surprised look on his face. I was the heaviest I had ever been. The floral cotton dirndl skirt made my hips look like *two axe handles across*. Jim kept his thoughts to himself that day. Years later he told me that he couldn't believe his eyes when he saw me waddling down the sidewalk. Jim was never one to appreciate a pleasingly plump figure.

We drove to Tupper Lake for a weekend of visiting relatives, dancing at the Waukesha, and looking at engagement rings. I kept changing my mind about being engaged.

(May 8) My dearest Jim, As soon as I get home, I'm going on a diet. The best I can do here is cut out the sweets. . . . I was so shook up all weekend when you mentioned a ring that I didn't know whether to be happy or sad, but I do know that I was confused. But, I've had time to think and I'm not confused anymore. I'm just happy. Don't forget when you get my ring that I'd like platinum. It will match my watch. Love always, Sue

(May 9) Dear Sue, I was lonesome when I dropped you off at your house. I hated to leave you. I miss dancing with you. You follow my steps better than anyone. . . . I went to the PX today to look at rings. I really want to get engaged this summer. I always planned on getting platinum rings. I'll do

my best to pick out something you'll like. Love and kisses, Jim

(May 12) Dear Sue, About the ring, honey. Well, I was a little confused and hurt. It was a foolish idea. We have much too long to wait . . . but actually we are nearly strangers. We've only been together about 10 days. It seems I don't deserve you. There goes my complex again. I love you, Jim

Although anxious to be discharged, Jim realized he had made a good decision when he enlisted. He said, "Going in the Corps gave me a chance to test my old girlfriend. It also gave me a chance to meet the type of girl I really need."

My savings account was almost empty by the end of the school year. I interviewed for a part-time nanny/housekeeper position.

(May 18) My dearest Jim, Summer school begins July 2 and ends August 24. I have a chance to live with a family. That would take care of my room and board. The house is three miles from school. I get room and board in exchange for some babysitting. I love you, Sue

In June of 1956, I was offered the position and moved into a private home on Harvard Avenue in Albany. The homeowner was a lawyer for New York State; his wife was a stay-at-home mother. They had a thirteen-year-old girl and a nine-year-old boy. The first sign of trouble came on the day I moved in, and their daughter found out I was to share her room. She was indignant that she had to give up one of her dresser drawers to me. I tried not to take offense and tossed it up to her age.

(June 5) My darling Jim, I just finished a big ironing. It took me about four hours. We all get along pretty well. I pray you get your leave. The family will be away on vacation, so I can come to Tupper and be with you for nine days. Did you hear about Evelyn and John? Love, Sue

(June 8) My darling Sue, Yes, Hon—I knew about the Dear John that Evelyn wrote. I knew it was wrong from the start. I just finished reading a book about Felix Mendelssohn. I've changed. Your advice was taken to heart. You seem to be pretty busy at the home. The work isn't too bad though, I don't imagine, because there is no pressure—like at Albany State Pen. In one wk & 1 day I should be home. Love You Forever, Jim

(June 11) Dear Jim, Today I changed the beds, cleaned the refrigerator and still have to do the ironing. The people are the type that are involved in every social club there is. They're wonderful and I think I'm going to like it here a lot. I'm going home to Oneida so pick me up there. Call me as soon as you get to NYC. I'll wait all day Saturday for your call. Bring a bathing suit so we can swim at Coney Beach. Remember the day you threw me in the water. I was all thrilled. Love always, Sue

My duties expanded to include dusting, vacuuming, helping prepare dinner, cleaning up the breakfast and dinner dishes, washing and ironing, and being available every night of the week to baby sit. For this, I shared a bedroom and received $3.50 a week. The ride to school by bus costs $4 a week.

A break from school and nanny duties over the July 4th holiday allowed me an opportunity to head for Tupper Lake. Mary and I were talking one evening when she said, "I don't think Jim is serious. I think he's playing the field."

I was seated on a bench in her living room and wearing a grey dress with a V-neckline, a wide white collar, a matching belt at the waist, and a pleated skirt. I crossed my legs, swung my high-heeled foot back and forth and said, "Oh really. Well, we'll see."

At the end of my visit, Jim and I once again said goodbye. He had a few days of leave before returning to Camp Lejeune.

(July 9) Dear Sue, I have something important to tell you. Friday night, I went out with Luke and Ann, Larry and Nancy and I took Pat out. We were

only out for a few hours and just danced. After, I took her right home. I'm sorry. I hope you don't get mad. It's bothered me since Friday night. You must have received my letter today or you will tomorrow. I can see you now. There will be no smile on your pretty face. I won't blame you. I love you very much, Jim

I couldn't believe my eyes. Why would Jim date his old flame as soon as I left Tupper Lake? I began to question his sincerity.
Maybe Mary is right.

(July 17). Jim, Did you know how much it would hurt me that you would take HER out? She isn't just anybody. How would you feel if I went out with Gary. I thought you were over her. Since we discussed this earlier, I haven't had any dates except those with you. Now it's up to you to decide. Sue

CHAPTER 6 - MOVIN' ON

Added to my stress over Jim's news, my living situation was becoming untenable. My opinion of Mrs. A. had changed. She spent hours volunteering at the Synagogue, playing Mahjong with friends, and knitting. A cleaning woman every other week did a thorough housecleaning. Otherwise, all other household duties and childcare fell upon me.

One evening, I overheard a major argument taking place in their family room. Mr. A. screamed, "You cannot expect one college student and a cleaning woman every other week to do everything that needs to be done around here. Every now and then, you need to do something besides knit and play Mahjong."

At dinnertime, their conversation was barely cordial, and I pretended that I hadn't heard anything. We had just finished eating when the phone rang. I answered. The caller was a friend inviting me to play tennis.

"Mrs. A., if you don't need me this evening, could I leave after supper to play tennis?"

She gave me a withering look. "That will be fine." Her voice sounded like icicles cracking.

"Okay, I'll meet you at the tennis courts in about half an hour." I placed the phone back in its cradle.

"NEVER do that again, Sue. You are not to make any plans without first clearing everything with us in advance."

It was the final straw. I made up my mind to leave as soon as summer school was over, find a part-time secretarial position, and share an apartment with other girls.

> *(July 18) Dear Jim, I can't stand living here any longer. I hunted for five hours for an apartment. Most of them are so crummy I wouldn't let my dog live in them. I can't wait to move. I hate to bring up unpleasant subjects, but are you sure you don't love Pat. You told me before that you were sure, but it seems now that you really weren't. Love, Sue*

> *(July 19). My dearest Sue, The past two weeks haven't been pleasant. I've been smoking two packs of cigarettes a day. I hope I never have another week like the past. I never cheated on you. I guess I bored her to death by talking all evening*

about my girl Suzzie. I love you very, very much,
Jim

(July 19) Dear Jim, Mr. A. tried to talk to me about staying with them through the school year. I am very unhappy here. I feel I'm treated like a poor woman. I have to share a room with their spoiled daughter. The daughter even told me her mother is an ogre and asked why I put up with her. Love, Sue

By late July, the rift had smoothed over, and we were back to joking in our letters.

(July 20, 1956). My dearest Sue, Larry received a box of home-made cookies from Nancy. We chowed down. They were really good. Of course, they don't beat your bacon and eggs. Ha, ha. Just joking. Why don't you come to North Carolina to visit me? Be mine always, Jim

(July 31) My darling Jim, Mrs. A. wants me to do an ironing again tonight. Honest honey, she's driving me to drink. I'll be glad to get out of here. Delores and I went apartment hunting tonight and found one for the right price on Madison Avenue. It costs $45 or $50 a month. We can have it after September 1. That means I only have 4 more weeks to suffer with Mrs. A. You know when I first got to college I didn't know for sure if I wanted to be a teacher. For the last few weeks, the thought of going to Canton and being a secretary made me decide I do want to be a teacher. I miss you, Love & kisses forever, Sue

(August 6) My sweet Sue, Honey, I'm sorry if the letters aren't coming but I'll square away after this field problem—if I'm alive. We have to march 10 miles on the way back with rifle, helmet &

equipment. . . . I'll give you all the scoop about the trip here and what there is to offer when I call you Thursday night. All my love and kisses forever, Jim

(August 15) My dearest Jim, I've made all the arrangements for my trip. I leave Albany on August 24 at 5:12 p.m. Arrive New York 8:05 p.m. Lv. New York 9:45 p.m. Arrive Rocky Mt. NC on the 25th at 8:25 a.m. I can't wait to see you. Make sure you're waiting for me. Love and kisses, Sue

The idea of traveling by myself out of New York State all the way to North Carolina left me jumpy as a frog for days. I didn't know what to pack or what to wear on the trip. Finally, I chose black corduroy Bermuda shorts, a white blouse, knee-high socks, and loafers and pulled my hair into a ponytail. All of my other clothes were squeezed into one suitcase. I rushed through my final exams and left Albany at 5:12 p.m. on August 24, 1956 headed for a new adventure. Farmlands, hills, and small towns along the Hudson River sped by as the train whistled towards New York City. By 10 p.m. I was in Penn Station, scouring boards to find the correct platform for the next leg of my journey. My head spun around, and I watched people scampering for their connections. I purchased a hot dog and cup of coffee for dinner. Once I found my train, I elbowed through the crowded aisles until I spotted an empty seat in the first car.

Then, I glanced around. I was the only white person in the car. Suddenly, my adventure took on a different tone. On the trip, I was to become aware of life in the Deep South in the 50s. I would also learn some lessons about myself. I was frightened. I can't explain why I was frightened as no one bothered me, made any rude remarks, brushed against me, or even acknowledged my presence. Nevertheless, I was nervous. For the first time in my life, I was a minority.

By 11 p.m., I was hoping to fall asleep, but the overhead lights were glaring. I turned to the woman next to me. "Excuse me. When do they turn the lights out?"

She heaved a sigh. "They stay on all night."

The train began its slow chug out of the station. I scrunched back into my seat trying to get into a comfortable position but couldn't fall asleep. When a white conductor came to check my ticket, I motioned to him with a crooked finger and whispered, "Are there any other white people on this train?"

"In the last car, there are three."

I picked up my suitcase, headed for the last car, and settled down next to the other white passengers.

After a sleepless night, I exited the train in Rocky Mountain, North Carolina. The oppressive heat and humidity felt like a blast furnace had erupted on my body. I looked around. Jim wasn't there. Tears were dancing on my lids ready to pour out at the slightest provocation. I didn't have a way to contact him and didn't know what to do. I was famished, needed a hug, and a shoulder to cry on. Fear was rapidly turning to anger. *If he is so anxious for me to visit, why isn't he here?* I paced up and down the platform looking for a familiar face. No sign of Jim.

I took my suitcase and headed for the nearest ladies' room. *Why are people staring at me?* Further compounding my ignorance, I was in the room with a sign "Colored Only" over the door.

An hour later when Jim arrived, he knew by the frantic look on my face that he was in deep trouble. He put his arms around my waist and pulled me to him. The skin on his arms was sweat sticky from the humidity, but I didn't care. I nuzzled into the security of his chest, and my anger slowly drifted away.

"I'm sorry, Hon. I couldn't get here sooner. Luke's car wouldn't start, and we had to get it jumped. Then, I got hassled by my commanding officer to do a few more chores. I drove as fast as I dared. You must be hungry. Let's get a bite to eat."

We stopped at a nearby diner and cuddled close together in a booth. When our order of hamburgers with a dill pickle and soda arrived, there was a strange looking item on the plate. "What in the world is this?" I asked and pushed the goop around with a fork.

"It's grits. They're made from corn." Jim put a generous chunk of butter and salt and pepper on them. "You'll have to learn to like grits if you're going to stay here for a week." He scooped a bit of grits onto the tines of my fork and placed it in my mouth.

I ran the gob around the roof of my mouth with my tongue. "Not bad. I could get used to these."

While we ate, we giggled and listened to the cadence of the lazy southern drawl and the lilt of the language of people in nearby booths. Their vowels slurred along their words. Afterwards, Jim drove me to an old motel near the base where he had reserved a room for me. Each day, I sunbathed, read books, and waited for Jim. After work, he used Luke's car to pick me up. We walked around Beaufort with arms entwined and admired the old homes, saw movies and ate popcorn, went out to dinner and to the beach.

On Sunday, we went for a picnic and swim at a lake near a small, white clapboard church. As we lay on a blanket sunning ourselves, I said,

"Listen to the sound of that beautiful hymn coming from the church." We closed our eyes and eavesdropped on the church choir belting out "Swing Low Sweet Chariot." The singing was getting closer, and people from the church suddenly surrounded us. I watched fascinated as a number of them walked into the water. They were fully dressed in suits, ties, shoes, and dresses.

"What're they doin?" I asked Jim.

"They're getting baptized."

The pastor raised his face to the heavens, placed his hand on a man's forehead, recited some prayers, and immersed the parishioner in the lake. I was intrigued. It was so different from the solemn baptisms at our Catholic churches.

My week's vacation in the south was over too quickly, and Jim and I were once again parting. He gave me a quick kiss. "Have a good trip back and write soon. Let me know when you get home." As if he were in a hurry to leave, he walked away. I knew from his letters that Jim hated goodbyes and never lingered.

I felt lonely before the train even began to move. I watched from the train window, hoping to catch one last glimpse, but Jim was already on his way back to the base. I slept part of the way back to Oneida, and within a few days, left for Albany to begin my fall semester.

On that trip, I had learned some lessons that stayed with me a long time. I gained a new appreciation of what it felt like to be a minority. I thought of my African American friends in high school. They were just accepted as part of our group. I never considered them different in any way, so why did I react the way I did? I had been alarmed by a new situation for no reason. For the first time, I realized how unsophisticated I was and that all of the United States wasn't just like my hometown. People, languages, and customs were different. How could I have studied civics in high school, watched news reports of sheriffs turning dogs and hoses on African American people for drinking from the wrong fountain, and still been so oblivious to conditions in the South? I came home with a new understanding of segregation and intolerance that no civics class could have taught me.

(September 5) My darling Jim, Well, I finally made it home. I got in Oneida around 3:30 p.m. yesterday. I didn't have much trouble on the way back. I only got about four hours sleep but it was better than nothing. As always, I met some interesting people. Write soon. Love always, Sue

(September 17) My dearest Sue, Guess what. The other day the Battery Clerk finished all my papers to release me from this outfit. Including today, just eleven more days. I have 9 hours and 15 minutes left on this day. I've just completed my physical. My blood work, chest x-ray, dental check are all okay. Starting Tuesday I'm relieved of all duty. Love and kisses, Jim

It was only two more weeks before Jim's discharge date. He didn't know what he was going to do after service, but he knew he wanted to get out. On their drive home, Jim and Luke stopped in New York City to attend a fellow Marine's stag party. They didn't realize the venue of the party was a strip club.

Luke said, "When we got in the place, we went to the bar to order a beer. When the floorshow started, floodlights came on, and the strippers came out. That was one big surprise, and we were in shock."

In the 1950s, professional strippers weren't part of the Tupper Lake scene.

On Sunday morning, September 30, 1956, Jim came from New York to Albany to see me. I was returning to my apartment from church. When I opened the door, he was sitting in an old green chair in our living room. His broad grin showed how ecstatic he was to be out of the Corps. I was happy that, at long last, we could see each other frequently—I thought.

It wasn't to be.

We were back to corresponding daily, and Jim was as lonesome as ever. His high school friends had moved out of town, gone to college, had careers, or married.

(October 16) Dearest Sue, I didn't start work on the Seaway on Monday. They aren't hiring any longer. I've been working in the shop. I've decided to do some more looking at rings. I hope to make my decision soon. I know you would like to help me pick it out, but I want to do it alone. I don't know why, but I'd like to have it that way. If you have a chance to come up, please do. I miss you. It won't be long before we won't have to say goodbye. Love always, Jim

He and Luke kept busy bowling, shooting pool, visiting friends and family. Still, Jim didn't have any goals.

(November 29) Dearest Sue, I'm getting sick of being alone all the time. Right now I'm the biggest lost soul in the world. Saturday is the big day. I'm afraid Sue that I don't have the smarts to pass the college entrance exam. I've forgotten everything I knew. Wish me luck, Jim

(December 1) My darling Jim, Good luck on your exam. I know you can do well. You've got a lot more upstairs than you give yourself credit for. Don't worry about getting into school. I have a lot of faith in you. You don't give yourself credit for anything. Love always, Sue

(December 4) My darling Jim, Just a short note to tell you that I love you. Don't worry about getting into Potsdam. I know you'll make it. Love always, Sue

To my dismay, his high school sweetheart was back in the picture. Sometimes she called the shop and asked him to come to her house to talk. I was jealous when I heard of the phone calls. After our date one night, Jim pulled the car in front of Mary and Sonny's house. I had been seething inside all evening. I finally said, "Jim, you have to make up your mind what you want. If you want your old girlfriend back, then go for it, and I'll be out of the picture. I am not going to play second fiddle to her. It's up to you to make a decision."

His head bent down as he listened. "We're just friends, Sue. I've already made the decision, and you're the one I want."

I hoped with all my heart that he was telling the truth.

(December 12) Dear Sue, I finished all my shopping yesterday and last night. I bought the rings. Everyone I've shown them to says that they are pretty. I only hope you like them as much as everyone else. I miss you. I guess I'll just waste some

more time at the movies tonight. All my love and kisses, Jim

Christmas Eve, 1956: We sat by the Christmas tree at my home in Oneida enjoying the quiet. Everyone had gone to bed. Jim's hands shook when he took the solitaire engagement ring from its box, slipped it on my finger, and proposed. I held my hand up turning it this way and that watching the lights of the tree sparkle off the diamond. I loved the ring. "Yes," I said and planted a kiss on his lips.

When my father came down to breakfast the following morning, I held my left hand in front of his face. "Look at this, Dad."

"What's that supposed to mean?"

"It means Jim and I are engaged."

"Humph." He sat down to his newspaper and breakfast.

After the excitement of our engagement settled and the holiday wrappings were tossed, it was time for Jim to return home. Although closer in miles, it was still difficult to spend time together.

(January 4, 1957) My darling Jim, I'm sorry I didn't write sooner but I've been so busy. I just wish you could be here with me. I hope we'll always be as close as we are now. The one thing I always dreaded about marriage is that it seems that after a couple is married for a few years, they get further and further apart. I hope that never happens to us. If and when I get a better paying job, maybe I can send you some money and we can order some furniture from Sonny. I could probably send $5 a week and you could add $5 and put it in the bank. I love you, Sue

(January 17) Dear Sue, A man from Canton ATI went to see Mr. Christie, the guidance counselor at the H.S. He received a telegram from Albany. It must have been the results from the entrance exam. I can't figure out why they would notify me by telegram. I probably flunked with such a low score they just wanted to let the H.S. know how stupid I was. I love you very much, Jim

(February 4) My dearest honey, Remember the rug cleaning business I spoke to you about. Luke and I have been doing a lot of research and writing. If a partnership like this is successful, we would be all set. Luke, Sonny and I went to Watertown to see the Duraclean rep. We checked everything out books, equipment, methods and asked a lot of questions. We're quite sure of starting soon. Love me as I love you, Jim

(February 11) Dearest Jim, What a day. As soon as I stepped my foot in the door at work, the big shot was calling me for dictation. I rushed in and tried to take down two pages of shorthand in between his mumble, sputtering, coughing, laughing, etc. Then Mr. Spencer called me and gave me a few letters plus I still had three on the book that Mr. Crocetta dictated at 8:45 last night. Then Mr. Silverman started yelling for me to hurry with another letter. Actually, no one yells. They're all nice but just in a hurry. I'm very lonesome. Maybe writing this letter will make me feel better. I've been thinking about the last year. I suffered through three long weeks of boredom before I saw you again. Then Thanksgiving vacation. I ate so much turkey I felt like one. The Junior Prom came before that didn't it? At the Junior prom, I was so proud of you. I was glad that you hadn't ordered my corsage because I had so much fun running around looking for one. Remember the fun we had shopping in Lake Placid in December. I was so proud to have you meet me at the train station. Remember how excited I was when you came home in May. Janeann and Palma had to pack for me I was so excited. I still have the crazy calendar I had on my door last year. And you drove 7 hours to get down here for the weekend before Christmas. It was a wonderful surprise. I was so thrilled to be going to North Carolina that it's a wonder I *passed my last two exams. Then at Christmas we were sitting in the living room in Oneida me in my PJs and Dad talking your ear off. I was hurt when you went hunting and then came back and said you were going out again. I'll never forget how nervous I was about my ring. When I got back to Albany, I just couldn't stay away from you but had to catch the next bus to Tupper Lake. I giggled to myself all the way to Glens Falls because I felt so sneaky. I feel better already after all this reminiscing. Love always, Sue*

(February 14) My honey, The long letter I just received was the nicest you have ever written. It was sweet, funny, serious and everything wrapped into one. I've never read such a nice letter. I love you, Jim

Jim borrowed Sonny's car on a few occasions and visited me in Albany. One night, while the car was parked outside my apartment, a drunk driver missed the corner, smashed into the side of the car, and left the scene. Our nosey neighbors, whose main entertainment was watching from their front window for any activity, got the driver's license plate number. Jim stayed an extra day to straighten out the mess.

(March 19) My sweetheart, I went to city court and talked to a lawyer. They have the guilty party. They said we could collect two or three hundred for our inconvenience if we don't press charges. This will be a hardship for Sonny and Mary. I drove the car home, but I had to tie the door shut with rope. Love me as I love you, Jim

(March 26) Dear Jim, I did talk to a lawyer and he said the longer my back hurts, the more money I'll get. I think it's going to hurt for a long time. Ha, Ha. Love, Sue

We were both upset when the check of $850 to Sonny and Mary wasn't enough to pay for another vehicle.

In anticipation of their new business venture, Luke and Jim rented an apartment in Saratoga, NY in the spring of 1957. "I don't have enough to pay Luke for my share of the investment. I need another $400," Jim said.

"I'll lend it to you. Once you're doing well, you can pay me back."

(April 12, 1957) Dearest Sue, We found an apartment on Main Street in Saratoga over a clothing store. We are going to work at the State Street Nursery to pick up some money until we get things going. The state pays $1.31 an hour. We're working an extra eight hours on Sunday. We've rented an old shop for our business. Our letterhead, calling cards and postcards arrived and I've squared our gear away and mixed all the concentrates. Please love me, Jim

The loan was never repaid. Over our many years of marriage, I often reminded him of that loan. He assured me, "While I haven't paid back the $400, by being married to you, I have paid plenty."

Luke and Jim tried to get the business off to a good start, but it was obvious that they couldn't make a decent living. When the rug cleaning business failed, Luke got a job driving a delivery truck for a local beer distributor. Jim continued his job at the nursery working with the local winos and drifters, pulling seedling trees, and bundling them for shipment. It was the lowest form of work and didn't do much to build his self-confidence. However, it did convince him he didn't want to do menial work all of his life.

By the end of the spring semester, we were working out the details of our wedding, but he still didn't value himself.

(June 15) My dear sweet Sue, I love you very much. Even though I'm worthless, mean, moody and many other bad faults, stick with me. Love, Jim

(June 18) My darling, Why are you always degrading yourself? You said some awful things about yourself. You aren't mean, moody or anything else that you said... If you were, I

wouldn't love you. . .I wish I knew what to say to make you feel better. I love you, Sue

I was 19 and Jim was 23. Once engaged, we squirreled away every spare cent for our wedding. Sunday August 25, between summer school and my fall semester, was a perfect day for the ceremony. We'd have time for a short honeymoon with a few days left over to settle our apartment. The thought that I was a too young for marriage never entered my mind. I had been on my own and supporting myself since I was seventeen. By January 1958, I would be a nineteen-year-old college senior and almost ready to begin my teaching career.

We began preparations for our wedding. One afternoon, I went to a bridal shop in Albany to try on wedding gowns. I slipped into an assortment of gowns and practiced walking down the aisle. With each dress, I twirled in front of the mirror and made an assessment. This one looks awful on me; this one is beautiful but over my budget; this one is too tight. Finally, I pulled one more gown from the rack and fell in love with the stunning frothy creation. When I put it on and looked in the mirror, I felt like a princess wrapped in white cotton candy. Made of organza over taffeta, it had a full skirt decorated with lace daisies, a sweetheart neckline, cap sleeves, and a short train. I twirled around and hummed "Autumn Leaves"—our song—the song we'd dance to at our wedding. The under $100 price was right. With a $20 down payment, the store agreed to put the gown on layaway

In June, Jim received a letter from Evelyn asking him to be her best man when she married Larry Willett on August 25. My face turned ghostly white, and I squinched my eyes to prevent tears from escaping. My voice quivered, "How can they do that? Don't they know that's the date we've selected? Are they just being mean? Whatever we do, I don't want a double wedding."

Jim was equally upset but kept a cooler head, "Don't cry, Sue. We'll schedule a date in November. That'll give us a little more time to prepare and save money."

By August, I was over my snit and glad we had more time to plan our nuptials, but the gown I'd selected earlier wasn't right for a fall wedding. I called the store and blubbered to the store manager, "I have to cancel the order for the gown I have on lay-away."

The manager was incensed. "Well, you really can't do that. We've already put it aside for you. You'll lose your deposit."

"You don't seem to understand," I pleaded. "There isn't going to be a wedding."

CHAPTER 7 - LIVING ON LOVE

Reflections: He had many nicknames—Sarge, Eagle Eye, Mr. Savard, Mr. Self-Discipline, The Social Director, The Renaissance Man, Jimmy, and even Mr. Pain in the Ass. Taken together, the names form a mosaic of a man named Jim—my husband and best friend.

******

November, over Thanksgiving break, was our new wedding date. Jim found work in Zig Kryevsky's upholstery shop, and we worked out a budget. His salary of $40 a week and my part-time job as a legal secretary meant things would be tight. Yet, we felt we could get by.

I still needed a gown. Over coffee at a local hangout, I commiserated with friends. "I could make my own gown and save money, but I don't have a sewing machine."

A married man from my class came to my rescue. "You can come to our apartment and use Jean's."

In between classes and work, I spent every spare minute in their apartment cutting, sewing, snipping, and fitting.

"We've never heard that machine buzz so fast," Jean said. "If you don't slow down, it's going to take off."

The satin brocade gown I was making from a Butterick pattern was plain and disappointing compared to the summer one I'd ordered. My design had a round neckline, a princess waistline, and a full skirt that required a hoop. The long sleeves with six small covered buttons ended in a point at my hand. To keep costs down, Mary donated her shoulder length-wedding veil and Janet, the hoop for my skirt. My father contributed $250 towards the event, but beyond that, we were on our own. Jim's parents were too poor to contribute financially.

We also needed a car. We pooled our money and purchased our first car—a 1951 gray Dodge two-door standard shift sedan—costing $450. I wrote: "I wired the money to you today. I didn't have enough money to pay for wire transfer, so they deducted $2.75 from the $150. I hope we're doing the right thing."

He responded. "I got the car tonight and called Mrs. Fortune for insurance. The car payments are $28.16 a month, and the insurance is $74 a year, but we have to have a car."

There was a slight problem. "I don't have a license and haven't driven since I took driver's ed in high school."

"That's okay. I'll teach you. You'll pick it up again."

When Jim gave me refresher-driving lessons, his face took on the hue of a fire engine, but he held his tongue until one afternoon when he came within seconds of exploding. I had a death grip on the steering wheel while stopped on a hill waiting for the light to turn green. I was deep in concentration.

Think Sue. Stay calm. It's all about timing. Move the right foot from the accelerator and press the brake to slow down; press the clutch to the floor with the left foot; shift into first; put on the signal light; slowly release the clutch until you feel it hold; move the right foot from the brake to the accelerator; press down.

STALL.

Several more times I tried, and each time the car jerked backwards and stalled. With the light going from green to red twice and the line of honking cars behind me, my stomach was in knots. Jim bit his lip to control his temper.

"Would you like me to come around and take over?"

"NO. I've got to learn to do this."

I gave one last effort to getting all the levers and pedals coordinated. The car jerked and bounced ahead. Jim pushed his hands against the dashboard for support, and we squealed around the corner. After a few more weeks of practice, I passed my driver's test. At long last, we didn't have to borrow anyone's car and could see each other on weekends.

Our next hurdle was finding an affordable apartment in Saratoga. At each one we visited, we were asked, "Are you a Saratogian?"

"What does that have to do with anything?" I asked. "The landlords don't seem to care about security deposits or steady jobs. If we weren't born and bred in Saratoga, they won't rent to us."

We kept searching until mid October, when we found a third-floor walkup above a clothing store on the corner of Main and Caroline Street. The owner agreed to hold it until we were married. The three-room apartment had hardwood floors throughout, including in the small kitchen. Our bedroom was on the left of a long hallway that led to a living room in the front, where two windows overlooked Main Street. It wasn't fancy, but we were thrilled with our selection—except for the kitchen floor.

"Who wants a hardwood floor in the kitchen? " I asked. "It's too dark. Once we move in, I'm going to ask the manager to cover the hardwood with some nice aqua and white linoleum squares."

(October 29) Sue, I would like to make final arrangements for the wedding. Friday when you leave for Saratoga, try to leave as soon as possible so that we can get squared away, eat, and leave for Tupper as early as possible. We'll be hopping

this weekend, I'm afraid. Well, it's worth it don't you think? When 2:30 p.m. arrives on November 24, 1957, I will be the happiest man alive even if we are poor. Love me always, Jim

An early storm hit northeastern New York that evening. The snow was wet and sticky. Few other cars were on the road as we drove from Saratoga to Tupper Lake. Jim drove cautiously, but driving was treacherous. Heavy snow covered the tree branches on either side of the highway, bending them into a white bridal canopy over the road. I was exhausted and snuggled close to Jim, resting my head on his shoulder (no seat belts in those days). It took hours to reach Tupper Lake, but we made it and spent the weekend finalizing all wedding plans.

Leon and Sonny surprised us. They had been busy building a couch and chair as a wedding gift. It was Scandinavian in design—not fancy—but functional. The base and back were made of plywood covered in thick foam rubber and upholstered in beige nylon frieze. Round, narrow legs screwed into the base for easy removal. Wrought iron arms with small arm resting pads also screwed into the plywood. My mother donated an old swivel rocker to the cause, and Sonny covered it in light green brocade. Leon salvaged another chair and upholstered it in dark brown Naugahyde. I purchased my sister Janet's blonde bedroom set, and my father gave us a black and white enamel table and kitchen chairs from one of his rental units.

Preparations for our momentous day were almost complete. The flowers, vocalist's song choices, and menu were selected. Everything was ready—except my gown. I was running Jean's sewing machine at super-sonic speed.

"I may be hemming my dress while I'm walking down the aisle," I joked to classmates.

School, work, and sewing kept me so busy that November sneaked up on me, and we were in Tupper Lake for our nuptials. The night before we married, I felt fear, joy, excitement, and concern all at the same time. To complicate matters, I was sick: coughing and sneezing, and when I swallowed, my throat felt like razors.

"What if I'm sick tomorrow for the wedding and on our honeymoon?" I complained to Mary.

"Here. Suck on these lozenges and gargle with salt water. That should help."

I did, and it did.

That night, thoughts ran through my mind as I struggled to sleep. I was tense and my nerves tight as piano wire. *Maybe I'm making a mistake. Am I too young? Should I wait until I graduate? Will we have enough money to live on? What am I thinking? TOMORROW'S THE WEDDING.*

In the morning, Jim came to the attic bedroom at Mary and Sonny's home to collect my luggage. He was wearing jeans and a plaid woolen shirt. With one look at him, all doubt vanished. My jitters, anxiety, and indecision were forgotten. I knew marrying him was the right thing to do.

My pulse raced and my hands shook when I dressed. I pulled a pearl necklace and matching earrings from a box and secured them on my neck and ears. I slid the Marine Corps garter on my leg for good luck. My gown and hoop hanging in the corner looked like a puffy cloud, but I hated the gown. I slipped it over my head, closed the side zipper, and smoothed the skirt over the hoop. When I looked in the mirror, I imagined the summer wedding dress I had originally selected and visualized how beautiful it would have looked on me. I forced those thoughts from my brain and headed for my father's car.

The day was cold, snowing, and gloomy when he drove me to the church. I exited his car and wet snow oozed over my white high-heeled sandals and in between my toes. I sloshed up the church steps. Most of the bridal party was waiting in the vestibule. My bouquet of an orchid encircled in white mums and Mary's of rust and gold mums lay on a table near the entrance. Mary looked stunning in a gold knee-length satin dress. But, where was Nancy, my bridesmaid and college friend? Randy, our flower girl, arrived with Gladys and Leon. She wore a floor length dress trimmed with rosebuds. Her strawberry blond curls bounced, and her small feet slapped against the flooring as she ran into the center aisle and announced in a loud voice, "Nancy just fell in the snow," sending muffled chuckles rippling through the church. The front of Nancy's satin gown was soaked, but she laughed it off as part of the day's adventure.

When the vocalist, Margaret Larkin, began to sing, I straightened my shoulders and gripped my father's arm. I peered from under my veil and forced myself to look directly down the aisle into Jim's eyes. In his black tux and carefully gelled hair, he stood ramrod straight. His eyes were shining and locked on me. I felt self-conscious during the endless walk past the staring rows of eyes, but when I stood next to him and put my arm through his, it felt so right.

At two p.m. on Sunday, November 24, 1957, we stood under a narrow white arch decorated with ferns and white flowers and exchanged vows at the Romanesque Holy Name Catholic Church in Tupper Lake. I felt dazed, as if I were watching the ceremony play out in front of me, until Jim slipped a plain, platinum wedding band on my finger and the priest pronounced us husband and wife. Then it was real. Jim squeezed my hand, and we turned. Guests clapped, light bulbs flashed, and a broad smile spread across my lips. Cold air rushing into the vestibule made goose bumps pucker on our arms and legs while we stood in the receiving line. People hurried from the church to the confines of their cars and honked and slid along the snow-covered roads to the Waukesha Grill.

The Waukesha Grill was a long, one-story log cabin with red trimmed fascia boards and windows. Jim held the door for me. We stepped in from the bone-numbing cold, and the crackle and smell of a wood fire burning in the large fieldstone fireplace welcomed us. Behind the bar, pictures of the town's servicemen were scotch taped to a large mirror. The bartender waved his arm in our direction. "Congratulations, Eagle Eye." Jim's blue eyes danced at the familiar name.

A few of our guests were already seated to the left of the entrance at a half circle booth covered in red leather. They were warming up with coffee and mixed drinks.

Our bridal party lined up. Jim trailed his fingers across my back and pulled me close for a quick kiss on the cheek. It seemed like such a short time ago that I was walking into the Riverside for Mary's reception, never dreaming that I would wed Jim less than four years later.

"Ladies and gentlemen. Please welcome Mr. and Mrs. James Savard."

Guests cheered and beat spoons against their drink glasses, signaling us to kiss.

"And now for the attendants, Mr. and Mrs. Sonny Savard and Ms. Nancy Catalfamo and Dick Savard. How about a nice round of applause, folks."

We all moved into the center of the room. White cloths covered the tables surrounding the dance floor, and the bandstand, made to look like a drum, was located at the far end of the room. Murals of Indian scenes painted by Ray Jackman, a famous local Adirondack artist, decorated the sidewalls. Jim and I held hands as we circulated and thanked people for sharing in our special day.

Soon the bandleader announced, "If the bridal party will please be seated, our waitresses are ready to begin serving."

The scratch of chairs being pulled out and a hum of noise floated overhead as people chatted, dishes clattered, and waitresses served.

Our wedding and reception were modest. Many of today's customs weren't expected in the 1950s. There were no favors, expensive linens, gifts for the wedding party, or rehearsal dinner. Even so, at $1.25 per plate for chicken ala king dinner for one hundred people, we were still stretching our budget.

Helen Bigrow, the local newspaper's photographer, earned $8 to shoot eight black and white pictures. Our legs pressed together under the table as we leaned on either side of our wedding cake for one shot. She took a few pictures of our bridal party, and one of us with our parents. Then she left.

From old to young, people in the 1950s loved to dance to live music. We had been frugal in planning our wedding, but refused to skimp on the band. It had to be the Waukesha band.

No words needed to be spoken when we heard the opening chords of "Autumn Leaves." The music filled the crowded room. Jim took my hand and guided me into the center of the dance floor. He slid his arm around my waist, and I snuggled my cheek against the softness of his tux. We danced as if no one was watching and let the song move our bodies and feet. For the first time in my life, I felt protected and cherished.

Couples, ignoring the snowstorm, partied and jitterbugged until the dance floor hummed and throbbed under their feet. By seven o'clock when we left for our honeymoon, snow was still falling. Driving was difficult, and the roads were slick. Jim drove as far as the Breezy Acres Motel in Malone before the roads became impassable.

In the morning, I drew the curtains back and glanced out upon drifts of powdery snow. "The roads look plowed, Jim. I think we can continue to Montreal. Let's have breakfast in the motel restaurant before we head out. I wonder if anyone will even suspect we're newlyweds."

We'd been too excited during our reception to eat, so we attacked our plates of bacon, eggs, home fries, toast, and coffee. Our shy and foolish smiles gave us away. When the owner brought our check, he said, "Have a wonderful life together."

So much for traveling incognito.

Our two-day honeymoon in Montreal brought our savings to rock bottom. We were exploring the city when I noticed a poster.

"Stop the car, Jim. I want to run across the street and read that poster." On my return, I said, "The *Firebird* ballet is being performed at eight tonight. I'm not familiar with it, but if it's ballet, I know I'll love the performance. Let's use our last bit of money to go."

Jim probably didn't care if he ever saw a ballet but pretended enthusiasm. Did he like the performance? I don't know, but he was kind enough to act as if it were fantastic. That was the beginning of getting Jim out of his comfort zone and expanding his world.

Four days after our wedding, we were in Saratoga celebrating our first Thanksgiving together. Determined to impress my new husband with my culinary skills, I planned a full dinner, even though I had rarely cooked anything. I got out my new <u>Betty Crocker's Picture Cook Book</u>

and skimmed through the section on roasting a turkey. The easy instructions and picture of a fully cooked turkey labeled "A Handsome Turkey All Ready To Be Served" gave me the courage to tackle the task. *How hard can this be?*

Deciding how large a bird, whether fresh or frozen, and what brand to buy was a new experience. I finally selected a small, fresh turkey—about twelve pounds—and returned to our apartment. Around noon, I added salt, pepper, and a touch of sage to the carcass and placed it in a cake pan—my only container large enough. My girlfriend Carol arrived just as I pulled the golden brown turkey from the oven and centered it on a platter. I was smug when I placed the platter, surrounded by bowls of mashed potatoes, dressing, squash, and cranberries, on our black and white enamel table.

"Betty Crocker's got nothin on me. This bird is perfect," I said and waited with much anticipation for Jim's approval.

Jim sharpened his carving knife and took one cut of the breast whereupon a soggy, gray bag of slimy parts oozed onto the platter.

"What the heck is that?" I asked.

"It seems you haven't quite bested Betty C yet," Jim said. "Those are the gizzards. You're supposed to use them to make gravy." He sensed my embarrassment and leaned over to give me a peck on the cheek. "Don't feel bad, Sue. It's going to taste great."

"Well, who would guess they'd stick all that junk under the neck skin?" Maybe that was the beginning of me getting out of my comfort zone.

Fifty-two years later, while on a trip with Carol, we both had a belly laugh when she reminded me of that incident.

In the next few days, I unpacked our wedding gifts. For my first task, I organized our linen closet.

"Honey, come look at the linen closet."

I forgot he was an ex-Marine. I was expecting praise.

"You don't have all the single folds to the front."

"Huh? What's a single fold?"

From his Marine Corps training, Jim impressed me by patiently demonstrating exactly how to organize linens. After his years of being raised in a cluttered, disorganized home, he relished a clean house and order in his life. For the remaining fifty-two years of our marriage, our linens were stacked with single folds to the front.

I continued to unpack our belongings and came upon a few pictures of Jim as a young boy. In one picture, he was about four-years old and attending our cousin Barbara's birthday party. He had inherited his father's love of nice clothing and wanted to look dapper. He was the only child in the picture wearing a dress hat.

Then I found his high school yearbook picture. He looked so handsome with his pompadour style hair mounded high in front and swept back from his forehead like the popular actors of the 1950s.

"Hon, look how cute you look in this picture. You've got the most beautiful blue eyes. How did you ever get your hair to stay in place like that?"

"Nothing to it. You know the song. You'd better use Wild Root Cream Oil, Charlie."

After a few weeks of marriage, Jim commented, "It's so nice to have a clean towel to use after a shower." I was stunned to learn that their home never had fresh towels, so he and his siblings often showered at school. It was then I realized how little I knew of his upbringing.

Forever a Marine, Jim spit shined his shoes and always wanted an unbroken razor-sharp crease in the front his trousers. He made a small fold in his shirt's fabric on either side of his waist so there would be no wrinkles across his belly. He walked with his shoulders back and his stomach held in, looking every bit the Sergeant ready for inspection.

Once our apartment was settled and for the next two months, I drove to Albany for school and work, often working on Saturdays. With only one car, juggling our schedules was crucial. I left Saratoga at 5:30 a.m. in order to make my 8 o'clock class and dropped Jim off on the way. His boss refused to give him a key. He stood in the cold until Zig showed up for work at 6:30 or 7.

An elderly woman and her unmarried elementary schoolteacher daughter were our next-door neighbors. They loved Saturdays. While I worked in Albany, they listened through the thin walls as Jim sang his favorite songs while cleaning the apartment. They became good friends, and we spent Saturday evenings in their apartment eating popcorn and watching the Lawrence Welk show.

On our first Christmas as Mr. and Mrs., we were without funds to travel home for the holidays and had no friends in Saratoga. We planned to spend a quiet holiday. We squeaked out enough money for a Christmas tree and a few ornaments from Woolworth's store on Main Street. I copied my mother's idea of red balls, blue lights, and mounds of silver tinsel (it was cheap). A bucket of sand held the tree, and when we finished decorating, we stood back to admire our work. Only one gift for each of us was under the tree. The smell of the fresh-cut tree and cookies baking in the oven filled our small apartment. Our peace was shattered when three rambunctious little boys who lived in the adjacent apartment smelled the freshly baked cookies. They paid a visit. "Would you like a cookie?" I asked.

They sat at the porcelain table, devouring cookies. Then they ran like a herd into the living room to admire our tree. The tree fell over, breaking most of the ornaments. An uncontrollable whimper escaped from my lips.

"We can't afford more ornaments," I complained to Jim. "Well, I guess we'll just have to spread things out a little more and make do with what we have."

On Christmas morning, we celebrated with a bacon and egg breakfast, and this time, the eggs were properly cooked. Jim's gift was a flannel shirt and mine, a wooden jewelry box with a decal on top.

> Sweetheart
> I thought that you would like to know
> That my thoughts go where you go
> That life is richer, sweeter far,
> For such a Sweetheart as you are.

That evening as we sat near the Christmas tree, I said, "I'm sorry we don't have more presents, Jim. The wedding and honeymoon took our last cent. Maybe next year we'll have more money."

"Don't feel bad, Hon. We never had any gifts under the tree when I was growing up. Dad made a big deal about Christmas. I remember the holiday as a happy time. My father took us into the woods to cut down a tree. He didn't care that the tree was on posted land. We dragged it home and added our meager decorations to it. Sometimes, welfare gave us extra food and a little candy at Christmas time."

He got a far-away look in his eyes as he reminisced about his Christmases in Tupper Lake and then continued.

"My family couldn't afford presents so Aunt Grace and Uncle Buck brought us each a gift. One year I received a new pair of socks. I was so tickled with the socks that I wore them every day and wouldn't take them off to be washed. Marie finally tackled me and took off my socks. They already had holes in them from being worn so long. That year, Evelyn's gift was a headscarf. Aunt Grace gave Sonny and Dick a 29-cent toy containing a fence with two little crows sitting on it and two popguns to shoot at the crows. That was one of the few times they had a real toy."

I was fascinated listening to Jim's stories and realized that, although my own family was poor, we weren't that poor.

In January, when I was assigned to student teach in Saratoga High School, we got a reprieve. We could save on gas. But, I had to stop working part-time so our budget was tighter than ever.

During my first week of student teaching, I observed. What I saw alarmed me. I was assigned to one of the weakest teachers in the school. His unprofessional appearance startled me. His shirts were wrinkled, and his one suit had a rip in the sleeve. He rarely stood up to teach but sat in his chair and, in a monotone voice, read his notes. His students were disrespectful and rude. One day a young female stood up and challenged him. "I'm not going to pay any attention to you. You don't know what you're talking about anyway." High school students in the 1950s generally didn't behave that way.

"You'd better sit down right now or else," he said.

*What will the **or else** be? What can I possibly learn about teaching and classroom management from him?*

Most of my students were seniors, and I was only nineteen. That meant they were my age. Although young, I was not a typical nineteen-year old. I was married and a senior in college. The students just assumed I must be older. Thank God. Had they known my true age, they would have made me into mincemeat.

I spent hours preparing typed lesson plans using an old Smith Carona portable typewriter. Erasable bond, whiteout, and computers weren't invented yet. The college required that all typed pages have two carbon copies. My college supervising teacher was a hard taskmaster. Because we were certified typing teachers, she took points off if we made too many typing corrections. I was stressed and began to lose weight.

The situation became intolerable. Over coffee one afternoon, my supervising teacher said, "Sue, you don't have to stay in this assignment. I'll find another placement for you."

I considered her offer for a brief moment.

"No. I'm going to stick it out. What if I graduate and get classes like these? I'll have to learn how to handle them."

That comment earned me an "A" in student teaching.

As a new wife, I was still struggling to learn to cook. One evening, I burned my hand while preparing dinner. Jim took my hand and held it under hot water.

"What are ya doin?" I cried.

"My mother said that'd chase the heat away."

I pulled my hand from his grip and ran it under cold water. "I don't care what your mother said. That's a stupid idea, and it hurts. Cold water feels a lot better. Your mother has a head full of those old wives tales and remedies."

"Oh, that's not all of it," he said.

"My family had home remedies for everything, and those took the place of doctor's visits. When I developed boils on the back of my neck, my grandfather, Randolph, cut a potato in half, rubbed the cut side on the boils, and threw the potato over his left shoulder. I don't know why it worked, but the boils healed."

That eased the tension, and we both laughed over Jim's family's quirky cures.

I completed student teaching and returned to college and work; our financial situation improved marginally. Although struggling, we were content being together and being crazy in love.

One crisp winter night, we held hands and walked down Saratoga's Main Street. Evergreen branches laden with heavy snow hung vertically, and our footsteps squeaked in the silver-dust snow covering the sidewalk. Lights on in the few stores remaining open cast a soft glow. The plows had pushed the snow into high banks on either side of the walk. Jim mentioned that he had ten cents in his pocket. Like a professional athlete, I spun around and tackled him, throwing him into the snow bank. He rolled around to dodge me, and I tried to get my hand in his pocket to steal the ten cents. We both giggled like little children as we tumbled in the soft snow, caring little if passers-by watched us.

"Where did you get ten cents?" I asked as I tickled him. "You're holding out on me."

He held me off like a warrior fighting for his kingdom, and I never got the ten cents. In 1957, ten cents could actually buy something—an ice cream cone, a cup of coffee or half a gallon of gas.

What a fun memory.

Usually Jim found evenings long while I was occupied studying, doing homework, or writing term papers. He didn't have hobbies, money, or maintenance projects in our small apartment, and we didn't have a circle of friends in town. To amuse himself, he bought two English parakeets, a cage, and bird feed. Their chests were green, and their wings had black and white markings. Jim fussed over the birds—Jimmy and Susie. Sometimes one of the birds sat on his shoulder as he shaved or watched television. With one or the other perched on his finger, Jim attempted to teach them to speak. At other times, he began to read more or went to Luke's apartment to visit.

From our living room window, we could see the magnificent four-story Adelphi Hotel. The turn-of-the-century Victorian hotel had stenciled walls, large potted plants, and dark mahogany wood trim. Our neighbor played piano and sang in the hotel's lounge. On Saturday evenings, if we had extra money, we went there to listen to her sing and to dance for a few hours.

By Easter vacation, it was time for a visit to Tupper Lake to see Mary and Sonny and Leon and Gladys. On a walk down Pine Street, Jim filled in bits and pieces of his young life.

"When I was growing up, Webb Row was a close-knit neighborhood. One hundred children occupied ten homes on the street. Most of the families were poor like us."

He pointed to an empty field across from his home.

"All of the Webb Row kids made that field into an athletic complex. We built a baseball diamond and track and field areas. I tacked the rim from a fishing net to a wall, and used an old Tommy ball to shoot hoops. We didn't have jackknives so we used sharpened sticks to play mumble-de-peg. After dinner, all the urchins from Webb Row descended on the athletic field and took part in the games, no matter their age or ability. It was a great time because we all participated, and there were no refs, rules, uniforms, or age limits."

We walked a little farther down the street, and Jim stopped to look at an empty field behind his old Webb Row house. A broad smile appeared when he saw the small lot, full of scrub bushes.

"Isn't it funny how our perspective changes when we grow up? All of the neighborhood kids thought that lot was big. We called it the *woods* and played cops and robbers using sticks for our weapons. We didn't have any toys, so we made our own fun. In the winter, when the ice truck passed by, we grabbed hold of the back of the truck and let it pull us along the icy roads."

"Was your upbringing the reason you're always so down on yourself?" I asked.

"My environment conditioned me to have a pretty poor self-image. We were the kids from the wrong side of town. One evening, I was in Roy's Restaurant with a friend when the friend's mother came into the restaurant. I always thought she acted a little snooty. She said rather loudly to her son, 'What are you doing with *him*?' I never forgot that remark. It made me feel pretty low. Unfortunately, that feeling has stayed with me."

By the end of my spring semester, I had a few weeks' reprieve from school. On Sundays, we were desperate for the out-of-doors and escaped to Kaydeross Park, south of Saratoga. We'd pack a picnic lunch and blanket, buy the Sunday paper, and spend the afternoon away from our stuffy apartment. Then, from early July until late August, I rode the bus back and forth to summer school. The summer of 1958 was unusually hot, and our apartment was unbearable. To escape the closeness, I sat in a beach chair on the tarpaper roof to do my homework.

I look back on those early years of our marriage as idyllic in many ways. We didn't have children to raise or a mortgage to pay. We were financially strapped but healthy and young, and a world of possibilities was ahead of us.

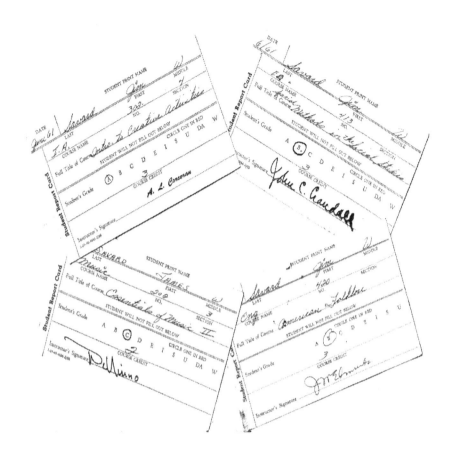

PART III

CHAPTER 8 - THE GREEN BEANIE

Reflections: There were three people in our marriage. My husband, the confident, self-assured and cool young man I'd married, me, and the inner Jim, about whom I knew little. Even though a few of his letters had mentioned his lack of confidence, I was too young and in love to realize how deep seated were his insecurities. I thought back to the struggle I'd had convincing him to attend college.

******

July 1958—seven months to go, and I would be a college graduate, ready to start my career.

My new husband was still in limbo, with no plans in sight. I was concerned. Jim couldn't decide upon a course of action for his life. Try as I might, I just couldn't understand his low self-image. To me, he was perfect in every way.

At times, he was quiet and withdrawn. I sensed that he felt isolated. When he'd lived at home, he'd been surrounded by the constant activity of his five brothers and two sisters. In high school, his athletic ability had made him feel special and important. As a Marine, he was part of an elite group whose every day was structured and organized. He didn't have to make any decisions.

Many changes had come Jim's way in a short time. He was newly married, away from family or friends, and working at a dead-end job. He was at a crossroads, and it was time for him to make a life-changing choice. But, his old insecurities from his background were haunting him. No one in his family valued education or encouraged him to attend college. He felt overwhelmed by the idea. I didn't know what he was thinking, but it seemed to me he was wasting his potential. I was determined to make him realize his full possibilities.

For me, life was hectic—driving to Albany for classes, working thirty hours a week as a legal secretary, and learning to be a housewife. From dinner to bedtime and again on weekends, I was buried in books and homework. He had a lot of idle time and time to fret.

I was getting frustrated with his lack of direction.

"It won't be long before I graduate. What da ya wanna to do?"

He gazed down at his shoes. "I think we should wait until you get a job, and then I'll decide."

"I can't apply for a job until I know where, or if, you want to go to school."

He could stretch his excuses no further. He was out of options and feeling trapped.

"I don't know, Sue. I just don't think I have what it takes for college."

How could I convince him otherwise?

"To be honest, I'm afraid."

"What's there to be afraid of? What's happened to my big, tough Marine? You have to believe in yourself."

His eyes had lost their merriment and showed the strain from the pressure I was putting on him. I slid my hand through his thick hair and tussled it. "No matter what you do, I'll love you, Honey."

Then, I took a deep breath and tried another tactic. "Let's say the rosary every night before bed. Maybe our prayers will give us divine guidance."

Each night, we kneeled against the side of our bed and fingered our rosary beads. "Hail Mary. . . "

For a while, I let the matter rest, but my semester was coming to a close, and his decision time was nearing. One evening, Jim sat on the couch with his feet propped on a footrest. I lay down next to him and placed my head in his lap. I looked up, held my gaze steady, and tried yet another approach.

"Why not give college a try? What do you have to lose? You shouldn't squander the opportunity to use your GI bill. I know you can do it."

Behind his every excuse was a nagging thought, "What if I fail?"

Finally, in the fall of 1958, I had worn him down. He began to make plans.

"I think I'd like to be a physical education teacher and Athletic Director like my coach, Len Perry. Ithaca and Brockport both have strong PE departments."

When the college catalog arrived, he looked through it and became paranoid when he read the PE curriculum. "Look at all the math and science required, Sue. I've never been good in math. If I have to take that much math, I'll surely fail. I'm going to change my major to history."

"Whatever you decide is all right with me—as long as you decide," I said.

He sent an application and scheduled an admission's test and interview at SUNY Brockport. While we waited in the Admissions Office for his results, he cracked his knuckles and thumbed through a magazine. Adelaide Brown called him to her office.

"Mr. Savard, your test results weren't great. It took me a while to convince the committee to give you a try. You impressed me during the interview, but you'll need to take remedial English and math. Don't disappoint me."

"I'll try not to," he promised.

His final college selection depended on where I'd get a job since I'd be the main breadwinner. In January 1959, teaching positions were plentiful. I didn't have to grovel for a job, only decide which one to accept. The superintendents and principals traveled to colleges in search of candidates for open positions in their schools. I crossed my fingers through the entire interview with Brockport's superintendent. It took place in the casual lounge of the stately Ten Eyck Hotel in Albany. We talked briefly about the opening and then the superintendent asked, "When can you start, Mrs. Savard? We've been covering the position since the fall with substitutes."

"I'll be there just as soon as my semester is over. My husband's been accepted at Brockport so we'll both be embarking on a new adventure." I was proud when I put a pen to paper to sign my first-ever teaching contract for $4,200 a year. The superintendent never mentioned that the first teacher of the year had left with a nervous breakdown.

Everything was falling into place.

We traveled to Brockport over a weekend to find an apartment and stayed at the Rose Motel—the only motel in town. To us, the quaint village of Brockport felt like coming home. Its business district reminded us of Tupper Lake's and the high school, resembling an English castle, was impressive. The best place to eat breakfast was Vinny's Village Restaurant in the center of town. We sat at the lunch counter.

"You folks new in town?" The owner asked.

"Yes," I replied. "We're moving here in a week, and we're looking for an apartment."

"Take my advice," he said. "Don't rent. Buy up every bit of land you can."

By the time we pay moving expenses, rent an apartment, and buy groceries, we'll be lucky if we have $40 left. I don't think I can buy much land for $40.

Looking back on how Brockport has expanded, it was good advice. Still, even in 1959, $40 wouldn't buy much.

We found a one-bedroom, second floor apartment a block from the college and a short distance from the high school. It had a small bedroom, a miniature kitchen, and a long narrow living room whose windows looked towards the college. The location and price were perfect.

Back in Saratoga, after work and classes, we packed our few belongings. I was excited, but he was apprehensive. "What if I flunk out, Sue?"

"Honey, you're going to prove to yourself that you can do this. That's more important than anything else."

Boxes and suitcases filled our car's interior, and a rented U-haul trailer stuffed with our furniture was attached to the back of our vehicle. Our two parakeets, perched in their cage on top of boxes, squawked happily, flapped their wings, and scattered seed all over us. Brockport, here we come.

"The roads are terrible, and the weather forecast isn't good," Jim said as we drove across the state. "Let's stop in Oneida for dinner with your parents. If things don't improve, we can always stay there overnight and head out again in the morning."

We ate dinner and pushed on. By 9 p.m., the roads were slick when we headed down the hill into the village of Brockport. The wipers slapped at the window, barely keeping up with the falling snow. Jim leaned forward in his seat, trying to follow tire tracks in the road. Halfway down, I heard a thump, then a frantic thump, thump as Jim's foot pressed on the brakes.

"Oh my God, our brakes just failed."

"What're ya gonna do? If our U-Haul jackknives, we could end up in a ditch."

"I'll keep my hand on the emergency brake lever in case we can't slow down. Pray that the stoplight at the base of the hill doesn't turn red. I may not be able to stop."

He leaned down and grabbed the brake, pulling it slowly to halt our downhill momentum. The car slowed to a crawl, and we inched the rest of the way to our apartment on the corner of Allen and Adams Streets. Jim yanked the brake lever. Our heads lurched forward, and the car jerked to a halt. I made the sign of the cross, and we both rested our heads on the back of our seats. I hoped this wasn't a sign of his failure.

We were tired and ready for bed. I knocked on the door of the elderly retired pharmacist and his wife who lived in the downstairs apartment.

"What're you doing here in this weather at this hour?" they asked.

"We're moving in," I replied. "Could we have the keys?"

He just shook his head in disbelief and handed me our keys.

I took the stairs two at a time and opened our door. Not expecting us, the owners had turned the heat down to fifty. The wind buffeted the loose windows until they rattled. I jacked up the heat and ran back down to help unload. I reached over the seat to retrieve the parakeets—my first concern—covered the cage with my jacket, and hurried upstairs. I placed the birdcage on a counter and made another trip down. Meanwhile, Jim had muscled our mattress from the trailer, and we hauled it up the narrow, steep staircase to our apartment. I made one more trip down to rummage around in the backseat for a box marked linens. We locked the car, made our bed, and listened to the wind whistling into our apartment as we snuggled down to get warm. We'd worry about the rest tomorrow.

There wasn't a moment to spare that weekend. On Monday, I was to start my new job, and a few days later, Jim was to register for classes. The brakes needed fixing, and our small savings account was almost empty.

"That's our last few dollars. Until I get a paycheck or your GI Bill arrives, we're destitute." In the morning, Jim unhooked the trailer and drove the car slowly to a mechanic's garage. He pleaded our case and convinced the friendly mechanic to repair the brakes and wait a week for payment.

I was exhausted from settling the apartment, but had to plow ahead and start my new job. For several days, I shadowed the current substitute. Rosie was short and very pregnant. In fact, I had arrived on the job none too soon. She barked orders in a gravelly voice like a drill sergeant's. She clapped her hands together the minute students entered her classroom. "Hurry up. Hurry and take your seats. We have a lot of work to cover today."

It was obvious there would be no fooling around in Rosie's classes. I could tell her students liked and respected her.

"I'm impressed, Rosie," I said during our planning period. "You really have good control of your classes."

"Students need to know who's in charge. Did you know I'm the fourth teacher they've had this year?" she asked. "The first teacher left with a nervous breakdown?"

What am I getting into? "No one warned me about that. These kids don't seem that bad."

"Don't worry. I've got them whipped into shape, and they really are nice kids. I just think teaching wasn't right for her."

That night, I couldn't sleep. What if teaching isn't right for me?

I was scheduled to take over from Rosie in one more day. I was getting panicky and watched Rosie's every move, hoping to pick up some tips. I took copious notes. I couldn't back down now, and I wouldn't let them sense my apprehension or my youth. Once again, many of my students were only a year or two younger than I.

Rosie's final words of advice stayed with me for all my years of teaching: "Remember Sue. Respect is earned, not demanded."

It was show time when I stepped into my first class. My stomach was in knots, and my knees were knocking. I straightened my shoulders, held my head high, and marched into the room with a sense of purpose. That day, I managed to keep everyone so busy they didn't have time to get into trouble. By the end of the week, I had convinced the students and myself that I was in charge and wasn't about to leave with a nervous breakdown.

Saturday was registration day for college classes. Jim paced back and forth and ate Tums to settle his stomach. In 1959, registration was done in person. Computers and pre-registration for classes didn't exist. Advisors and faculty were stationed at large tables around the college gym. Cardboard signs taped on the front of each table indicated the various departments. Students hurried from table to table filling out registration cards, hoping to get into a class before it was closed. Once closed, there was no alternative but to sign up for whatever other course was listed in the catalogue.

Jim wasn't in a hurry to leave the apartment. I had no doubt my Marine would fight like a tiger in the face of an enemy, but he was a pussycat in the face of college registration.

I took his hand. "C'mon. If you don't hurry, you won't get in the classes you need. I'll go with you."

We walked to the college gymnasium, and he moved from line to line (nothing new for a Marine) signing up for classes. While he was busy registering, I watched the crowd of people. I noticed a slender, pretty blonde girl wandering around aimlessly with a vacant look on her face.

"Watch that blonde, Jim. I wonder what she's doing. She doesn't seem to be registering."

"Yeah, I noticed her. She certainly looks lost."

Later, we strolled around campus locating his classrooms and getting acclimated, and in the evening, we attended a social hour in the gymnasium for new registrants. We stood chatting with a man we'd met at registration

"Did you notice that dizzy blonde walking around in the gym all afternoon?" I asked.

"Yeah, that's my sister," he replied.

Whoops. Big foot in big mouth.

At last, my husband was a college student. In 1959, it was the custom that freshmen wear green beanies to announce they were newbies. Upperclassmen could ask a freshman to do tasks such as carry their books.

It wasn't long before an unsuspecting sophomore spotted Jim. Since it was such a small college, the young man assumed Jim was a freshman.

The sophomore slapped Jim on the shoulder. "Where's your beanie, freshman?"

Jim turned, glared at the student, and got inches from his face. "Get out of here you little twerp. If you think I've spent three years in the Marine Corps only to run around wearing a little green beanie, you're nuts. Scram before I beat the tar out of you." The sophomore hurried away, never to be seen again.

SUNY Brockport's campus consisted of a cluster of buildings around Hartwell Hall that serviced a few thousand students. Often, Jim's Saturday morning classes were held in Quonset huts left over from WWII and located next to a busy railroad track. The huts were like his home on Webb Row—poorly heated, cramped, and noisy. In the middle of lectures, professors automatically stopped speaking when trains passed.

The college was so friendly that faculty and students became well acquainted. Whether Jim was in their class or not, professors stopped us on the street to chat. The president lived in a Victorian home on the college grounds, a block from our apartment. He often greeted us as we passed on an evening walk.

In spite of the welcoming atmosphere, college was a time for Jim to confront his self-doubt. In his first semester, he realized there would be no more wheedling his way out of doing the work. His first history teacher was a man named Jack Crandall who dressed in well-tailored suits and a signature bow tie.

"You wouldn't believe my one professor. He uses words I've never heard before. He's so smart that he makes me realize how little I know about anything. I think the dictionary is going to be my best friend."

Jack was quick to pick up on Jim's speech. After talking to him for a few minutes, Jack said, "You're from the Adirondacks aren't you?"

"I don't think I have an accent. Do you?" Jim asked that night. "Dr. Crandall picked up on it right away."

"People from the Adirondacks have a definite accent. You don't use those hard A's that I do, like when I say Rah-ah-ah-chester."

My insecure husband was swimming against the current—out of his element. He never raised his hand to comment and was too shy to speak up in groups. Although an average student in high school, he had poor study habits and an intellectually deprived background. If he'd brought a book home and tried to read, his father would yell, "Put that away, and stop wasting time. Get in the shop and work."

Jim's grammar needed work. It wasn't unusual for him to say he drug a deer out of the woods or clumb a tree. To him, these were legitimate words—ones he'd often heard. He mispronounced other words, such as preformance for performance. I tried to correct him without hurting his feelings. By the end of the semester, when his grades were posted, he was elated that he'd passed everything—even remedial English and math.

That summer, we answered an ad for an apartment in the country, five miles from school. The homeowners lived downstairs with their two young sons. We followed the landlord up a long stairway at the back of the house onto a small porch. He opened the main door, and we stepped into a large kitchen with new cupboards and black and green floor tiles.

"Look at all these cupboards," I said. "This is a huge kitchen."

We walked around the apartment and poked our heads into each room.

"What do you think, Jim? We could put our bedroom right next to the bathroom, and use that smaller room for an office?"

"I like that idea. If we put our living room in the front, we'll be able to watch the sunset through those big windows."

The landlord watched and listened to our discussion. Then he said, "You should put your living room on the other end of the apartment. You're putting your bedroom right over our fighting area."

To our peril, we ignored his remark.

Once moved, Jim suggested, "Now that we're in the country, I'd like a hunting dog."

Neither of us knew much about the different breeds, but my father had owned a Brittany spaniel, and we saw an ad for a new litter for sale.

"What do you think of that one over there?" Jim pointed to a feisty pup. "He has a natural docked tail, and he's spunky." He picked up the dog and nuzzled his nose into the wiggling bundle of soft rust and white colored fur.

"I can see you've made a choice. That one's fine with me."

"How much are you charging for the dogs?" I asked the breeders.

"Twenty-five."

When Romeo heard how much we'd paid, he was annoyed knowing we couldn't afford that much money. He was right.

"Let's name him Chipper after my father's Brittany."

Chipper and Jim became inseparable. He spent hours playing with the dog and training him to hunt pheasant.

By the fall semester, Jim regretted wiggling his way out of his senior speech in high school. Somehow, he had convinced his high school teacher he didn't have to do the speech, even though it was required for graduation. In college, a whole semester of speech was mandatory, and there was no way to finesse the instructor. On days he presented his speeches, he perspired so profusely his shirt was wet from his armpits to his waist. He gradually gained confidence in his ability to speak in front of a group.

His learning curve was steep. His only exposure to good literature or poetry was in high school English courses. At home, poetry consisted of listening to his mother's ditties. One he laughed about went like this:

"Ladies and gentlemen take my advice. Pull down you pants and slide on the ice."

Now, he was faced with Walt Whitman and Robert Frost. He persevered, learned to appreciate poetry, and could recite some of his favorites. His grades continued to improve, but that nagging feeling of inferiority persisted.

Learning to play the piano was the next hurdle. He dreaded the days when he had to perform in front of the class. To get practice time, he went to the college at 6 a.m. and struggled to get through "The Old Sow Took To Measles and She Died In The Spring."

"My hands lock up, and I just can't make my left and right hands do two different things. Some of the people in class have taken years of lessons, and they can play "The Old Sow" and make it sound like a concert piece. Somehow I'll pass, but I pray I never have to play the piano as a teacher."

One semester, he was having a difficult time starting his term papers. "I can't seem to get the first paragraph written. I've started over and over again, but it just isn't right."

"Okay, I'll write the first paragraph, and you write the remainder," I offered.

When the professor returned it with a grade, he had written: "This would have been an "A" paper, but the first paragraph isn't your writing."

Although stressed keeping up with homework, Jim still needed a part-time job. He found work, stocking shelves from 9 p.m. until 1 a.m. at the A & P grocery store. Our apartment was on a lonely country road; we had one car and no phone. One evening I needed the car, so I drove him to work.

"I can get a ride home with one of the other guys," he said.

"No, Sweetheart, I won't be able to sleep without you to snuggle against. I'll pick you up."

"Are you sure? It's going to be late."

"Absolutely. I'll miss you too much to sleep."

When quitting time came, Jim stood in front of the store.

"Hey Savard, ya need a ride home?" colleagues called from their car.

"No thanks. Sue's picking me up."

After a half hour, Jim began the five-mile walk home.

He watched a number of cars drive by.

After a mile, he began to wonder if I had been in an accident.

Once out of the village, there were no streetlights, and not even a moon to light the road. One mile, two miles, three miles—still he saw no sign of our car.

He turned onto the final stretch of road, and it was darker yet. He could barely make out the way home. A junkyard German shepherd barked, growled, and strained at his chain. Shivers rippled down Jim's spine, and the hair on his neck went up. He thought of the time when he was young and the stray dog had left scars on his arm.

By three a.m., he was home. The door was locked.

I was in a *dead-to-the-world* sleep.

Pound. Pound. Pound on the door. No response from me.

In desperation and in the pitch dark, he climbed on the roof of a porch and banged on the bathroom window.

At last, I stirred. "Who is it?"

"It's Jim."

"Jim who?"

At that, he gritted his teeth and yelled, "Jim. Your husband, Jim. Now, God damn it, let me in."

I exploded from the bed and ran down the hall. Still dazed and befuddled, I unbolted the door. "Oh, my God. I'm so sorry. I slept right through the alarm."

"Yeah, yeah. So, you wouldn't be able to sleep without me. Hah."

"I'm sorry, Honey."

"To make matters worse," he said, "when I passed the junkyard, I thought that German shepherd was going to attack me. Thank God, he was chained."

He stumbled down the hallway towards our bedroom.

"I'm going to bed."

For that whole weekend, no apology was good enough. But, I did rework our finances to afford a phone. He gradually forgave me, and for many years, the incident made for a good story.

Jim was half way through his sophomore year when, on December 4, 1960, the phone rang at 3:30 a.m.—never a good thing.

"You'd better come home right away. Dad had a heart attack and died this evening," Sonny said.

He was silent, unable to think, but finally blurted out, "What happened?"

"Well, Dad was drinking all night and watching the middleweight fight between Fullmer and Sugar Ray. By the fifteenth round, Dad got so excited he started to vomit and then passed out. Mom called the ambulance right away, and she and Don rode to the hospital with him. There was nothing the doctors could do. Major heart attack."

"Okay. We'll get our things together and leave as fast as we can. We probably won't be there until late tomorrow night."

He hung up the phone, and began to cry. We hugged, and I tried to console him.

"I don't know what to do," he said.

"Well, in the morning, you'll go to the college to explain the situation to your professors. I'll call the school to let the principal know and get my plans together for a substitute."

Looking back on that night, I now know he meant, "I don't know how to feel." The man who had been so dominant in Jim's life was gone. Was my husband happy, sad, angry, or confused? He rarely verbalized his feelings, and his face gave nothing away. But, I believe it was all of those emotions wrapped into one.

We straightened out our affairs in the morning and headed for Tupper Lake.

After the funeral, Jim's siblings brought us up to date on the events as they had transpired.

Don said, "On the ride in the ambulance, Dad said he was sorry for the way he'd treated me. You know, his apology was a little too late. I'll never treat my children the way he treated us."

It seemed everyone had a story to tell.

"Fate was with me that night," Roy said. "I came home on a surprise leave. When I got to the house, I found that Dad was in the hospital. By the time I got there, he was gone."

Dick shook his head upon hearing Roy's story.

"It is funny how things happen, isn't it?" Dick said. "I was working on the seaway project in Plattsburgh that night. Theresa called me at work. She was frantic. She didn't have any money for food. It was hard for me to get to a bank and I couldn't get my paycheck home. The minute Theresa phoned, I told my boss I was leaving work and that I'd be back after I gave her my paycheck. It turned out Dad died that night."

Marie stayed for a few days after the funeral to help Gladys wrap up Leon's affairs.

"How do you feel Mom?" she asked.

"Peaceful," was Gladys's only response.

We returned home from the funeral and resumed our busy lives of college and teaching. It was our third Christmas together, and we realized that neither of us had any established holiday traditions.

"My mother always baked beautiful cookies and made a delicious Christmas dinner, but that was the extent of the holiday," I said.

"Christmas at my home usually meant that my mother and father were fighting and weren't speaking to one another. Mom loved Christmas, but our family was poor, and Dad resented that Mom had spent a little money for presents. She purchased one big item, such as a pair of skates, and one small item, maybe a purse or shirt, for each of us. Even that made my father's blood boil, and he took no part in the joy of the holiday."

"I remember Christmas as a big deal," Jim said. "Dad was usually drunk, so he was in a good mood. Aren't you going to do anything special to get ready for the holiday?"

"Such as?"

"Well, maybe make stuffed dates or special cookies?"

I opened my cookbook and selected some cookie recipes to bake over the weekend. After that year, we made more and more preparations for Christmas. Special cookies, large parties, and decorations galore became part of our celebration.

By the spring semester, Jim was gaining confidence as a college student. When his school year ended, he worked for my father for two weeks painting houses. I stayed in Brockport with Chipper, our new and naughty puppy.

I wrote Jim, "When I came home from school, Chipper was so ready to see me. What a mess he'd made. He tore the paper I had laid on the floor; he had two nice poops and had wet all over. He'd knocked down the broom and mop and thrown the birdseed from one end of the hall to the other. He's played out now and taking a nap, but he'll probably be up during the night."

My summer vacation was approaching, and I was stunned to learn I wouldn't have an income. Teachers could elect to be paid ten or twelve months of the year. I had inadvertently checked ten months when I filled out payroll information.

What are we going to do? I'm the main breadwinner. Maybe I can work as a secretary for the county.

I called the local head of a political party who lived next door to my superintendent.

"This is Sue Savard. I teach at Brockport High School, and I was wondering if the county hires extra help over the summer months?"

"Sometimes we do," he said. "How do you vote?"

I was speechless. When I found my voice again, I said, "I don't really know. I've never voted. I just turned 21."

There was a moment of silence as if he couldn't understand how a teacher could be so young. "I doubt we'll have any openings," he said.

The next day, I ran into the superintendent in the hall. I told him what had happened. "Can you believe it? He didn't even ask me if I could type or take shorthand. He just wanted to know how I voted. Is that even legal?"

I had to find a job. After my disappointment with Monroe County, I secured a secretarial position at the local hospital. A few days later, there was a knock on our door. It was the local official. He shuffled his feet and turned his head away.

"I'm sorry. I spoke too quickly, and I'd like to talk with you about a job over the summer months."

"Thank you, but I found a job and won't be interviewing with the county."

He left.

By the winter of 1961, we realized we had made a mistake moving to our country apartment. Our landlord was a mean drunk who abused his wife. Sometimes, I saw her with black eyes and bruises, and she confided in me that she wanted to leave him but felt trapped. She was sweet natured, but didn't work, couldn't drive, and spent every day cleaning and taking care of her two boys. Late one night, we heard screaming and crying coming from the landlord's apartment directly below our bedroom. She was pleading for him stop hitting her, but he continued. Then we heard the sound of furniture breaking. I was terrified for her safety.

"This sounds just like my house on Webb Row," Jim said. " The old man was always slapping Mom around. It sends chills up my spine just to listen what's going on downstairs."

"I'm calling the state troopers."

When the troopers arrived, our landlord was surprised and angry. He knew we had reported the incident. The next day he turned off our heat.

"We have to move," I said. "I don't want to listen to their arguments any longer, and she's apparently going to stay with the brute."

Plans quickly percolated, and we found an apartment close to both schools at 206 Utica Street.

Chipper was growing rapidly and was an incredible bird dog. Pheasant hunting became Jim's new hobby. Often after school, he'd change clothes, grab the dog, and head into nearby fields in search of pheasant (in plentiful supply in the 1950s). Almost every evening when he returned, a pheasant's tail feathers stuck out of his game pouch. I collected the feathers and stuck them in a crock. After a successful hunt, Chipper collapsed on the floor from the exertion and slept the evening away. When money ran out at the end of the month, we joked, "We're dining on pheasant under glass like the rich."

It was time for Jim to leave the comfort of college classes to embark on his next assignment—student teaching. He was assigned to Gladys Queen at Brockport's Middle School. For two weeks, he sat in the back of her room and observed. Gladys was quirky but devoted to her students. He was amused when he saw her snapping her garter while she sat on the edge of her desk and lectured. He had yet to actually teach a class by himself.

One afternoon, he came home from his day of OBSERVING and said, "I don't know why you complain about teaching. I'm having fun." That remark earned him a cold stare. I shrugged my shoulder, turned away, and began cooking supper.

"You'll find out," I said.

In preparation for teaching his very first class, he prepared meticulous lesson plans. So that he wouldn't be jittery, he abandoned his usual morning coffee. He didn't smoke before leaving for school. He walked into the classroom, straight-backed, immaculately dressed, and in command. The students couldn't see the butterflies in his stomach. He began his lesson. Gladys was supposed to sit in the back of the room and observe. Instead, she was reading a magazine, and something in it struck her as a brilliant idea.

She stood up just as her unsuspecting student teacher was warming up, waved her arm in the air, and said, "Stop right now. This is what we're going to do."

And with that, Jim's lesson plans went into the trash, but he had learned to be flexible.

CHAPTER 9 - BIRDS ON A WIRE

Reflection: Our lives went along in what seemed like a jumble of random activities with no clear pattern. But when I created this chapter, I realized that world events and our lives intermingled and formed a wealth of stories. From these threads of stories, I wove a tapestry. When I stepped back to admire the results, I found myself yearning to return to those years.

****

1960 - HEADLINE NEWS - JFK (Sen-D-Mass) beats VP Richard Nixon (R) for 35th US president.[i]

The period of the early 1960s brought about big changes in our lives. The country was going through a transformation.

Our attention to politics crystallized when Jack Kennedy became President in 1960. We were mesmerized by his inaugural address and the words, "Ask not what your country can do for you but what you can do for your country."[ii]

"Jacqueline and Jack are so attractive, don't you think? She's young and pretty, and he's a knockout."

We were taken in by the excitement and glamour the Kennedy's brought to the White House. Times sizzled as if France had come to Washington.

After the dull years of the Eisenhower's, the *Camelot* years of the new administration brought a sense of optimism and promise to us and to the nation. We were excited by Kennedy's determination to land a man on the moon. I watched the evening news and, like every other woman in America, admired Jackie Kennedy's elegant fashions. Her signature pillbox hat became the rage, and I wanted one.

"Why can't we make our own pillbox hats?" I asked the girls in my craft group. "We can buy a hat form at the hat shop on Maiden Lane and use pheasant feathers to cover it." I proudly wore my new hat to church on Sunday mornings.

With the purchase of each dress pattern, I selected designs that emulated her elegant style. Sleeveless A-line dresses, low-heeled pumps, and triple-strand pearl necklaces became my dream wardrobe. If we visited Tupper Lake, I made a beeline to the new dress factory and purchased fabric remnants. Fifty cents could buy a pattern and a dollar, a yard of fabric. The minute we returned home, I went to work with scissors, pins, and my sewing machine to create a "Jackie" look-alike outfit.

1961 - HEADLINE NEWS - Bishop Burke of Buffalo Catholic diocese declares Chubby Checker's "Twist" to be impure & bans it from all Catholic schools.

Chubby Checker and the Twist were hot in the 60s. In 1961, on the last day of classes before Christmas vacation, my students heard a party going on in the social studies class next door. "Mrs. Savard, can we join them? Please. It's Christmas."

"Sure. Why not?"

I finished straightening my desk and hurried to the next classroom.

My students were doing the Twist—a new dance. I was horrified. With their pelvises pushed forward and their buns pushed back, they twitched their hips side to side and wiggled low to the floor.

"Come back to class right away," I said. "That dance is way too suggestive for high school students. It's disgusting."

"Oh, c'mon Mrs. Savard. It's fun," they begged.

"No way." I held my ground.

I never imagined then that one day we would add the Twist to our evenings of dancing. Now, I look back with nostalgia on the New Year's Eve parties we attended and did our very best to bend our knees and twist our backsides with the rest of the revelers. It was no longer the evil dance.

January 1962, within three years of beginning college, Jim graduated with a B.S. degree in history. The young man from Tupper Lake, who never dreamed he would go beyond high school, was exhilarated. We both loved to party, and his graduation gave us a good excuse for a gathering.

"We've got to celebrate my husband's graduation. Can you help?" I asked our good friends Avis and Sal Randazzo.

We rented the GE Clubhouse, and with their help, prepared spaghetti dinner for forty. After dinner was over, everyone circled around to watch Jim open gifts. Sal and I carried two large wrapped boxes into the room and laid them at the new graduate's feet. To receive such a large gift was a new experience for Jim. He looked at me with a question in his eyes and then began to rip off the wrapping paper. I had surprised him with a DeWalt radial arm saw I had purchased through the industrial arts teacher at school, paying a little on it each month. He couldn't wait to set it up in our basement and begin projects.

Until Jim found a teaching position, our income remained stagnant. Each night we prayed that he would soon have a job; we saw visions of two paychecks; we would be rich. By the end of January, he had accepted a sixth-grade teaching position at Kendall Central School. He signed the contract. $4,800 a year spread out over ten months was the most money he'd ever earned. The insecure boy from Tupper Lake was now a teacher. He stood tall with pride when his students addressed him as Mr. Savard.

As a teacher, Jim dressed professionally. He enjoyed nice clothing like his father, and it made him feel more secure. But, he still felt uncertain of his ability. His lack of confidence caused him to bristle quickly at students and fellow teachers. There were times, however, when he knew enough to remain quiet.

One day in the faculty room, he overheard a conversation between two teachers.

"Hey. Da ya wanna to go to the flea market this Saturday?"

He had never heard that expression. When he came home he said, "Boy, it's a good thing I kept quiet today. These two teachers were talking about going to a flea market. I was wondering why anyone would buy fleas. I finally figured out what it was all about. As old Abe said, 'Better to remain silent and be thought a fool than to speak out and remove all doubt.'iii I'm sure glad I was silent this time."

When John Glenn orbited the earth in February of that year, the event was broadcast over my school's PA systems. Administrators, teachers, students, and maintenance staff stopped work. All talk and activity ceased, and we sat glued to our chairs. A cheer went up when liftoff was announced and then, absolute quiet returned. Not another sound could be heard throughout the building. There was a sense of awe and a renewed pride in America for days afterward.

At home, Jim and I were about to launch our own new adventure. In mid-March, morning sickness, exhaustion, and tears reminded me daily that I was pregnant.

Once pregnant, my job ended with the end of the school year—so much for two salaries. Pregnant women, even though married, couldn't teach, and maternity leaves weren't even considered in 1962.

I stormed around our kitchen.

"Can you believe it Jim? The board turned down my request for a leave of absence. Just because I'm pregnant, I'll lose my job," I grumbled. "It's really unfair."

But, I resigned myself to the inevitability of being unemployed.

Our lives were about to change in other ways.

1962 - HEADLINE NEWS – The average cost of a new house was $12,500 and the average income per year $5,556.

We lived frugally while Jim was in college and saved toward the purchase of a starter home.

"Honey, with the money we've saved from your GI bill, we've got the 20% we need for a down payment. It's time for us to become part of the American dream."

We spent weekends searching for a house, scouting for-sale signs, checking the Penny Saver, and asking around. That's the way it was done back then. An old cobblestone house on the market for $16,000 intrigued us. A sense of timelessness surrounded the home as we walked around the peaceful yard. It had a large barn and one hundred rolling acres with frontage on two roads. The asking price was fair and cheap by today's standards. But, the house needed major renovations: a new kitchen, wiring, furnace, and an indoor bathroom.

"Let's buy that cobblestone house, sweetheart. I adore it," I whined like a spoiled teenager.

We calculated mortgage payments and costs for renovation during the day and lay awake nights trying to finagle a way to buy the house. What was I thinking? I was pregnant. Outhouses were fun when we rented cottages in Tupper Lake, but did I really want a house without indoor plumbing? We came to terms with reality and accepted the obvious fact that we could afford the house, but not the renovations. We continued to look.

We drove the village streets and spotted a for-sale sign on a small, tidy ranch house and made an appointment for a tour. The price of the house was within our budget. It was well constructed, didn't need any repairs, sat on a sizeable lot, and had an indoor bathroom. The house would be perfect for our growing family. It had three small bedrooms, a kitchen with a tiny eating area, a small living room with a picture window, one bathroom, and hardwood floors throughout. It felt spacious and cozy compared to our apartment. I was thankful to see hookups in the cellar for a washer and dryer—no more visits to the Laundromat. The small garden in the back yard beckoned me to dig in the dirt. Not normally given to food cravings, I ate three toasted peanut butter sandwiches as we sat with the realtor in a friend's kitchen and nervously signed the purchase offer.

It was accepted.

In 1962 final walk-throughs, home inspections, warranties and exact date of occupancy weren't part of the home-buying experience. Nor did my salary count in determining our mortgage approval. The house cost $15,000. The bank approved a $12,500 mortgage based on Jim's salary.

"Can you believe it?" I beamed. "Our first house. I can't wait to move in."

Each evening after work, we packed boxes in preparation for the big move. The homeowner kept changing the date on which we could take possession.

"Next Friday," said the owner, Mr. Lydig. "I'll be out by then."

We loaded the car.

He changed his mind.

For two weeks, we drove around with the car packed to the ceiling. Jim called the owner. "Would you mind if I begin painting this weekend?"

While he painted the living room ceiling pure white, Mr. Lydig appeared grumpy. "My wife and I preferred off white on the ceiling," he said.

I didn't understand. *After all, it's not his house anymore.*

We finally moved on a Saturday. A few days later, a new neighbor phoned. "We'd love to have you folks join us on Friday for a backyard picnic. You'll get a chance to meet your new neighbors."

"That invitation sounds fantastic," I responded, "but we're Catholic and don't eat meat on Friday."

"Don't worry," he said. "I'll fix something besides hots and hamburgers for you."

We feasted on lobster while the remaining guests had the hots and hamburgers. The neighborhood of college professors, nurses, retired seniors, and a TV repairman accepted us like old friends. We felt welcomed and comfortable with them and immediately connected with this friendly group.

1962 - HEADLINE NEWS - October 16 - Cuban missile crisis began as JFK becomes aware of missiles in Cuba.

Our euphoria over the Camelot Years ended in October with the Cuban Missile Crisis. I puttered around the house while listening to President Kennedy's radio address "the purpose of these bases in Cuba can be none other than to provide a nuclear strike capability against the Western Hemisphere."iv

How would our new young president and his advisors handle the mess?

One afternoon while sewing, I turned on the radio to get the latest update. I was so tense and edgy, I lost my concentration and ran the sewing machine needle clear through my finger. I eased the balance wheel back to raise the needle, drew my hand away, and sucked my finger to stop the bleeding and pain. Later that day, while I was in our cellar, an airplane flying faster than the speed of sound created a sonic boom. I dove under a table. My throat was dry, and I could feel my heart beating in my neck. My reaction brought home to me just how scared I was. When the crisis came to an end without a bang, I thanked the Lord. The atmosphere of foreboding was gone, but for me, so was some of the glamour.

As my belly grew larger, loose dresses became my new style. My former students surprised me with a baby shower; I sewed nightgowns and a christening dress; I read Dr. Spock's book, <u>A Baby's First Year</u>. It gave a common-sense approach to child rearing and stressed the importance of showing love and affection.

We wouldn't know the sex of our baby until it was born, so Jim applied a neutral green paint to the nursery walls. We painted a used rocking chair black and hung white cafe curtains at the windows. Pictures of nursery rhymes decorated the walls. For our living room, Jim built a cradle from plywood, cut the ends heart-shaped, painted it white, and padded the inside with fabric and thin foam. I provided the finishing touch by sewing a coverlet. We were almost ready.

But, we still needed to select a name and poured over lists of baby names in a book, laughing at some of the suggestions.

"How about Cinderella or Artemesia?" I giggled.

We scoured the Saturday newspapers, which always carried pictures of newborn babies with their names.

"Don't you remember the letter I sent you when I was in the Marines?" he asked. "I suggested the name Desiree if we ever had a daughter. We should name her Desiree. Do you like it?"

Yuck. I hate that name.

As the due date approached, my determined husband was still partial to Desiree and gave the name a last-ditch effort.

I couldn't be convinced. We continued to negotiate.

After weeks of mulling over names, we reached a final compromise—Shelly for a girl and David for a boy.

Shelly was anxious to make her appearance when Jim rushed me the few blocks to the hospital. I had expected unbearable pain during childbirth, but I didn't have to work at it for very long. Jim eyes bore into mine, and he held my hand while I grunted through labor pains. I gripped his hand hard and stared at him.

"I love your beautiful blue eyes. They're the prettiest eyes I've ever seen," I said between contractions. Our daughter arrived at 11 p.m. on

November 13, 1962. Early the next morning, the nurses brought her to me.

"Here's your beautiful daughter all washed and swaddled."

They had scotch taped a pink bow to her bald head. I caressed her, marveling at her little rosebud mouth, turned up nose, and tiny fingers. Delirious with joy, I was convinced I was the only woman in the world who had ever produced such a miracle.

At school the following day, tender excitement showed on Jim's face, "Our daughter Sherry was born last night. Wanna cigar?"

That was the expected practice for new fathers.

When he came to visit me after school and mentioned Sherry, I said, "Honey, her name isn't Sherry. It's Shelly."

Jim's colleagues teased but forgave the new papa when he later admitted his mistake.

We brought Shelly home, and Jim immediately became a hands-on father. At night, he'd rock back and forth slowly and croon his own version of a lullaby: "Rock abye my baby, rock abye my honey, rock abye Daddy's little baby girl."

He didn't want to miss seeing her in the morning before he went to school so, much to my chagrin, woke her from a sound sleep.

1963 - HEADLINE NEWS - "Camelot" closes at Majestic Theater NYC after 873 performances.

Before long, reality set in. We were down to one salary. Our mortgage payment of $106 was one-third of his paycheck. Catastrophe struck whenever our car needed repairs, the washing machine broke down, or Shelly was ill. Each month, I put aside at least one bill we couldn't meet.

"How're we going to make it?" I sobbed while trying to stretch his $333 a month salary to cover our expenses.

The pain on Jim's face showed when he saw me in tears. "When you're crying over bills, Sue, I feel as if I'm not doing my part to support our family."

Thinking back, I now realize he was doing all he could. He was struggling as a first-year teacher and taking graduate courses at night.

We had to do something.

I signed up to substitute teach to take the burden off my husband. A second solution arrived in the form of a married graduate student Jim had met during summer school. He paid us $10 a week to rent our spare bedroom. Ten dollars could buy a week's groceries and put a little extra meat in the freezer.

Once Shelly became part of our family, we'd place her in a nip n' nap on the kitchen table as the three of us ate dinner while admiring her every move or twitch. Our renter, Lloyd, didn't have any children, but he was fascinated with Shelly.

"Yes sir. I can just see it now. You'll be lining up little Savards like birds on a wire."

Jim chuckled. "I'm not sure of that Lloyd, but I think there'll be at least another one. We have to have a boy."

Lloyd had a storehouse of stories to tell and entertained us in the evening by playing the harmonica and guitar or spoons at the same time. We lost our privacy during the week, but on weekends, he returned to his home and wife in Buffalo. He stayed with us for a full school year.

Shelly was growing rapidly and rattles were her only toys. I went shopping for new ones and spotted a Barbie Doll—a new phenomenon to hit American culture.

"Jim, they're making dolls that are anatomically correct. I'll never buy our darling daughter one of those. I want her to play with baby dolls that she can wrap in soft blankets, dress in little baby nightgowns, and pretend to feed with a plastic bottle."

I never expected that someday I would have a box of Barbie Dolls for our daughters to dress.

The next year, I accepted a half-day teaching position in Brockport. My income helped us stay ahead of the sheriff and allowed me to spend a major portion of each day being a mom. A nearby neighbor provided childcare in her home. She was warm and loving, and we always knew she cared for Shelly as if she were one of her own.

Arriving from school one afternoon just as Shelly was waking from her nap, I was quite amused when I opened the bedroom door. The sitter had placed pink rollers in our daughter's skimpy hair and covered it with a hair net. It would have made a great picture.

In the spring, my sister called. "Sue, if you're free this weekend, we thought we'd come down and bring Gladys with us. She wants to stay a few days with you and then fly to Michigan to see Don."

"Sure. You're all welcome anytime."

They arrived with Gladys and her overnight case full of medicine bottles. Seeing her supply of drugs brought a vivid scene to my mind of Gladys with her three sisters. After Sunday mass, they often gathered in a semi-circle in Gladys's kitchen. They were all hypochondriacs and relished an opportunity to compare illnesses and drugs. Each was certain her suffering was the greatest and longest. They traded medications back and forth with no thought about the consequences. We never knew what drugs Gladys was taking or if they were prescribed or acquired from her sisters, friends, or neighbors.

While my mother-in-law was visiting, a brilliant idea struck Jim. "Mom, would you like to baby sit Shelly for a few days, and we'll pay you?" he asked. "You'll just have to get her lunch and tuck her in for a nap. Sue'll be home by the time she wakes up."

"No." she answered. "I can't do that."

So each day, I took Shelly to the neighbor's home, and Gladys sat and watched TV. On the following weekend, we planned activities for Gladys, knowing that she rarely had an opportunity to go to the movies or shopping.

"We've hired a babysitter tonight, Gladys," I said. "The *Sound of Music* is playing, and it's supposed to be terrific."

At the end of the movie, Gladys said, "That was okay, but I don't care if I ever see it again."

I took her shopping in Rochester to Sibleys, McCurdys, and Formans. She couldn't wait to get back to Brockport. I realized she was content to sit in our rocker, smoke cigarettes, and watch television all day. When she left for Don's home, I noticed the philodendron plant on top of the TV was completely burned from the heat of the television.

1963 - HEADLINE NEWS - President Kennedy raised the minimum wage from $1.15 to $1.25 per hour.

In the summer of 1963, Jim worked nights at a processing plant. Never a sound sleeper, he tried sleeping in the cellar with dark curtains over the windows. It didn't help. Invariably, he could hear the *whir, whir, whir* of a neighbor's lawnmower as he struggled to sleep. It was a long summer for Jim, but playing with Shelly and showing her off helped make up for his sleepless days.

In preparation for the winter, we purchased a steel runner sled to which Jim added a three-sided plywood box. He painted the box red and attached decals spelling out the name Friendship 7 after John Glenn's mission. On brisk winter days, I'd bundle her in a warm snowsuit, wrap her in a blanket, and pull her along the snow-covered sidewalks.

Jim was considering what to do for the next summer's employment. "Let's paint houses this coming summer," he suggested to his friend, Bill Draper. "If we get some contracts, we'll make more money than we can by working other summer jobs."

The two men merged their talents to create what Bill's wife, Betty, and I affectionately dubbed "Slob and Dob" painting service. Word of mouth spread, and they had a full summer schedule contracted.

When Slob and Dob started their first painting job, I began a part-time teaching position in Rochester, and Betty babysat Shelly. After work I arrived to pick up Shelly, and Betty greeted me at the door.

"We had a near disaster today. Jim didn't want me to call you at work. He was afraid you'd rush home and have an accident on the way."

My stomach did flips. "Why? What's wrong? Where is he?"

"He's in the bedroom. He was struggling with his aluminum ladder when a strong wind hurled it against a live wire. A jolt of electricity hit him like a train, traveled through his body, and exited his toe. Bill heard Jim scream and kicked the ladder away. An ambulance rushed him to the hospital. The doctors were astonished because his only injury was a small burn mark on his toe. As soon as he was discharged, he came here and said, 'I want to see my daughter.' He woke her from her nap. I never saw him hug Shelly so tightly before."

Fear stabbed through my heart. He was right. Had I known, I probably would have had an accident getting to him. I ran to the bedroom to see Jim hugging Shelly to his chest. He was visibly scared; his lips quivered.

The revelation of what had almost happened left me trembling.
Maybe this painting idea isn't so great.

The next morning, Jim returned to the job with a newfound respect for electricity and a prayer, thanking God for his survival.

On another painting job, Slob and Dob used eighteen gallons of white paint just on the trim of a large Victorian house. As they reached to paint the 2 ½ foot overhangs, they were perilously close to falling from their ladders. They finished the job and stepped back to admire their work.

"That trim looks kinda pink," Jim said. "What if the owner notices? I never wanna paint this one again."

When confronted, the storeowner and manufacturer denied there was anything wrong with their company's paint. Slob and Dob persisted.

The manufacturer researched the problem. "You're right. Our mixing vat wasn't properly cleaned after a batch of red paint was mixed. We'll give you eighteen gallons free."

"No way," they said. "If the owner complains, you can paint the trim again."

1964 - HEADLINE NEWS – 1st government report warning smoking may be hazardous to one's health

Jim became concerned when articles appeared in newspapers linking smoking to cancer. That scare, the increased cost of smoking, and his penchant for self-discipline made him determined to control his cigarette addiction.

"I hate the fact I'm so addicted to cigarettes, I run to the faculty room between classes to get a few puffs."

"If you quit, you can have the $3.50 a week you're spending on a carton of cigarettes," I said.

It was the added incentive he needed. Over time, he quit but never got his $3.50 a week. Diapers, formula, and baby food soon gobbled up the money. Sometimes he reminded me of my broken promise, even calculating how many dollars that promise was worth.

As the years went by, the tears shed over our financial state dried up. We were accustomed to being poor, and the love we shared overshadowed our poverty. Towards the end June of 1964, we were on high alert because another addition to our family was due to arrive. In the early evening of June 29, 1964, rapid labor pains announced that it was time to grab my suitcase and head around the corner to the hospital. Our baby boy was in a big hurry to make his grand entrance. He arrived two hours later.

When I finally had a chance to see him, I was amazed. "He's 22 1/2 inches long and almost nine pounds," the nurse said.

"I've never heard of such a long baby. His legs are so long and skinny, his father will call them ramrod legs."

Jim, the proud papa, was thrilled that we now had the perfect, all-American family—one girl and one boy.

This time there was little argument about a name. John Kennedy's assassination was fresh in our minds when we named our son Kerry Kennedy. I called my mother and father to blab the news.

"Why in the world did you name him that?' my father asked.

"Well, I could have named him Romeo Felix after you." That ended the discussion.

Late that evening, the nurses wheeled me into a room, Jim headed home, and I snuggled in for what I hoped would be a good night's rest.

The night proved to be anything but restful. I had a pounding headache. By two a.m. I could stand it no longer. I got out of bed and dragged myself to the nurse's station. "I can't sleep. My headache is keeping me awake."

"Here, Mrs. Savard. Take a few aspirin. That should help," the nurse said.

It didn't. I couldn't sleep and tried more aspirin.

The night seemed endless, and my headache worsened. Six thirty arrived all too soon, and the staff started their rounds. I was exhausted and hungry. When the meal of juice, cereal, and coffee arrived, the nurse's aide raised the head of my bed and wheeled an adjustable food table over me. After one bite, my arms and body flailed against the tray, food flew everywhere, and my tray clattered to the floor.

A new mother in the next bed screamed, "Nurse. Nurse. Help."

I'd had toxemia after delivery, a very rare condition that caused a seizure. Chaos ensued in the room, but I was unaware of anything around me. I have no memory or knowledge of that day or the next. I found out later that it was serious, and my life was almost extinguished. By the third day, I began to respond.

Jim was holding my hand and sitting by my side when I opened my eyes. I was dizzy and puzzled. His eyes were dark with worry; his jaw set.

"What's wrong, Jim? Why am I in the hospital?"

"You had a baby boy."

"I did. I don't remember. Is he all right?"

"Yes. He's fine, and he's been waiting for you to wake up."

"Is something's wrong? I don't remember feeling this way after Shelly was born."

"Well, you've had a little problem," he said, "but you're all right now."

"What's his name?"

"Kerry Kennedy."

On day four, I was sent me home with blood pressure medicine, even though my blood pressure was no longer elevated.

With an eighteen-month old and a new baby to care for, I didn't have time to worry about my condition. Each morning, I felt normal and took my blood pressure medicine, and Jim went to work. Within an hour, I was shaky, anxious, afraid to be alone, and depressed. I didn't know what was happening. I needed help, but no one came. Then, I became livid with my mother. *Why am I always on my own with no help? Just once, couldn't she understand and offer some assistance?*

Several days of these roller coaster feelings followed until I began to put the pieces together. "Jim, I'm not taking that medicine any more. I feel fine until I take it, and then I'm miserable."

My energy and mood improved immediately, and I poured myself into being a mother again. Shelly, at eighteen months, was fascinated with her new baby brother and watched his every move. One morning I said, "Well, it looks as if your brother's diapers need changing."

Shelly ran into his bedroom and came back with a diaper. I looked at her as if she had grown into a toddler overnight. My little girl wasn't verbalizing much but understood far more than I had realized. She was a little people.

With my health crisis over, our life settled down into sleepless nights, formulas, diapers, and bedtime stories.

An opportunity for Jim to teach closer to home presented itself when the woman for whom he had student taught retired from Brockport. He was hired to teach eighth grade social studies. At the beginning of the school year, he was lonesome for the familiar safety net of his Kendall colleagues. "I don't know any of the Brockport faculty, and I don't feel part of the group," he complained that fall.

"Give it a little while. You're new in the school. You'll make friends in no time and feel welcome." My counsel was right. He drew people to him with his quick wit and ready smile.

Our sphere of friends increased in September when Bill Visick, a teacher from England, traded positions and houses with a Brockport teacher. "I'd love for you and Peg to join us for Jim's surprise birthday party."

We were the first people to include them, and they happily accepted. Bill Draper was put in charge of keeping Jim occupied for an hour. They drove around town on useless errands until Bill could stall no longer.

"Sh. Sh. Here he comes," we whispered and waited to yell SURPRISE. Things didn't go smoothly. The birthday boy hurried into the garage, banged on the door, and yelled, "Sue, open the door. I've got to pee."

I don't know if Jim were more surprised or more mortified to see the large crowd.

By Thanksgiving, Jim was settled into teaching in Brockport. He taught a half day on the Wednesday before Thanksgiving and planned on spending a good share of his vacation deer hunting.

"As long as you're going hunting, I'm going to Oneida with Shelly and Kerry and spend the holiday with my parents, brothers, and sisters. I'll be back on Friday." On Wednesday morning, I left for home, leaving him a love note on the kitchen table.

> Jim,
> I am always thinking of you.
> I am always looking for you.
> And I know you are always with me and taking care of me.
> I love you very much. Have a good day.

When I returned on Friday, I found the following:

*As I cleaned the kitchen after you
left for home - You were on my mind.*

*I prepared for tomorrow's hunt with the things I
need - You were on my mind*

*As I made the bed with the new flannel
sheets you bought - you were on my mind*

*I crawled into bed - reached for you
You were on my mind.*

*Early in the morning - frost on the ground.
In the deer stand before nature awakes -
You were on my mind.*

*Sitting here with pen in hand - and the
phone in view - I'm still thinking of you
You are on my mind*

1966 - HEADLINE NEWS – Forecasters are warning that some areas of upstate New York could get more than 100 inches of snow before the cold wave ends.

    The blizzard of 1966 brought sixty miles per hour winds that blew the heavy snowfall into deep drifts and clogged roads. Frigid temperatures and constant snow across western New York caused the thruway, schools, and businesses to close. Road crews worked round the clock to clear roads, but for four days the snow continued to fall making roads impassible. People we rarely saw came out to shovel their driveways and chat about the weather. A neighbor served hot chocolate to anyone braving the cold.
    Shelly stood on the couch, looked through the window, and watched the older neighborhood children scrambling up the snowdrifts for a lively game of King of the Mountain. Kerry, at one and a half, snuggled deeper into his soft blankets and slept through the whole event.
    Our back door was banked to the top with drifted snow. "We need to let the dog out to romp. I think I'll dig a tunnel from our back door to the yard," Jim said.

When the tunnel was complete, I dressed Shelly in her pink snowsuit with a fur trimmed hood, her boots, scarf, and pink mittens connected with an idiot string.

"C'mon, Shelly. Here Chipper. Let's have an adventure." He crawled through the tunnel heading to the yard with Shelly and Chipper at his heels.

We spent our days playing games with the children and evenings playing cards with neighbors.

My mother called, "What're ya doin? Isn't this awful?"

I hated to admit that we had been having a wonderful time.

1968 - HEADLINE NEWS – Punxatawney Phil saw his shadow this morning!

On February 2, 1968 our family again expanded. Certain our new baby would be a girl, we never selected a boy's name.

On the delivery table I said, "Well, doctor. This one had better be a girl. Otherwise, we'll have to call him Hey You.

Shortly thereafter, I heard the doctor's pronouncement, "Welcome, Hey You."

I was dumbstruck.

We stared in wonder at our new son. He had chubby pink cheeks, peach-fuzz blonde hair, and puffy eyes. I couldn't stop laughing. "He looks like a miniature old Eagle Eye."

Our baby was strong and healthy, but we were stuck on a name.

"How about Seth Savard? I like the alliteration." I suggested.

Jim vetoed that, along with every other name I tossed around.

On the day of my discharge, a nurse stepped into my room. "You two have to select a name. I refuse to put Hey You on this birth certificate."

We were driven to action. We chose the name Tracy Thomas and headed home with our pink cheeked, fuzz blonde bundle, and a completed birth certificate.

I was surprised three weeks later by my husband's announcement. "There's a social studies position open in Ausable Forks. I'd like to move back to the Adirondacks."

The thought of moving and uprooting our family shot dread through me. *Is he serious? Does he really want to live in the Adirondacks again?* I was uneasy but didn't want to discourage him.

"Why not check it out?"

After applying and scheduling an interview, he headed for Ausable Forks, a few hour's drive from Tupper Lake. On the morning of the interview, Jim ate breakfast at the local diner. He was offered the job after his interview, and he politely declined. He had changed too much to return to his roots.

"I've changed my mind," he said when he returned. "I don't want to move."

I sucked in a deep breath and said, "Good."

We lived in a good neighborhood, and we had established a group of friends through our work. They were mainly teachers who, like us, struggled financially. Keeping up with the Jones's was not a problem. Our friends shared our values and raised their children in much the same way. Weekend nights, we often gathered for a spirited game of cards with pennies supplying the jackpot. Unable to afford a babysitter, we'd bundle our children into the car, put them to bed at a friend's home, play cards, and then late at night, whisk them back to the security of their own beds.

1969 - HEADLINE NEWS – US population reaches 200 million.

By 1969, our small ranch house was bulging at the seams, and Jim wanted to live in the country.

"I know a perfect spot. I often hunt there. I think it belongs to the secretary at your school. When you get to work Monday, ask her if they'll consider selling a lot."

The land had been in the White family since the area was first settled. Herb and Florence did a little soul searching and agreed to sell us five acres for $3,000. The sprawling expanse had a small hill, stone walls, and faced west for a panoramic view of sunsets. Not one tree was on the property.

Our married life can be charted in phases, and 1969 was our home building phase. Builders invited us to visit their model houses, and we looked at books of home designs. I worried over our tight budget. We could swing the mortgage, but there was no wiggle room for unanticipated changes.

"Green around the ears" proclaimed the imaginary sign around our necks. We didn't know what we were doing and selected an unscrupulous contractor.

On the night we signed the contract, the builder said, "These are our samples of cupboards and flooring. Pick what you want."

I felt pressured.

We have no idea what we want. We just signed the contract. We haven't had a chance to think about anything.

"We have so little time to make decisions," I complained to Jim. "With our ranch already sold, we only have three months for our new home to be completed. Besides, we can't afford any upgrades. We're going to have to settle for minimum quality fixtures, cupboards, and flooring."

From the first day when the cellar was dug, Jim checked after work on the builder's progress. He was livid when he saw the shoddy workmanship. He argued with the builder. "You can't leave that insulation so poorly stapled, and that wall is crooked." It was to no avail. The poor workmanship continued.

Many mornings, Tracy and I took a ride into the country to check on the house. At 1 ½- years old, he was fascinated with a field of grazing cows at a neighbor's farm. He watched from his car seat, and as soon as we passed the first hill on West Sweden Road, his index finger shot upward ready to point.

"What do you see Tracy? Are those cows? What do the cows say?"

"Moo, moo," he responded with a satisfied grin.

"That's right. Moo, moo."

When we arrived one morning at our almost completed home, our brand new dark wood cupboards had been installed. They seemed so much richer than the white metal Youngstown cupboards in our ranch house. While I looked into another room, Tracy spotted a paintbrush in a container of white paint, grabbed it, and proceeded to apply the paint to the side of a dark cupboard. I was so stunned, I couldn't think what to do. I came to my senses, found a rag, dipped it in turpentine, and wiped the cupboard clean before the paint dried. Calamity solved.

In spite of the terrible workmanship, our new house felt unexpectedly grand. It was twice the size of our ranch house, had a fireplace, a large kitchen, four bedrooms, 1 ½ bathrooms, and plenty of land. In order to save money, Jim spent every night after school painting the interior. Before the house was totally completed, we planned a surprise.

"Get your PJs on kids. We're gonna have a picnic in our new house," Jim said.

He built a fire in the fireplace, and we set up lawn chairs in the family room. After roasting marshmallows with our three children, they went to bed in sleeping bags on the floor of what was to be their new bedroom.

"Isn't this grand, Sweetheart?" I asked as we basked in the glow of the cozy fire and contemplated our good fortune. The shoddy workmanship was but a distant memory.

In 1970, the first summer in our new home, we purchased 1,000 Douglas fir seedlings. Heeling in the seedlings occupied two full weekends of hard work.

"This reminds me of the days I spent with the local winos pulling and bundling seedlings," Jim said. "I like being on the planting end of things."

I wondered how many of the trees would live. To my delight, most of them survived.

1970 - HEADLINE NEWS – This year's Disco fashion is bright and showy, designed to pop under the dance lights.

Double-knit polyester leisure suits were the new men's wear in the 1970s. My clothes-savvy husband was quick to grab on to the new fashion. He wore wide-collared, open-neck shirts and no tie for his new, casual style. The suits were comfortable to wear and wrinkle free, but polyester made him, and everyone else who wore them, sweat profusely in the summer and freeze in the winter.

Never wealthy enough to spend a lot on clothing, I did my best to keep up with the fashions of the day. Bell-bottom pants in knits, jersey and polyester were the in thing. With them, I wore patterned blouses, knitted cardigans, or crocheted vests.

Disco Dancing took nightclubs by storm, and we tried to emulate what we saw on TV. The beat of the music was strong as we moved to the rhythm and added our own flourishes. A spinning mirrored disco ball added to the effect, making us look better than we were. Whenever we returned to the Waukesha in Tupper Lake, however, jitterbugging was still our dance of choice.

Dancing and cooking were always part of our lives. The aroma of food cooking came from the kitchen whenever Jim was home. He liked to experiment with new recipes and create his own concoctions. Often on Saturday mornings, he surprised me with breakfast in bed and, in summer, added fresh picked flowers to the breakfast tray. I relished the chance to be spoiled and the opportunity to snuggle in bed for an extra few minutes.

Even at school, Jim and his colleagues would spend their entire lunch period sharing cooking stories and family recipes.

"Why don't we start a gourmet club," suggested a colleague.

John Izzo, Rudy Aceto, Andy Nazzaro and Don Clarke, four co-workers, jumped at the proposition.

"Let's do a practice dinner and see how the evening goes."

In the spring of 1971, over wine, crackers and cheese, Donna, Joan, Pat, Carol, and I planned the first dinner. We consulted cookbooks, looked over magazines, and bantered ideas about, finally settling on a French menu.

> 1st meal – July '71 at Izzo's on Campbell Rd.
> French
>
> Appetizer: Carol – Onions Monaco Style
> Salad: Donna – Wine + Fruit (Banana)
> Main: Sue – Stuffed Lamb Shoulder
> Vegetables: Joan – Artichokes
> Dessert: Pat – Frappe coffee
> Crepe Suzettes (Flambée – Code 5 John with fire helmet)

We divided responsibilities. Host couple: set tables, prepare a menu and salad, select and purchase the wines and other beverages.

Guest couples: prepare one of the dinner courses and keep a tally of money spent.

Anticipation was high on the appointed evening. Oo's and ah's abounded as we all stuffed our bellies full. The meal was a huge success until dessert was served—Crepe Suzettes. When the liquor was poured and lit, a whoosh of flame spiraled towards the ceiling. John grabbed his fireman's hat and extinguisher to douse the flame, but it had already burned out. The drama added the final FLARE of the evening.

After dinner, Donna, our math teacher, added the amounts spent by each couple, divided by five and gave an accounting. Depending on their outlay, a couple either received a kickback or paid additional money. Pretending to lick the end of the pencil and swirling it around in the air like a magician, she announced, "You owe $5.25 or you get back $15." Including beverages, the total per couple was around $20. What a steal.

"I say we take a vote. How many want to continue the gourmet club?" asked Andy.

All hands went up.

"Okay," said Rudy. "Then let's have a dinner every other month, each time focusing on a different country's cuisine and rotating the location and course prepared."

That was the beginning of the gourmet-dining phase of our lives.

Gourmet club nights lasted until the wee hours of the morning with everyone telling stories and laughing until our sides hurt. From time to time, we even dressed in costume.

One year it was our turn to host the Christmas dinner. The wives selected a meal from Gourmet Magazine. As the evening drew near, Jim headed for the liquor store to purchase the wines suggested by the menu's author.

"Wow, the wines cost $120," he said.

"That's way too much. It's Christmas time, and everyone will be short of cash. Maybe you can return the wine and select something less expensive," I said.

Jim called the other couples to get their opinion.

"No problem," they all agreed. "We only do this a few times a year."

I was voted the official *Gourmet Club Tightwad* that night.

Our club was exclusive—guests not welcome—until one New Year's Eve. We were the hosts. It was decided that each couple invite one other pair, and the theme would be Vickers and Tarts.

The invitation read: "Come appropriately dressed."

On New Year's Eve, our home was filled with an amazing gathering of saintly Vickers and naughty tarts. There was enough wickedness and hilarity to make the good parsons blush.

In forty years, no one has ever quit the group. In 2009, our club was still going strong with a few adjustments. Now we eat at 6:30 and leave for home by 10:00. We no longer consume as much wine or food, and we don't really like to drive after dark. We don't dress in costume because it's too much trouble. Instead of talking about teaching or childrearing, we discuss politics, the possibility of Medicare being changed, or the latest technology for hip replacements. We only meet three times a year since two couples have moved farther away, and one couple goes to Florida for the winter.

In spite of these changes, we still enjoy spending an evening with long-time friends, and laughing at silly stories is our main ingredient.

1971 - HEADLINE NEWS – In June of 1971 a non-binding resolution passed in the U.S. Senate urges the removal of all American troops from Vietnam by year's end.

By 1971, the USA's involvement in the Vietnam War was being questioned. I had just finished reading Pearl Buck's book, The Good Earth, and many articles in newspapers reported the plight of the

Amerasian children in Vietnam. They were outcasts, abandoned, and sometimes killed.

I wanted another daughter and felt strongly we should adopt a mixed-race baby from Vietnam. Jim wasn't convinced. We were still struggling financially, and he felt three children were his limit.

"No room at the inn," became his favorite song.

"We can always squeeze in another bed and chair."

It's impossible for me to explain the depths of my passion about adopting. Maybe it started when I was young and saw pictures of Asian children in magazines. I was drawn to them as if somehow they belonged to me. Whatever the reason, it was an avenue I felt we should pursue.

"Let's look into it and see where it leads, Sue."

My heart skipped a beat when I heard those words.

We researched the process, and were stunned to learn that the Vietnamese hated us so much they cut off all adoptions by American families.

"Well, if we can't adopt an Amerasian child, let's look into Korean adoption," I suggested.

Jim stopped putting up roadblocks and became committed to the whole idea. We sent to Holt Adoption, a Christian-based agency in Oregon, for information about Korean adoption. "It says in this brochure that a home study has to be done by Monroe County. I'll call and get an appointment as soon as possible," I said.

We filled out an application, turned over our income tax information, and scheduled an appointment with a county social worker. That was just the start.

"In the next few months, you will be asked to attend several meetings with other potential adoptive families," the facilitator said. "That'll give you a chance to ask questions, meet other interested couples, and decide if you really want to go through with foreign adoption. At some point, a home visit will be scheduled. Also, we require letters of recommendations from friends and your clergy and an essay from each of you about your faith."

We felt overwhelmed by all of the paperwork, but continued to push forward. Completing all of the necessary steps took over a year. Maybe that was the county's weeding out process. The cost of adoption was based on our income—still under $10,000 a year.

We were attending our final interview when the social worker bent her head forward, looked over her glasses and said, "Are you sure you can afford a fourth child? Your salary is quite low."

We exchanged puzzled looks. *Did she think we weren't well aware of that fact?*

"Believe me we know that, but I think we can always squeeze one more baby into our home and hearts," I said. At long last, every requirement was fulfilled, and we began a yearlong waiting period.

While we waited, our life returned to its usual hectic routine of work, family, and friends. Although we weren't addicted to television, in 1971 a new sitcom was introduced that revolutionized TV viewing and caught our attention. *All In the Family* was brash and irreverent and pushed the boundaries of acceptable topics. By today's standards, the script was mild. We howled with laughter at the antics of Archie, Edith, Gloria and Meathead. When Archie made racist statements, we shook our heads in disbelief and hoped we wouldn't hear similar things about our Korean child. We nicknamed our friend, Bill Draper "Archie," because of his red-necked comments. I think many Americans changed their thinking when they saw a little bit of Archie in themselves.

Waiting for news of our adoption seemed to go on forever. Every now and then, I called Holt Adoption Agency to check on the status. "These things take time. We'll notify you as soon as a child is selected."

1972 - HEADLINE NEWS - Families may vacation closer to home this summer now that the average price for a gallon of gas is 55 cents.

Each summer after Jim's painting jobs were finished, we headed for the Adirondacks towing a used pop-up camper. For two weeks, relatives and friends surrounded us. Betty and Bill, by now called Aunt Benny and Uncle Boo by our children, rented a nearby cottage and shared in our family's activities.

When I speak of family, I mean a *really big family*. From ten to thirty children were around at all times. Each day, the cousins swam, played ball, hiked, held hula-hoop and footsie contests, and hunted for crayfish. Each night, we organized an activity around the campfire.

One night, making stick-bread was the plan. Stick bread is biscuit dough wrapped around a stick, cooked over an open fire, and filled with jam. Jim and our boys had the task of finding the perfect sticks—long, fat, and sturdy enough to hold the dough without breaking.

On popcorn night we cooked Jiffy Pop, a relatively new product, over an open fire.

The crowning celebration was homemade ice cream night. The outside of our green ice cream maker was made of a composite material; the center stainless steel container held the cream and flavoring. We sprinkled salt liberally on the ice packed between the inside and outside walls. It wasn't electric—its handle had to be physically cranked.

As dusk settled, I announced. "We're making ice cream tonight. If you want to have some, you have to take a turn cranking. The rule is no crankie, no eatie."

From the youngest to the oldest, nieces, nephews, and friends turned the handle and anxiously awaited Uncle Jim's declaration.

"The ice cream is finished."

Children licked their lips and stood in line, arms outstretched, their small hands holding paper cups and plastic spoons. Somehow we always adopted new family members—children belonging to nearby campers.

"Can I have some too, Aunt Sue?" they'd ask. "How could I refuse those big eyes and sad pleas?"

Afterwards, adults tucked children into bed and then sat around the campfire.

Added to our list of camping activity was mountain climbing.

"Let's do Mt. Amerpsand this year," someone recommended.

Tracy was four years old and wanted to participate. It was his first big climb. Part way up the mountain, he lifted his arms for his father to carry him the remainder of the way.

"I could carry you, but then you won't be able to say you climbed a mountain. You'll be a lot prouder of yourself if you make this hike on your own."

With that, Tracy trudged up the mountain. At the top, Jim lifted his son into his arms and said, "I knew you could do it all by yourself. I'm proud you."

Anyone who expected a relaxing vacation was soon disappointed. Not used to so much family and activity, Bill started each day by saying, "What's on the activity wheel today? It never stops spinning."

Canoe trips across Middle Saranac or Tupper Lake usually occupied one afternoon and playing cards while sitting under a tarp on a rainy day, another. One year, we tried our skill at tennis. As hard as I worked at the game, I just didn't have the eye/hand coordination. The racket and ball rarely connected.

"Honey, this is no fun at all. I'm terrible, and I just can't play tennis. And, besides, I don't have to do everything. I quit." We chalked that activity up to a lost cause. There was always something else to try.

One afternoon, a neighboring camper asked, "Would anyone like to water ski?"

"Sure," we responded.

My sister, Janet, was the first to volunteer. Try as she might, she just couldn't get up on the skis. She kept falling forward into the water.

"Let me show you," I suggested. "I've water skied a few times before."

I jumped in the lake, jeans and all, to give her a quick lesson.

"When Sue says she is going to do something," Jim said, "she really means it."

Janet still couldn't get the hang of water skiing and gave up.

1973 - HEADLINE NEWS - Pearl Buck passes away. She is famous for vivid, compassionate novels about life in China. *The Good Earth* (1931; Pulitzer Prize), considered her finest work.

Days turned into weeks and then into months, and still no word about our new daughter. From time to time, friends asked for an update. "No news yet, and it doesn't do any good to call the agency. We just have to be patient," I responded.

In February 1973, Tracy celebrated his fifth birthday with a luncheon party. The children made paper hats and played Duck, Duck Goose and Ring Around the Rosie. I baked a cutout cake shaped like a space shuttle in keeping with the nation's fascination with the space program. After a rousing rendition of "Happy Birthday" in several keys, the children played while we mothers chatted.

Once Tracy turned five, he expected to attend school with his older sister and brother. When his father arrived home, Tracy ran to greet him. "Dad—FIVE," and held up his fingers.

On the following day when the big yellow bus didn't whisk him off to school, Tracy was disappointed.

Jim and I continued to be discouraged about the lack of news regarding our adoption plans. Our resolve began to slip. *Do we really want to start over with another infant? Now that Tracy is five, he'll be heading to school in the fall.*

Was a higher power reading my thoughts? February 1973: I was busy with supper dishes when the phone rang. It was a female's voice.

"Hello. Is this Mrs. Savard?"

"Yes, it is."

"I'm calling from the Holt Adoption Agency. You'll be receiving a picture of a three month-old girl in the next few days. After you and your family have a chance to talk things over, please call back and let us know if this child will be acceptable to you."

"I can't believe it. We had just about given up hope. I can't wait to see the picture."

Jim was in the yard cutting wood. My legs sprouted wings, and I ran to the back yard yelling, "They're sending us a picture of our new baby."

With that call, our hesitation was replaced with wonder. *What will she look like? How soon will she arrive? Will our children accept her?*

A few days later, a grainy photocopy of a picture of Kang Myung Ja arrived. We felt drawn to her and knew we would love her as much as our biological children, no matter what she looked like. Once again, we began to discuss names. Only this time, three children's votes had to be considered.

"I like Suelyn. What do you think?" I asked the family.

Thumbs down.

More ideas were tossed around.

The final decision—Kim Myung Savard. The fact that our niece was also Kim Savard or that Kim is the most popular surname in Korea didn't matter. We just liked the name.

We mailed our $1,000 check immediately, depleting our savings to less than $200. Only one of us could fly to New York to meet her—but which one?

Instead of sleeping at night, I worried and stewed about all the possibilities. If I go and there's an accident, how will Jim manage to work and take care of three children? If he goes and something happens, how will I support three children?

"I'm nervous as a cat about flying, but I just have to be the one to go to New York. I won't be able to stand the suspense. Do you mind?"

"Go ahead, Sue. I know how excited you are."

"Everything should work like clockwork. She'll arrive at eight p.m. and I'll return on the ten p.m. flight. You and the kids can pick me up at eleven in Rochester."

I packed a diaper bag with bottles of formula, disposable diapers, a fresh outfit, and a baby blanket. I fumbled my way through the check-in routine and waved goodbye with deep trepidation. My stomach tightened in knots when I boarded the plane for my first-ever airplane ride. The minute I sat in the seat, I clipped the seat belt closed and yanked it tight. When the plane taxied for take off, my back pressed into the seat, and I white knuckled its arms. As the flight attendant went through her safety spiel about oxygen masks and life preservers, I paid close attention to every word and followed along in the instruction pamphlet. Then I prayed the plane would land safely. To distract myself, I looked out the window and marveled at the patchwork quilt of colored squares and aligned rows of trees. It all looked so organized and planned. The hour-long flight seemed endless. But once there, I was sure things would move along quickly.

At the airport, I waited and waited and waited. Eight o'clock came and went with no sign of her flight. Frequently I checked the marquee. *Flight delayed* flashed on the screen. The twenty-four hour flight she was aboard and the long delay made me concerned about who was caring for our daughter. I only knew she was being looked after by someone who had received a free flight in exchange for tending to several children. Grandparents, relatives, adoptive parents, and I paced the floor. We checked the marquee, drank coffee, engaged in small talk, and waited. I was alone in a sea of wound-up families and wished Jim and our children were there to share in the excitement. When the plane finally arrived at midnight, passengers began to deplane. Everyone jammed forward to be first to catch a glimpse of his or her new family member. Older Korean children held tightly to their caretakers' hands and looked with startled, tired eyes at the assembled crowd at the exit ramp. Balloons, cheers and hugs added to the confusion. The caregiver handed Kim to me. Drained and anxious, I looked lovingly on our new daughter as I held her for the first time. I marveled at her beautiful almond eyes and satin skin. Her face was scrubbed clean, but her ears were dirty and a red sore encircled her neck. She was bald and chunky and dressed in a white knitted hat, sweater, and pants. She was the most beautiful baby I'd ever seen. Chaos ensued as paperwork was straightened out and signed, ensuring that the correct child was placed with the right family. By one a.m., I learned no more flights to Rochester were scheduled.

I called Jim at two a.m. from an airport pay phone. "She's beautiful, Honey. You should see her long delicate fingers. I'm stuck here until tomorrow morning. I'll get in Rochester at ten a.m. I can't wait to show her off to everyone tomorrow morning."

An adrenaline rush kept me from falling asleep, and I sat on a wooden bench all night in the airport staring in wonder at our new baby as if I'd birthed her myself. Our long wait was over.

The next morning, Jim, Shelly, Kerry, and Tracy fidgeted as they waited to greet Kim. Not one moment of rejection from her siblings occurred when she joined our family. Although exhausted, I bathed her and dressed her in one of the new outfits I'd received as a gift. Our home again settled down to a daily routine of bottles, diapers, and sleepless nights.

For several days, Kim seemed unusually quiet and observant of her new surroundings. I assumed that was her nature.

"I should have sent our other three children to Korea for a few months. Maybe they would be as quiet as Kim," I joked.

According to her paperwork, our daughter had been in a foster home with three brothers—never in an orphanage—and had been fed rice milk. What the heck is rice milk?

She hungered for solid foods and eagerly tasted everything on my plate. As the days turned to weeks, I understood her quietness was culture shock. She was adjusting to our touch, the smells in our home, the sounds of our voices, and the cadence of our language.

The information packet also warned: "When she gets upset (for no apparent reason), she will hold her breath until she turns blue." She quite often did exactly that. Jim was shocked the first time he saw her turn blue.

"She'll calm down shortly," I said. "Eventually she'll have to catch her breath." And she did.

Our biological children were enamored of Kim. They kept her entertained, and after school, Kerry took over. He sat on the couch with his feet propped on an old buckboard, turned on *People's Court*, and held a bottle to her lips.

Kim's arrival opened a new world to us. When Arlene Kim, one of Jim's students, heard him brag about his new adopted daughter, she told her mother. One afternoon, Arlene's mother came to visit.

In broken English she said, "I have brought you a gift of one of Arlene's Korean dresses and a pair of her shoes. I want you to have them."

"Thank you so much. The dress is exquisite. Please come in and meet our new daughter."

The vividly embroidered, bright red traditional hanbok consisted of a blouse shirt or jacket and wrap-around full skirt. The shoes were made of brightly colored plastic and came to a turned-up point at the end. Soon we were sharing dinners with the Kims, learning Korean board games, and joining an International Adoption group.

Another surprise: "The Rochester's Korean community invites your family to Aa-Ga-Pah day or Parent Love Child day."

We weren't certain what to expect but looked forward to a new experience. A Korean dinner of bulgogi, rice, kimchi, steamed vegetables, soup, tea, milk, and small boxes of hard candy plus afternoon entertainment became an annual event. The food was delicious until dessert arrived—rice cakes. Unlike the sweet confections we were used to, we all agreed it tasted like squares of wallpaper paste topped with a sweet nut.

CHAPTER 10 - SALVAGED SNIPPETS

Reflections: Snapshots of events from our years together came flooding back to me when I least expected them. Recollections filtered through my mind like whispers from the past, bringing me pleasure and reminding me of happy times. When I closed my eyes and thought of these memories, I could picture my husband, with his smiling eyes, teasing me or holding me as we danced.

****

Two months after Kim's arrival, Jim headed to Washington, D.C. for the annual eighth grade, six-day field trip. The trip was the highlight of the school year. For months, students worked to raise money by selling sundries door to door, doing odd jobs for their parents, and babysitting for neighbors. The chaperones came home late on Saturday evening with tired bones, sore feet, and stories of students' broken friendships and broken hearts.

For me, the week was a break from the daily routine and from cooking complete meals. Instead, I'd say, "How about pancakes and bacon for supper? Or "Let's have hotdogs and Campbell's pork and beans."

After the children went to bed, I did projects I couldn't get done when Jim was home. On the night of his return, I began a tradition of feeding the children early, putting them to bed, and preparing a midnight candlelight dinner for the two of us complete with linen tablecloth and napkins. I looked for new recipes and fussed over the menu.

On his return trip, when the busses stopped for dinner, my husband ordered coffee.

"Savard's got a heavy date tonight," his colleagues teased.

When busses rolled into the school's parking lot at ten p.m., parents and spouses cheered a greeting to the returning students and teachers. Jim pulled me into his arms for a hug, and his warm smile told me he was glad to be home. At midnight, we sat down for dinner and caught up on the family news without the constant interruptions of four noisy children. Bathed in the warm glow of candlelight, we rekindled the special bond we shared.

1973 - HEADLINE NEWS - When the Twister game was featured on 'The Tonight Show', the presenter, Johnny Carson, had to climb over Eva Gabor, who was on her hands and knees and wearing a short skirt. Milton Bradley (MB) was accused of selling "sex in a box" by its competitors.

After a week to recuperate, the chaperones were ready to party at our house. Everyone brought a dish to share and stories of the trip to recount. The hot party game was Twister. At the time, our friends could still bend without hurting their backs or crying about their knees. Laughter filled our home as arms, legs, and bodies entangled and stretched from one color circle to the next. We never thought of Twister as sex in a box.

The limbo dance craze was also going strong, and a few teachers did their best to bend backwards and slither under a broomstick. Our children slept through the whole commotion.

When summer arrived, we planned a trip to Tupper Lake to attend Jim's high school reunion. Because graduating classes were small, each reunion combined several years of graduates. I was at ease since a number of the attendees were my first or second cousins. Once there, he became Eagle Eye again and swapped high school memories and sports stories with old friends. After the dinner and speeches had concluded, we danced the night away.

Many people believed Jim had married his high school sweetheart. She was my height and weight and had dark hair and eyes like mine. At one reunion, a man sitting behind me tapped my shoulder and said, "Pat."

"No, She's the one he dated. I'm Sue. I'm the one he married."

The man looked down at his hands. When he heard me chuckle, he realized I was enjoying the mix-up. After all, it gave me new material for a story.

Summertime was gardening time, and we planted and tended an acre of corn, tomatoes, squash, melon, peas, and beans. Shelly, Kerry, and Tracy helped us weed the garden and pick the produce. Canning and freezing the excess consumed hours of our time and provided us food for the winter months.

"When I was little, my father had a garden in Uncle Buck's back yard," Jim said. "We had to weed it and pick the vegetables. I hated every minute of that chore. I can't believe I like it now."

One day, as I watched Jim fussing over his garden, I yelled from the kitchen window, "Leon would be proud of you."

It was during corn season, when two boys from another teacher's family joined us for dinner. There were five children in their household, and their parents didn't plant a garden. I placed on the table a large platter filled with freshly picked, golden yellow corn. "Have as much as you want boys. I've got more in the pot."

The boys told their parents, "Savards are rich."

"Why do you say that?" their mother asked, knowing full well that the Savards weren't rich.

"Because, their kids can have all the corn on the cob they want."

Our activity wheel didn't stop spinning in the winters. We looked for cheap entertainment. Our house sat on a hill just high enough for good sledding. On Sundays, friends arrived with their bundled up children and plastic sleds to enjoy an afternoon of winter fun. When the sun began to set and the air became chilly, we all retired to our family room to drink hot chocolate and socialize by a warm fire.

1974 - HEADLINE NEWS - Barbra Striesand's First #1 hit, "The Way We Were"

"Hon, your 40th birthday is approaching. What'dah ya want?" I asked.

"I'm going to buy my own early birthday present."

He'd never owned a bike—his family couldn't afford such luxuries. He checked prices and models and purchased his very first bike. "Let's go on a bike ride," he said to Kerry and Tracy. The three rode past our neighbor's horse corral. Kerry spotted a stallion with a full erection.

"Dad, Dad. Did you see that horse?" Kerry asked. "It's got five legs."

Jim was so amused over the five-legged horse that he nearly crashed his new bike. It was time to have a *man talk* with his son. When I heard the story, I hooted. Another yarn was added to the Savard Family Chronicles.

Summertime slipped by and melded into fall, school, and holidays. It was after Thanksgiving, when Jim decided to make turkey soup. He wrapped the bones in a cheesecloth bag, added water, and began to prepare the stock. While the stock simmered on the stove, he cut a slab of suet into slices to make a snack for our bird friends.

Our children were watching their father and complaining about lunch. It wasn't unusual to hear, "Yuck—I don't like that." Or, "Do we have to eat these vegetables?"

"So—you don't want to eat the good food your mother's prepared for you, huh? Well, how about rag soup and fat sandwiches for dinner?" he said in his best actor's voice. With that, he used tongs to hold up the greasy, gray bag of turkey bones. Then he took a slice of suet and threw it between two pieces of bread.

"Yes, sir, this is what we're serving for dinner. Rag soup and fat sandwiches."

Kerry burst into tears. "You don't *lub* us. You're making us eat rag soup and fat sandwiches."

When I smiled, the kids settled back and realized their father was just being dramatic. The story of the rag soup and fat sandwiches became a classic to be retold again and again over the years.

Santa appeared at our home that year with cross-country skis for everyone. Acres of empty farmland surrounded our house—great for cross-country skiing. Jim led the entourage and cut the trails as we glided behind. At two, Kim enjoyed the sport by riding in a child carrier on her father's back. Downhill skiing had to wait until much later in life. It was way too expensive. Instead, we skated, went sledding, canoed, climbed mountains, cross-country skied, rode bikes, went on picnics, played baseball, and fished. In the process, our children were exposed to a greater variety of activities and a healthier lifestyle than many of their more affluent friends.

Since Jim sang in the church choir on Sundays, we sat in the balcony. Our two boys struggled to sit through an hour-long mass. They vied for an opportunity to bring money downstairs to the collection basket. One day, it was Tracy's turn. He was six years old.

"Here, Tracy. It's your turn today," I said. "Wait quietly in the back of the church for the usher to come by with the basket."

My eyes popped a few seconds later. I looked over the railing and spotted Tracy running full speed down the center aisle, taking a sharp turn at the altar, running the full length of the side aisle, and back to the balcony. I put my head down and stifled an embarrassed snicker. His sprint was so funny that we didn't have the heart to scold him.

On another Sunday at breakfast, Kerry pulled a fake $50 bill from his pocket.

"Boy, Father Lintz would like to see a $50 bill in the collection basket," I said.

At the end of the mass, the priest announced, "I would like to thank the generous person for the $50 donation in today's basket."

Oh, oh.

After mass, I stopped the priest. "I hope you were serious that someone actually gave you $50." Then, I told him about my comment to Kerry.

"No, no, it wasn't fake. I really did get a $50 donation."

I think even priests tell little white lies when the occasion warrants.

Our income remained low, and our children had few toys. They used their imaginations in creative ways. GI Joe was one of Kerry's favorites.

In Kerry's hands, GI Joe became a real action figure. Kerry's bedroom window was directly above our kitchen sink window. Often the boys tied a rope around GI Joe's neck, dangled the doll from the second story window and passed it before my eyes as I did the dishes.

"There's GI Joe making a fast getaway again," I said as the doll went by.

In the wintertime, Kerry used his vinyl slipper and duct tape to create a sled for GI Joe. When the snow was hard and crusty, GI Joe could be seen sailing at full speed down our hill.

In the spring and summer, an old cherry tree in our backyard became the staging area for Kerry's and Tracy's alter-egos to begin combat operations. They'd climb up, nestle into a crotch of the tree, and using sticks for guns, try to shoot down the crop dusters.

"Ratta, tat, tat. Did you get that one, Joe?" asked Kerry.

"Yeah, Mike," responded Tracy.

1975 HEADLINE NEWS - A 1974 television commercial for Post Grape-Nuts cereal featured Euell Gibbons asking viewers "Ever eat a pine tree? Many parts are edible."

One Sunday in 1975, our local paper carried a long article about Euell Gibbons.

"Honey, did you see the article on Euell Gibbons in the paper? I'm going to get his book, Stalking the Wild Asparagus. He's an authority on North American edible wild plants."

I plunged into the book. He touched a chord with the back-to-nature crowd, including me. I studied his book from cover to cover.

"Let's host a wild foods dinner," I suggested.

A new chapter began. Once a year we hosted a wild foods dinner for carefully selected, adventuresome friends. Menus included fish or game Jim caught and a variety of foods gathered from the fields. We served milkweed, dandelions, burdock, purslane, cattails, day lilies, wild berries, and amaranth.

"What're we eating?" guests asked.

"Oh, no you don't. It's not that easy. First try to guess."

The year of the gooseberry pie caused quite a sensation. Some wild gooseberries are spiny, and some are not. The spines will soften as the pie cooks, I thought as I prepared the dessert. Wrong.

We heard "Ouch, ouch" when our guests ate the pie, and their mouths got pricked with semi-hard thorns. Everyone teased me. The account of the spiked pie episode provided fodder for the Monday morning faculty room gathering.

Our list of down-home activities continued to expand when we added cider-making day. Herb, our neighbor, had an antique cider press sitting unused in his barn for decades.

"Herb, do you mind if we borrow the cider press for a few days? We're going to have an old-fashioned cider making day."

"No problem. We're glad to have someone use it," he said.

We called friends. "C'mon over on Saturday for cider making. Bring a bag of apples, some jugs, strong arms, and your children. Sue's going to make homemade doughnuts using her mother's famous recipe."

While other parents pressed apples, Jim was busy. "Hop in kids. I'll give you a ride around the yard in my hay wagon (his tractor cart filled with straw).

The children's task was to frost the doughnuts or shake them in a bag of cinnamon and sugar. On a bright fall day, nothing is quite so memorable as biting into a warm doughnut fresh from the frying pan and sipping a cup of new cider. Our slice of Americana became a yearly tradition. The cider press found a new home with us and never returned to our neighbor's barn.

Kim carries on cider making day with a new twist. The day includes a jump house, pizza, a hay bale mountain, and pony rides. I still make the doughnuts.

1976 - HEADLINE NEWS - *My Fair Lady* runs at St. James Theater NYC for 384 performances.

The newspaper reported that *Bubbling Brown Sugar, Candide,* and *My Fair Lady* were enjoying long runs on Broadway.

Brockport's Middle School had its own version of Broadway. Two devoted middle school teachers, John Izzo and Andy Nazzaro, directed and cast a play using sixth, seventh, and eighth graders. The play was the major event of the middle school.

"We're doing *Music Man* this year and we need a barbershop quartet," John said. "C'mon, Savard. You can sing baritone."

"Are you kidding me? I've never been in a play before."

"We need you. You can do it."

"I'll give it a shot, but I'm not confident of my singing voice."

Meanwhile, tryouts were announced, and students vied for key roles. As an eighth grader, Shelly auditioned for and was chosen to play Gertrude Britt, one of the ladies in the Grecian Urn scene. Late night rehearsals went on for months, and tickets were sold out three weeks in advance. The whole school was abuzz with excitement. As the time drew near, Jim got cold feet.

He returned home from rehearsal late one evening and said, "Tonight I wanted to quit the play, but for once in my life, I'm not going to back out."

I was bursting with pride and knew the real Jim was emerging from his blanket of self-doubt. On opening night, Jim paced back and forth worrying about missing his queues or notes. Once on stage, he settled into the part.

"That was the most fun I've had in a long time," he said. "I didn't think I could do it, but I actually loved the evening—especially when I heard the audience clapping."

He was hooked. Barbershop singing became his new hobby. Jim joined a local chorus and rarely missed rehearsal night. After the first few meetings, Jim smugly announced, "Guess what? Now I'm president of the local chapter."

For the next thirteen years, Jim rehearsed weekly with the chorus and twice a year participated in sectional competitions. He got braver. "I'm going to form my own quartet. After all, SPEBSQSA means barbershop quartet singing, not chorus singing. We're going to get an act together and take part in the spring quartet competition."

The night of the competition, he felt as if a brick hit his stomach when he walked out on stage. From the audience, I could see his pant legs shaking, but he resorted to his *Never Quit* Marine Corps training and finished the songs. When his quartet won the Novice Trophy, his chest expanded five sizes.

"I've never been so nervous in my life, but I got through it. I can't even put into words how it made me feel to win that trophy. I guess my voice isn't so bad after all."

Spring and fall conventions gave us a chance to make new friends with people who shared a love of singing. After each show, the host chorus sponsored an *After Glow* party with plenty of food and drinks. Singing continued until two or three in the morning as quartets wandered the hotel's halls, stopping into rooms, singing a few songs, and then moving on to the next room.

1977 - HEADLINE NEWS - In the 1970s and 1980s, Julia Child was the star of numerous television programs, including *Julia Child & Company*.

For the first twenty years of marriage, I baked bread every week. We purchased hundred pound bags of flour from a nearby mill. After mixing the ingredients, I'd punch my fists into great mounds of stretchy dough and mush it around until my hands were covered in goop. Our friend,

Jane, joked, "You'll know you're done kneading when your fanny sweats."

When the bread came from the oven, the comforting aroma permeated our house. While it was warm, we couldn't resist sinking our teeth into thick slices spread with generous slabs of butter.

"Honey, could you teach me to make bread?" Jim asked.

I gave him one lesson after which he became our official bread maker, experimenting with French bread, English muffins, salt-rising bread, and bagels.

Suddenly, our children forgot my years of bread making. One day, I heard Kerry tell a friend, "Dad always makes our homemade bread."

"Wait a minute. Did you forget that I made all the bread for the first twenty years of our marriage?" I asked.

Our fascination with cooking continued to evolve.

"Let's make maple syrup," I suggested. "I found spigots at an antique shop, and we can use plastic buckets. Call Herb and ask if we can tap his big maple trees."

When the air was crisp and the sap running, we collected pails of the sweet liquid. Jim cooked the sap over an open fire—forty to one ratio of sap to syrup. Our children played outside, kept the fire stoked, and learned something of what the pioneers endured.

I wondered what all that effort was for when, many years later, my husband announced, "I prefer Mrs. Butterworth's."

By 1977, some of our evergreens were tall and full enough to be cut for our Christmas tree. We made a ritual of selecting the perfect tree.

"C'mon. It's time to select our tree." I announced.

"Put on your snow pants and boots," we reminded the children and all headed to the back acres.

"How about this one?" I asked.

"No, maybe this is better. That one has a crooked trunk."

And so it went until the perfect specimen was selected.

Jim was in charge of trimming extra branches, screwing the tree into the stand, and arranging the white lights. Afterwards, we placed on the tree the remaining red balls purchased during our first years of marriage. Homemade and antique ornaments followed until the tree was crammed with memories. An angel topper and quilted tree skirt provided the finishing touches. When completed, we turned out the room lights and admired the warm glow cast by the lighted tree. Still today, the smell of an evergreen tree brings to mind Christmas, family, laughter, and friends.

When our evergreens became too large for our home, we donated them to local churches so they could continue to provide Christmas pleasure.

1978 - HEADLINE NEWS - 600,000 attend "Summer Jam" rock festival, Watkins Glen.

Our *summer jam* officially started when we hosted an end-of-the-year party at our house for one hundred or more teachers and their partners. We had the perfect location—twelve acres and no close neighbors. Music, laughter, and singing wouldn't bother anyone. Jim and I emptied the garage of clutter, swept and washed the floor, mowed the lawn, and prepared wood for a bonfire.

The teachers were ready to relieve the tension of dealing with middle schoolers and consumed wine, beer, pop, hots, hamburgers, and salads at an alarming rate. After dark, they stood around the bonfire rehashing school stories and telling of their summer plans. The year the party fell on Kerry's birthday, he pretended to be embarrassed when a hundred teachers serenaded him with "Happy Birthday."

By July, we were heading to Little Wolf Pond in Tupper Lake to camp with our multitude of relatives. On arrival, Kerry, Tracy, and their cousin wanted to fish, and they headed across the lake in our canoe. They dug down deep with the oars until they reached the middle and heard their father's whistle. He had a powerful whistle that seemed to carry for miles. He'd pucker his lips and whistle between his teeth. That whistle meant: "Come back immediately from wherever you are."

"We've got to go back," Tracy said. "Dad's whistling."

"What'da ya mean?" Tom asked. "We just got here."

"I know, but when Dad whistles, we'd better respond."

They paddled back to shore.

"What're you guys doin?" Jim asked.

"We're fishin."

"Oh. Okay. Have fun."

"Jeez. What was that all about?" Tom asked as the boys paddled back and began to fish.

1980 - HEADLINE NEWS - President Jimmy Carter announces US boycott of Olympics in Moscow

My husband liked challenges. The track and field coach spotted Jim leaving school one afternoon. He called, "Mr. Savard, I remember your telling me that you were pretty good at pole vaulting when you were in high school. I'm having trouble explaining to the kids how to pole vault. Can you help me out a little?"

It was true. In high school, he had won awards for pole-vaulting. However, he was 16 at the time. Now, at 45, he still imagined he could pole vault.

Removing his sports coat and grabbing the pole, my Superman took off on a dead run and demonstrated the skill. When he came home, he never mentioned the episode to me.

The next day, we were in our garden planting a row of beans.

"Boy, I don't feel very well. I ache all over," Jim said.

"Well, maybe you're coming down with the flu. You should go to bed. I'll finish up here."

"I don't have the flu. I didn't want to tell you, but I was pole vaulting yesterday."

No longer sympathetic, I said, "You idiot. What are you doing at your age, pole vaulting? Are you crazy?"

He had pulled every muscle in his upper body. That ended his pole-vaulting career.

In 1980, at the age of eight, Kim became fascinated with séances. We were stymied.

Where in the world did this idea come from? Did she read about séances or hear about them on TV?

To prepare for a séance, Kim's costume consisted of a white blouse with large blue polka dots, a wide belt, a first communion veil, sunglasses, two or three necklaces, and high heels. Her invented character, Velma Dean, was ready.

A tablecloth-covered footstool with an unlit candle in the center became her altar. A glass of water represented wine, and a dish of dried bread provided SACK-red bread (as she pronounced it). Arms outstretched, back and forth Kim swayed and called her medium.

"Cleaman. Cleaman. Where are you? Come to me, Cleaman."

Late one evening, Jim's fun-loving side kicked in, and he decided to play along. At dark, he stood outside the living room window with everything but his face covered by a white sheet. The way he held the flashlight at his chest, shining upwards on his face, made his face ghostly white.

"Cleaman. Cleaman. Where are you?" Kim chanted.

"Hoo-o-o. hoo-o-o. I am here. I am here," came the sound from outside.

Turning around and seeing Jim's ghost-like face sent Kim six feet into the air screaming bloody murder and running headlong into the safety of our kitchen.

Laugh lines appeared on her father's face and crow's feet around his eyes. He doubled over with laughter and thought that was the most fun ever. It was just one more of his adventures.

That year, a milestone occurred for our family. Shelly graduated from high school. In the fall, she planned to enter St. John Fisher College—only thirty minutes from home. Over the summer, we purchased bedding, lamps, a hot pot, and all the essentials for a college freshman. All summer, I noticed that Shelly was testy. She wanted to go to college but was ambivalent about leaving home. We hadn't predicted our reaction to her leaving. When I actually began helping Shelly unload her closet and pack boxes with her belongings, the shock hit me.

Where had the years gone? How dare she grow up? Would our home be the same without her? Why didn't I spend more quality time with her? Was she leaving us for good?

The thoughts swirled around in my head, but I tried hiding my misgivings. I wanted Shelly to make a smooth transition to college. On the day we unloaded our daughter and her belongings at the dorm, we drove home in silence.

"This is ridiculous," I chided myself. "After all, she is only thirty minutes away. She's going to college, not war, for God's sake."

Her absence was sharp, and I felt such sadness when I looked in her closet, and her clothes were missing. Hot tears danced on my eyelashes. I began a cleaning frenzy, thinking that keeping busy was the answer to my sense of loss. I started in the cellar by reorganizing the shelves. Jim came down to help.

"What's in this?" he asked when he spotted an old gym bag.

"Those are all the letters and some of the cards we exchanged over the years."

"Burn those things."

"I will not. They're mine, and I want to keep them. Just put the bag back up on the shelf."

We both forgot about the letters, and they languished in the gym bag until 2010.

Eventually, we adjusted to having only three children at home, and our lives settled down.

We celebrated Tracy's thirteenth birthday in the winter of 1981 by inviting friends for dinner, followed by cake and ice cream and a round of "Happy Birthday." I purposely placed twelve candles on the cake.

"Mom, I'm thirteen this year," Tracy said.

"I know that, Tracy, but I refuse to have three teenagers in our house at the same time. Don't worry. Next year Shelly will be twenty, so you can become a teenager then."

Tracy just smiled and blew out his twelve candles.

It was about then that we decided to raise Rhode Island Red chickens, housing them in an old chicken house on our back lot. With the excess eggs, Jim was certain he'd earn enough money to pay for chicken feed. When my handsome husband dressed for work in his navy blue pinstripe suit and carrying a briefcase, he looked like a senator. Once in the faculty room, he thoroughly blew his senatorial image by opening his briefcase to reveal a few dozen eggs for sale.

Our chickens were free range, and Kim was afraid of all birds—especially our chickens. They greeted her as she departed the school bus and chased her up the driveway. With hair flying and eyes bugging, she screamed, "Get away, get away," and ran for the protection of our house. When fall drew near, we planned to kill our chickens, clean and freeze them for winter. On a bike ride past a friend's home, we stopped for a glass of water.

"Tomorrow morning is chicken-pluckin day," Jim said. "We're going to start killing our chickens around seven a.m."

The colleague's children were intrigued and awakened their parents the following day.

"Wake up. Wake up. It's chicken-pluckin day at Savards."

"Go back to bed. It's only 6:30 in the morning."

"We know. Get up. We don't wanna be late."

The knife was sharpened, the water boiling, there was excitement in the air—for a while. Jim was in charge of killing and gutting; I was in charge of defeathering. He grabbed a chicken, tucked its head under a wing, spun it around, plunked it down on a stump, and swiftly decapitated it. The carcass twitched on the ground, and blood pumped from its neck. The smell of wet feathers, innards, and blood made everyone's stomach queasy.

"I never guessed how messy this would be," I moaned.

After the children had satisfied their penchant for gore, they were bored with the whole activity, and went off to play. By the end of the day, our chickens were wrapped in the freezer, and we swore off ever having another chicken-pluckin day. On Monday, Jim regaled his lunchroom companions with his story of chicken-pluckin day.

Sue Etta, an expensively dressed, sophisticated science teacher asked, "How did you kill them?"

"I did what I thought I should do: tucked their heads under their wings, spun them around, then laid their necks across a stump, and chopped off their heads. Isn't that the right way?"

"Heck, no. I'm from Iowa. Out there, we just step on their heads and yank on their legs."

1983 - HEADLINE NEWS - On October 20, 1982, Korczak Ziolkowski, sculptor of the Crazy Horse monument, died unexpectedly at the age of 74. His family vows to continue the project.

One by one, our children were leaving the nest. By June 1983, Kerry was enrolled in a two-year college in upstate New York. It would seem strange to have him so far away. In both middle and high school, he'd played basketball which kept us busy shuttling him to practices or games. On weekends, we attended his games and cheered his successes.
What would we do with our spare time?
We would be down to two children after September. That summer, Shelly was home and working at McDonald's, earning money for her senior year. Kerry was looking for a summer job to help with college expenses. Jim and I were planning a three-week trip west with Tracy and Kim. We'd saved our money and read books about travel in the U.S. We were prepared.

"I've laid out our itinerary. It'll be exciting to see the Rockies, the national parks, and the monuments—all those things you teach about in your classes. I'll pack our cooler with enough food, snacks, paper products, and drinks to last several days," I said. "We can eat breakfast and lunch on the road and go to local restaurants for dinner. I think I'll throw in our electric fry pan. If necessary, I can use it to prepare dinner. We'll camp sometimes and stay in cheap motels other nights. I've packed our tent, camp stove, sleeping bags, and lanterns in the trunk."

A list of places of interest and AAA books with a route plotted were in our glove compartment. It was a dream realized. Concern about leaving Shelly and Kerry alone was on both of our minds. I tried to reassure myself.

After all, Shelly is 21 and Kerry 19. It's time to trust them. Besides they need money for college.

"We'll call and check on you. Water the plants, and keep an eye on the place while we're gone. Remember. No big parties. You know we always find out."

We left Brockport at 8:05 a.m. in our used, 1980 green Chevy Caprice. The sedan's seats were wide as a boat, easily accommodating three people across. Jim agreed to be our trip journalist, and the Falcon Inn in Detroit was first destination.

Journal entry 7/1/83: Found Falcon Inn - no trouble. Sue insisted the kids sneak in without paying. Sue spilled her milk. Went to a ballgame with brother Don's family. Baltimore won 9-5. 40,000 plus in attendance.

Journal entry 7/2: Dearborn Village; Arrived at Dearborn and bought tickets for two days. 1871 school room w/ Mr. Chapman played role to the hilt. Kids went to Don's house. Sue and I went to Detroit to the music festival. Wow - multitudes of people - numerous weirdoes. Temp hot; crowds oppressive.

Journal entry 7/4: Happy B.D. Amer. 4:00 a.m. on the road. Surprised by the flat lands of Mich. & Ill. Arrived DesMoines 4:15 p.m.

Around every turn in the road, we were met with another revelation—one of which was the number of miles between villages and towns. Jim drove long stretches of flat land—sometimes 120 miles—without seeing another car or community. One hamlet's sign made us laugh: Population, 10. The 10 was crossed out and replaced by 11. A new baby must have entered the world. Although the human population was low, the prairie dogs seemed to be experiencing a baby boom. Every few feet, the heads of the cuddly looking creatures popped out of holes.

Everything was more expansive than in the east. For the first time, I understood the term *big sky*. The canopy of blue was unbroken by clouds, and the terrain was flat and uninterrupted by buildings so that we spotted rolling hills and mountains miles before we got to them. The car's tires continued to slap against the blistering highway for hours until we finally arrived at the hills.

At times, I thought the car's air conditioner wasn't working until I stepped out of and realized it couldn't keep up with the sweltering heat.

Journal entry 7/6: Followed J. McKenna's directions perfectly. Arrived McKenna's, Omaha, Neb., 11:30 a.m. Great to see them. Regret not having planned more time with them. Went to Aquarium, Louisville Rec Beach for a swim, returned to McKenna's for strip steak dinner, visited till 11:30 p.m.

Journal entry 7/7: Tracy and I drove through part of the Badlands, found a trail and climbed to the summit. Breathtaking, not to mention scary. Kim and Sue took a trail ride. Kim rode Peanuts, and Sue rode Charlie Brown. Returned at noon. Sue is burning up - outside temp is 110°.

I never understood panic attacks until our visit to the Badlands. I had a rip-roaring one. After dinner, we all climbed the same summit Jim and Tracy had climbed earlier. When I turned to descend, I froze. I couldn't move a muscle. Jim, Tracy, and Kim ran down the hill and called, "C'mon, Mom. What's the matter?"

"There is nothing to grab onto if I fall. I can't move. The dirt is like tiny marbles. I'm afraid."

"There's nothing to be afraid of, Sue," Jim said and demonstrated by running up and down the hill. It didn't help.

When his coaxing failed, my savior climbed to where I was standing and told me to turn around and get on my hands and knees. He grabbed my ankles. Then one leg at a time, inch by inch, he navigated me down the hill. I was as stunned as Jim at my reaction. I'd climbed Adirondack Mountains many times before and never been afraid. There was always a rock or branch of a tree to grab, but these mountains were different.

> Journal entry 7/7: On our trip back down over smooth curved area adjacent to an 80' sheer drop, Sue got vertigo! It took me some time to get her back down. I tried to make light of the situation, but I was very worried.

The following day, we drove to Mt. Rushmore.

> Journal entry 7/8: Man's endurance over the power of nature—an inconceivable achievement—a feeling of national pride. I'll have to take issue with Dr. John McKenna's comment that Mt. Rushmore is overrated. Found a camp site in Custer State Park—kids swam—Tracy tried to drown me. Residents moved in next to us w/3 dogs, 4 adults and 7 kids-yuck.

The never-ending and always changing natural beauty of the countryside astonished us as we traveled from state to state. The meadows and mountains were alive with color and animals we'd never seen before.

> Journal entry 7/9: Found a nice camp site—Rafter Bar J Ranch—a few miles from Crazy Horse Mt. Korczak's plans and achievements at Crazy Horse make me feel very small. I have achieved nothing during my lifetime

> *in relation to this man. I hope this incredible dream is finished in my lifetime.*
>
> *Journal entry 7/10: After eggs and buttermilk biscuits, we drove to Little Big Horn battle site. I am always very moved to be on the land where some powerful historical events took place.*

Everything went smoothly until we reached the Black Hills on July 11. Our car overheated and billowing steam rose from under the hood. We were in a desolated area, and cell phones weren't in use yet. What to do?

"You stay here with the kids, and I'll walk until I find a place to call a local garage."

> *Journal entry, 7/11: Our first mechanical problem. Walked to Burgess Junction, which was just that - not a building of any type. Finally found a lodge, called a garage. $4.56 for a cap; $20 for delivery.*

At Burgess Junction, Jim used a pay phone to dial an auto repair shop and a woman sitting nearby overheard him. She said to her husband, "We should help this young man out. He seems trustworthy. Let's drive him back to his car."

We all thanked the kind strangers profusely, waited for the repairs to be made, and continued on our way.

Upon entry into Yellowstone National Park at six p.m., we realized that the Roosevelt Lodge where we had reservations was still seventy miles away.

> *Journal entry 7/11: Stopped in Cody for supplies - lunch in the school park - visit to Wm. Cody museum - Indian culture bldg. super. Arrived Yellowstone at 6:00. Scenes were breathtaking. Some treacherous turns were made even more so by the fact that I was trying to view the scenery and locate game. We spotted moose, buffalo, elk, and sheep (not confirmed by the rest of the family).*

The following day, we drove through part of the park. Our plans for lodging changed when I spotted the Old Faithful Inn.

"Look at that beautiful old inn, Jim. Let's see if a room is available and stay there tonight."

We secured a room in the spectacular log and limb structure built in 1903-04. From our window, we watched Old Faithful erupt every hour. I felt special to be staying the night in such a historic inn, a far cry from the tent lodging we'd stay in at our next stop - Colter Bay.

Journal entry 7/15: Cutting firewood for tonight. Weather cool. Tent breezy. Colder than a miner's buns in the Yukon. Reservations made for raft trip on Snake River tomorrow.

Journal entry 7/16: Sue and kids took off. I took 89 south to Alpine Junction. Met family. Found an A-frame restaurant. Homemade vegetable beef soup, bread, coffee, milk, pie.

When we reached Salt Lake City, we expected to hear the Mormon Tabernacle Choir. My careful planning fell short.

"We're too late to be seated inside the Tabernacle. I'm so disappointed," I said.

Tracy and Kim were relieved. From the steps outside, we caught part of the performance. The acoustics of the Tabernacle and the perfection of the voices made us realize why the chorus is called *America's Choir*.

Jim lost his enthusiasm for journalizing.

Final entry 7/18: Dinosaur National Park. Ranger was very enthusiastic. Great report on this period of history. Toured Josie Morris's cabin—friend of Butch Cassidy. Very dry—sandwiches dry in seconds. Enjoyed the afternoon playing Crazy 8's and reading.

Off to Colorado, where we consulted our niece, Paula, about the best places to eat. "The Casa Bonita Mexican Restaurant in Denver is a must do."

A juggler walking on the highest stilts we'd ever seen greeted us at the door. Once inside and seated, our heads pivoted from one performance to the next. A deep diving pool in the center of the restaurant accommodated the indoor cliff divers. Cowboys put on an old west show and Mexican dancers performed. The fun atmosphere made up for the quality of the food.

Alas, three weeks of traveling, camping and living out of suitcases proved long enough. "Let's head home," I said. "I'm anxious to see Shelly and Kerry and sleep in my own bed. We'll make one final stop—Abraham Lincoln's twelve-room Greek revival home in Springfield, Illinois."

We had hoped Shelly and Kerry had kept things at home under control. They hadn't. The garden looked unattended, the car had a dented fender, and Kerry hadn't secured a full-time summer job. We reminded ourselves that no serious catastrophe had happened; gardening was never his or her thing; everyone was in one piece; it was delightful to be home.

Our busy household took on a slower pace after Kerry left for college. With only two children home, we could finally afford a Friday night fish fry. We made fewer trips to shuttle children to and from school events or part-time jobs. Jim and I had time to pursue our own interests. We read books, played cards, and watched movies. In the winter, we ice-skated at Churchville Park and cross-country skied. We took clogging lessons—a type of Appalachian Mountain dance that combines European, African American, and Cherokee dancing. We purchased taps for our shoes, went to weekly lessons, and practiced our steps in our basement during the week. With Jim's natural rhythm and ability, he was quick to pick up the steps. Clogging was a new style of dance for me after years of ballet and jazz lessons. A few times, we performed with our group. I dressed in a red and white checked shirt and navy blue square dancing skirt with a crinoline underneath; Jim dressed in a matching shirt and jeans.

1984 - HEADLINE NEWS - "Let's Go Crazy" by Prince & Revolution peaks at #1.

September 1984: Jim turned fifty—reason enough to invite forty people for a surprise party. He relished being the center of attention as friends teased and roasted him with stories of his antics.

Part way through the party, a stranger appeared at the door. Cat calls and cheers bounced off the ceiling when she entered. The new arrival, adorned in a black and gold beaded costume, glided into the room. A navel jewel punctuated the smooth skin of her midriff. A sheer veil covered the lower portion of her face giving her a mysterious aura. Unbeknownst to me, his friends from school had hired a belly dancer for Jim's entertainment. The party was about to get more interesting.

Middle Eastern music played, and she began her dance. A mixture of shock and pleasure registered on the birthday boy's face while he watched her undulating arms and her hips sway to a beat coaxed from her finger cymbals. With her warm body inches from him, she circled Jim in a sensual dance and placed grapes, one by one, into his waiting mouth. Then she placed her upside-down mug-shaped hat topped with a yellow feather on Jim's head and drew him to the dance floor. His blue eyes glistened with joy, so tantalized was he by her slow, rhythmic movements.

Maybe I should take up belly dancing.

1984 - HEADLINE NEWS - With the award of the 1984 Olympic Winter Games to Sarajevo in 1978, the International Olympic Committee was bringing the Winter festival to the Eastern Bloc for the first time.

Tracy was halfway through his sophomore year when he burst through the door after school, anxious to tell me about the morning's announcement.

"The science teacher is getting a group together for a day of skiing at Swain. Can I go? He said we're gonna sell candy to help pay for the tickets."

"That sounds great. I'll even buy a few candy bars to get you started."

Tracy was on a crusade and sold his candy bars in a matter of days.

I was happy for our son but a bit jealous—I wanted to try downhill skiing.

"I've packed your lunch and some money for a snack. Have fun, but don't try anything crazy."

In no time at all, Tracy could parallel ski through sharp turns on black diamond slopes with the smoothness and elegance of a weathered skier. He had found his sport.

"How'd ya do Tracy? Was it fun?" I asked when he returned.

"It was great, Mom. I never even stopped for lunch or the bathroom. I skied eight hours straight and ate my lunch on the way home."

With every muscle worn and barely a goodnight, he collapsed into bed.

That week, an ad blared over the radio. "Ten dollars for ski rental, a lesson, and an eight-hour lift ticket."

"Hon, I've always wanted to try downhill skiing. Let's try it. Swain is offering a great package for $10."

"That's an expensive sport. We can't afford it."

"Well, maybe we can't ski very often, but I can afford $10 this Saturday."

Off I went by myself, a little apprehensive, but certain I'd be fine.

Tracy said skiing is easy. I should be able to handle it.

After a one-hour lesson, I was on my own and could barely snowplow. I struggled to get on the chairlift; I struggled even more to get off the lift; I did a face plant on the bunny hill to the cheers and cat calls of the overhead skiers; I took off my skis and walked down the slope after I attempted to navigate an intermediate run.

By the end of the day, my legs were rubbery—almost too tired to drive home.

Downhill skiing is undoubtedly going to be a challenge, but I know I can do it. I just have to try harder the next time.

Jim heard the same ad the following week.

"If you're going to get involved in this sport, I might as well give it a try," he said. "I'll ask Bolthouse if he wants to go with me."

After a day on the slopes, they were both hooked.

On Christmas morning, Jim held his camera ready. The picture of Tracy wearing his bathrobe and caressing his new skis was the only thanks we needed. We would have to wait till the following Christmas to purchase our own equipment.

For the next five years, downhill skiing was added to our activity wheel.

1985 - Nicholas Mark Sanders (England) begins circumnavigation of globe, covering 13,035 road miles in 78 days, 3 hr, 30 min

I was on my own circumnavigation mission—planning and saving for a trip to Europe. For as long as I could remember, my bucket list contained travel in Europe. I hinted at the possibility several times to Jim.

He ignored me.

By the end of the school year in 1985, we would be down to two children. Shelly and Kerry were out of college and beginning jobs. Tracy was a junior and Kim a freshman. It was a perfect time for us to take a trip to Europe with our two youngest.

Maybe my dream can be realized.

One evening, I broached the subject of Europe again. "Hon, I'm ferreting as much money away as I can and reading Frommer's book, Europe on $25 a Day. I think we'll have the money by June to take a trip to Europe."

"We can't afford to go to Europe. We should wait a few more years until everyone's out of college."

Damn it, I grumbled to myself. Here we go again being negative. Why can't he just once be excited about a trip? It's those old insecurities showing up again.

Over the next few months, I persisted.

"I've got quite a bit saved, and the trip will be a great experience for us and Tracy and Kim."

He let the comment hang in the air like a frozen glob.

As summer vacation got closer, I was no closer to changing his mind.

One night in frustration, I said, "Remember Dr. Buscaglia's story about the professor's wife who wanted to wear a red dress to a party, and he wouldn't let her. Then she died, and he buried her in a red dress. Buscaglia said not to wait for your red dress. If you want it, the time is now. I won't force you into a trip you don't want to take. However, please understand that Tracy, Kim, and I will be in Europe during the month of July. We'll see you in August. I'm not waiting for my red dress."

Shocked at my statement, he said, "I guess I'm going to Europe this summer."

"I think that would be a good idea."

Thank the Lord. I breathed a sigh of relief. It was a threat I never would carry out, but it worked.

Once I had a tepid agreement from Jim, I moved into full-scale planning mode and laid out a trip on a map of Europe. We'd land in Amsterdam, drive to Paris, on to Nice, cross to Milan, then Munich, and back to Amsterdam. The anticipation of a month-long trip to Europe was almost more than I could endure. Until the end of the school year, each day of teaching was drudgery. I typed lists of everything: places to see, places to avoid, what to say, what not to say, what to pack, what to leave home. My fingers flew over the keyboard. As our day of departure drew closer, we narrowed down our clothing choices. We'd each carry one small soft bag, pack all dark, mix-and-match clothing, take only items easy to wash and fast to dry. The evening before our departure, well-wishers called. My mother, Mary and Sonny, Shelly, Kerry, John McKenna, John Izzo, and the Fitzgeralds all phoned. "Have fun and a safe journey. Send a card from wherever. We'll see you in August."

Disbelief replaced the worrying, waiting, and planning of the past months. We were actually heading for Europe. At the Toronto airport, we paced the waiting area for our flight announcement only to be informed that it would be delayed due to a bomb scare. The announcement didn't help settle Jim's nerves. I looked at him—uncertainty showed in his face. I kept quiet, afraid he would suggest we scrap the whole trip.

"If our World Ways plane lands and has propellers," Tracy said, "I'm scalping my ticket."

Two hours later, we boarded our plane and lifted off. Forget sleep. Besides nerves, stimulation, and excitement, the two men behind us talked all night. On July 8, at 3:05 a.m. our time, we exited the plane and walked towards the custom's desk. Machine-gun totting soldiers lined the hallway.

What have I had gotten us into? Will this be the usual site in Europe?

Jim, our designated driver, found maneuvering the rented Ford Escort along Amsterdam's narrow streets, with one-way bridges over the canal every half-mile, and crowds of people on bicycles (800,000 people/600,000 bikes) especially challenging. But, in spite of it all, after two hours of being lost, we found the Casa Cara Pensione ($43.44 a night), where we had reservations for our first two nights. The hearty breakfast of assorted breads, hard-boiled eggs, cheeses, sliced meats, orange juice, and dark coffee carried us through the day. The Van Gogh Museum, Rijksmuseum, and Anne Frank's house were must-sees in Amsterdam.

Once Jim realized we could find our way around, he settled into the spirit of the trip. He was glad I'd cajoled him into it until 326 miles later when we arrived in Paris's Arch of Triomphe. He pulled into the roundabout. "Damn. It's rush hour and these people drive like maniacs."

I was scrambling to figure out which one of the twelve exits off the circle we needed to take. Round and round we went at a dizzying speed, waved on each time by a female traffic guard. By the fifth or sixth time around, she began to laugh as she signaled us with her gloved hand. Jim could take it no more. He did a suicide maneuver across traffic, made a mad dash out of the circle, jumped a curb with the car, and turned off the engine. His hands were shaking.

"I've got to calm down," he said. "I'm a nervous wreck in this traffic."

An elegantly dressed Parisian man was exiting a men's club and saw our confusion.

"Could I help you?" (Who says Parisian's aren't nice to Americans?)

Jim laid our map across the car's hood. "We're trying to get here." He pointed at the left-bank area.

"Ah, follow my car, and I'll point you to the right exit," our French friend said in understandable English.

Jim pulled into traffic behind the Parisian's black car. We followed him for a short distance; our savior's arm came out his window; he pointed over the top of his car towards an exit. We said a quiet thank you for our helpful stranger and left the Arche behind. Once in the correct area, Jim parked the car on a side street and began to decompress. For the next four days, we took the subway.

Kim and I walked blocks, stopping at Pensiones to inquire about vacancies. At long last, two rooms at the Hotel Gerson were available ($24 a night). The mattresses felt like plywood and the sheets like burlap, but we were in Paris. What could be better? That night, we tried to sleep, but couldn't. We listened to two French women arguing for hours. The only words we understood were f___ y__. I guess some words are just universal. In the morning, we planned our route, figured out the subway system, and headed for Notre Dame Cathedral. We rode the subway for twenty minutes, exited at the correct stop, and congratulated ourselves that we had located the church. The cathedral was everything we expected. Tracy and I climbed to the top of the tower for an overview of the city. The next morning, I looked out our bedroom window, and we could see the cathedral only two blocks from our hotel. Oh well, we had learned how to navigate the subway system.

For me, strolling the streets of Paris, sitting in cafes eating omelets, munching croissants drizzled in chocolate, listening to the cadence of the language, and calculating the exchange rate was as intriguing as visiting the Eiffel Tower or the Louvre.

"Jim, pinch me. I can't believe I'm in Paris."

We had so much fun seeing the sights that late one evening, Jim and I linked arms and danced down the street singing "We ain't got a barrel of money" as our embarrassed children hung back and distanced themselves from us.

For the remainder of the trip, we took a meandering course following instinct. We had a general idea of places we wanted to see, but not a specific itinerary.

Arles on the Mediterranean, where we experienced our first stand-up urinal, was our next stop. Impressions of feet on the floor indicated proper placement in order to get a direct hit. Kim held out for a while, but nature finally intervened. Our stomachs and sense of time were still on Eastern Standard. France's was not. There would be no more five p.m. dinner hours. The French restaurants didn't open until 7:30 p.m., and customers were still drinking and chatting in the outside cafes at 11 p.m. What a life.

By chance one evening, we stumbled upon a comic bullfight where local boys taunted a bull by trying to remove a ribbon from its horns. It looked quite dangerous to me, but the crowd was not concerned about safety and cheered the boys (or bull) on. In a mad, every-man-for-himself melee, the angry bull chased the young men around the arena until the boys jumped over a fence to escape.

A complete European experience wouldn't be complete without enjoying sunbathing on the Riviera. That is, Kim and I enjoyed the sun, and Jim and Tracy enjoyed the topless women. They weren't all model material. I watched one woman, about 65 and 225 pounds, lift her large sagging-to-her-ample-stomach breasts, one boob at a time, and apply suntan lotion underneath. I wondered how the sun would get to that spot.

We relaxed on our towels on a long jetty, soaked up some rays, and listened to the multitude of foreign languages around us. We felt certain we were the only Americans within miles. A small, annoying dog nipped and barked at Jim's feet. He gave a gentle nudge to shoo it away, but the dog was relentless. Finally, Jim said, "Get out of here you little bastard," assured that no one near would understand his words.

"My feelings exactly," said the well-endowed, topless young girl from Chicago on the next towel over. Jim was embarrassed; she was amused.

On we meandered past Monaco, through the tunnels and bridges of the Apennine Mountains, and past acres of grape vines. We planned a few days in Milan. Our plan unraveled rapidly when we couldn't locate a Pensione. I was sticky from the heat, and Jim short-tempered from driving around the same block several times.

"Pull over a minute, Hon. I'll see if I can find someone who speaks English to give us directions."

I stopped a tall, dark haired woman wearing a sundress who could speak broken English.

"Where is Pensione?" I asked, pointing to the name in the book.

She raised her arm shoulder height and pointed out the direction, exposing an unshaved armpit of dark hair.

I anticipated Kim's reaction.

"Yuck. Did you see that hair under her arm?" announced Kim, grossed out by the hairy armpits. "It's disgusting."

"Get used to it. Things are a little different from home. It's all part of the experience."

Jim pulled into traffic. "You know what, Jim. To hell with Italy. Let's head for Austria. It's too darn hot here."

Plan B took shape.

Dusk was settling when we crossed the border into Austria. The mountains, cool air, and scent of evergreens reminded us of the Adirondacks. The scenery was so like that in *The Sound of Music* film, we couldn't squelch our urge to sing "Do-Re-Mi" as Jim drove along the winding road.

By 9 p.m., we were knocking on the door of a Pensione in Innsbruck.

"I've no vacancy," the owner said in halting English. "I'm so sorry."

"Oh, no. We're exhausted. Do you know of any other?" I begged.

"One moment."

She called her sister-in-law who had a room. The woman who greeted us looked as if she'd been plucked from the pages of an Austrian travel magazine. She was short and stout and wore a gathered skirt overlaid with an apron. Blonde hair wound round in braids adorned either side of her face. Her dancing blue eyes, rosy cheeks, and happy smile made us feel welcome. She motioned for us to follow. We watched her butt cheeks jiggle as she bounded up the stairs to our rooms—more like a small apartment on the third floor. It had a large central hall, a sitting area with a dining section, one bedroom (Tracy had a couch and Kim the floor), and a balcony overlooking the mountains. The large bathroom was in the basement. Another bedroom would be available in the morning, but for now, we had a place to call home.

Each morning, breakfast of soft-boiled eggs wrapped in cloth napkins, sliced ham and bologna, a basket of breads, juice, and coffee or hot chocolate appeared on our breakfast table as if by magic.

"How does she do that?" Jim asked. "We're so quiet in the morning. How does she get everything here at just the right time and temperature?"

"I have no idea. She seems to sense when we're dressed and ready."

It's hard to compare the beauty of the countries we visited. Each had its own. The mountains in Austria were like the Adirondacks, Black Hills, and Grand Tetons all jumbled together. White houses decorated with elaborate paintings and balconies spilling over with a profusion of brilliant flowers made the scenery sparkle with vivid color. There was so much to see and experience, and each country offered a smorgasbord of delectable delights.

A brief stop in Hallein for a trip into the salt mines offered a change of pace and a break from museums. We were each given a miner's shirt and a leather apron to wear over our backsides to protect us from splinters when we slid down a long wooden chute into a mine in the bowels of the earth. We boarded a rowboat, and a guide steered us through the underground river. Our heads spun around absorbing everything we saw.

We picked up a brochure of local attractions and decided Salzburg and a tour of Hallbrunn Castle should be next on our list. Built by an Archbishop with a quirky sense of humor and money to indulge it, the entire place was rigged with trick water sprays. When we headed down the stairs towards the grotto, hidden waterspouts sprinkled the backs of our ankles and birdcalls created by water pressure surrounded us. We giggled and laughed at the ingenuity of the designer.

Off we went to Prien in the Bavarian section of Germany where our neighbor's sister and brother-in-law lived. We planned to call them to say hello, but they wouldn't hear of us staying in a hotel. Fritz greeted us at the entrance to his home. "My home is your home in Germany."

His large two-story home sat on a small lot. It had solid oak wood doors throughout, a winding stairway with wrought iron railings, a garage floor covered in ceramic tile, and a comfortable patio under a vine-laced pergola. We didn't question how they could afford such an extravagant home, just enjoyed their hospitality. Our next-door neighbor, Ermgard was visiting and acted as our interpreter (thank goodness). The dinner of sauerbraten, potato dumplings, noodles, salad, wine and beer was better than anything we had tasted on our entire trip.

Fritz became our tour guide, and between broken English and hand signals, opened our minds and eyes to things we would have missed on our own. He took Kim on a ride on his two-seater bike and showed Jim and Tracy a cold fountain in the center of town where they soaked their feet to improve circulation. With a great deal of fanfare, he mixed Radlers (part Pilsner-style beer and part lemon-lime soda) for us to try.

We hated to say goodbye to our hosts but still had miles to cover. Jim wanted to see Dachau. I didn't.

"Sue, we've done everything you wanted to do on this trip. I teach social studies. I want to see Dachau."

"Okay, okay, but I really don't want to do this."

Tribute, silence, tears, reverence, disbelief. Enough said.

During our one-day stay in Zurich, Jim left to find a bank and a safe place to park the car. Kim chose to rest and read. Tracy and I went in search of a beach. We took a three-mile walk, hoping to locate a sandy beach. Instead, we found a park with three pools. I didn't have any money with me, but convinced the clerk to let us in. On our first dive, we heard the lifeguard's whistle. We ignored it. He stormed over to us and began to rattle in German. "English, English," I said and pointed to my chest. "Slow down. Slow down," he said and pointed to me. After much hand signaling and puzzled looks, I realized all swimmers had to wear a rubber swim cap. Again, somehow I convinced him to lend us two hats. We began to swim across the pool. The lifeguard blew his whistle again and approached us—not too pleasantly. More hand signals. We couldn't swim across; we had to swim lengthwise. It's a lot of work to swim in German pools.

Jim didn't have much better luck. He was dressed in shorts, t-shirt, and sandals when he headed for the sign "Spiel Bank" on top of a nearby building—a perfect place to exchange a few traveler's checks—he thought. When he walked in, two muscle-bound men dressed in tuxedos greeted him. They folded their arms across their chests and denied him entry. Not understanding, he shook his head and held out two traveler's checks. They shook their heads NO. They pointed to his outfit. He looked down at his shorts. More confusion, head shaking, and pantomiming. Jim was in a gambling parlor.

Our dream trip was drawing to a close. We turned the car towards Amsterdam. A month of touring, sleeping in strange beds, and struggling to understand different languages and currency, and we were ready for familiar surroundings. On August 3, $5,000 poorer and 2,600 miles of adventure richer, an uneventful flight, and a drive from Toronto to Brockport brought an end to our odyssey.

1986 - HEADLINE NEWS - Tennis ace John McEnroe marries actress Tatum O'Neal.

A stack of accumulated mail awaited our return. We divided the pile into junk and bills.

Jim opened a wedding invitation. "Oh, oh. The Miller wedding is this Saturday, and we didn't RSVP in time." He placed the invitation on the stack of opened mail.

"That's all right. They know we've been away for a month. They'll be expecting us."

On the day of the wedding, Jim was still experiencing jet lag.

"Let's skip the wedding and just go to the reception," he moaned. "I'm too tired to drive into Rochester for the wedding."

We lounged over a leisurely breakfast of bacon, egg, juice and coffee, took our time dressing, gathered up the gift, and headed for the reception. After placing our gift on a table, we enjoyed a quiet drink at the open bar and waited for the bridal couple to arrive.

"What a perfect day for a wedding. The bridal party can get great pictures in front of the gazebo," I said.

"You know," Jim said, "I don't recognize any of these people."

"That's all right. After all, we don't know the groom or his family. I'll go to the car and check the invitation to make certain we're in the right place."

I passed the bride and groom as I headed for the car. I didn't know them.

"You're right. I just passed the bridal couple. We're in the wrong place. I'm going to retrieve the gift. I can't leave a gift for someone I don't even know. Maybe the reception is in another location."

We checked the invitation. We were a week early.

In town, Betty bumped into a colleague's wife. "Are the Savards back from Europe yet?"

"Yes, got home last night," Betty said. "They're at the Miller wedding today."

"You must be joking. The Miller wedding is next week."

"Oh, I just spoke with them. They're at the reception."

The acquaintance quickly spread our mistake to all of Jim's co-workers and, it seemed, everyone else in town. A few days later, Jim went for a haircut.

A flush crept across my husband's face when the beautician said, "I hear you've been crashing weddings."

On the actual wedding day, we were up in time to attend the ceremony. When we entered the church, a ripple of snickers and elbow jabs went from person to person. We took a lot of ribbing at the reception, and for months afterwards. The story made for interesting comments amongst Jim's colleagues.

1986 HEADLINE NEWS – Jan. 28, *Challenger* Space Shuttle: exploded 73 seconds after liftoff, killing all 7 crew members including schoolteacher Christa McAuliffe.

I was in the faculty room at school when the health teacher burst into the room.

"The Challenger just exploded. Turn on the TV."

A pall descended on me. Over the years, I had become somewhat complacent about the space program—interested, but no longer sitting on the edge of my seat as I had during the earlier space shuttle missions.

"It doesn't seem possible. I was so enthused about this mission. Even though I didn't know Christa, I feel as if I've lost a friend."

For the next few weeks, I hung on the news waiting for any scrap of information about what had happened and why.

On the home front, our life was about to experience our own loss. In the fall of 1986, Tracy began a criminal justice program at a community college in Canandaigua.

Tracy was our tradition child. He took it upon himself to nag me, "It's December 1, Mom. I circled the date on the calendar so you'd get going on Christmas baking."

When I didn't bake my traditional selection of cookies, he scolded, "What? No chocolate slices this year?"

If I placed a Christmas decoration in a new spot, Tracy moved it back to its appointed location.

Each time another child left home, we felt the emptiness.

"I hate seeing Tracy's bedroom vacant. Our children are leaving the nest, Jim. It's so quiet around here. I miss all the hustle and bustle."

Kim, on the other hand, looked forward to four years of being an only child. No more sharing a bedroom with her sister; no more fighting to use the only full bathroom. The TV was hers to enjoy whenever she chose. She could talk on the phone for hours without interruption. The empty nest didn't bother her. She was queen of the homefront.

Little did we know that children leaving he nest was the least of our worries.

CHAPTER 11 - FAMILY ALBUM

Tupper Lake and Woodsmen's Field Day Scenes

Tupper Lake Main Street

The Junction station was a hub of activity with trains arriving daily from Utica, Montreal and Ottawa.

Horse Pulling Contest

Logging truck in parade

1947 Wedding - Marie & Bob

Log debarking

Savards in front of Webb Row home. Gladys, Leon, Marie, Sonny, Dick, Jim (about 13), Evelyn, Ed, Roy, Don.

(top) Marie, (middle) Jim - about 10, Dick, Sonny, (in front) Evelyn

Jim's school picture - at 13

Jim at 4 at cousin Barbara's birthday party

From left, Jim, Evelyn, Don LaBarge (friend), Janet LaPlante, Sonny, Mary, Rene (cousin), Sue LaPlante, Dick Savard, Barbara Savard (cousin)

July 4, 1955 Sue, Joan, Diane ready for walk on the boulevard.

Sue at 12 at Coney Beach

Jim (Eagle Eye) in the first row next to his mentor, Len Perry
Luke #19 in back row

1953 - Jim's high school graduation

1953 - Jim at Vieques Island

New Year's Eve, 1956, at the Waukesha
Sue, Jim, Mary and Sonny

Age 18 - Engagement Photo -
In Oneida Daily Dispatch

1955 Sue in hand-knit dress and Diane Peters

Jim - 1955 - Vieques Island

WE WERE YOUNG ONCE

11/24/1957 - Sonny Savard, Nancy Catalfamo, Dick Savard, Sue, Jim, Mary (LaPlante) Savard,, Armand LaPlante

Sue with father, Romeo, 1957

Randy, Age 4

THE WAUKESHA GRILL AND MENU

Appetizers

Fresh Shrimp Cocktail	.75
Antipasto	.50
Half Grapefruit	.20
Chilled Honeydew	.25
Chilled Cantelope	.25
Chilled Tomato Juice	.20
Chilled Grapefruit Juice	.20
Chilled Orange Juice	.20
Chilled Pineapple Juice	.20
Chilled Prune Juice	.20
Celery and Olives	.35
French Onion Soup	.30
Soup Du Jour	.20
Jellied Consomme	.20

Sea Food

ALL SEAFOOD LISTED BELOW MAY BE HAD AS A COMPLETE DINNER FOR AN ADDITIONAL 75c

Deep Sea Scallops — Tartar Sauce	1.35
Broiled Eastern Halibut Steak — Lemon Butter Sauce	1.35
Broiled South African Lobster Tail — with Drawn Butter	1.65
Fried Selected Shrimp — Tartar or Cocktail Sauce	1.45
Broiled Block Island Swordfish — Butter or Tartar Sauce	1.35
Pan Broiled Whole Brook Trout — Tartar Sauce	1.65
Assorted Sea Food Platter	1.35

Served with French Fries, Cole Slaw, Homemade Roll and Butter as Priced

Meats

MEATS LISTED BELOW MAY BE HAD IN COMPLETE DINNER SOUP or JUICE, RELISH TRAY, COFFEE and DESSERT—ADDITIONAL 75c

Broiled Thick Lamb Chops, Mint Jelly	2.00
Broiled Jersey Pork Chops, Apple Sauce	1.60
Genuine Chicken Livers and Bacon	1.65
Broiled ½ Native Chicken-Milk Fed — with Cranberry Jelly	1.60
Broiled Ham Steak, Pineapple Ring	1.60
Broiled New York Club Steak Plate	2.50
Roast Turkey with Dressing, Cranberry Sauce	1.75
Roast Prime Ribs of Beef, Au Jus	2.25
Broiled Heavy T-Bone Steak — Medium Size on Sizzling Platter	2.75

1957 - Honeymoon in Monreal

1959 - Sue's college graduation
with
Bev Rahn and Nancy Catalfamo

In neighbor's apartment in Saratoga - 1959

1962 - College yearbook picture

Jim in his leisure suit - about 1970

Velma Dean ready for seance

Quartet for "Music Man" -
Andy Nazzaro, Jim, Ed Miller,
John Izzo

Gourmet Club
1989 - Vickers & Tarts -
Jim & Sue, Larry & Marva McCracken

Paul J. Erhart at Coney Beach in T. L. to meet his family

Jim at 50th birthday party with belly dancer

Leon in his prime, at about age 20

Gladys & Sonny (3)

OUR LEGACY

Roberts Family
Mackenzie, Katie, Don, Shelly,
Christopher, Dylan

Savard Family
Kristin, Tracy, Jake, Michelle

Condon Family
Jason, Kieran, Talia, Nolan, Kim

Savard Family
Kerry and Vicki

PART IV

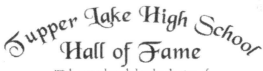

Tupper Lake High School
Hall of Fame
Wishes to acknowledge the election of
James Savard
as an
Outstanding Athlete
for the years
1949–53
awarded the 28th day of January 2000

Selection Committee
Chairman

Athletic Director

CHAPTER 12 - SHATTERED DREAMS

*Reflection: I never understood the word **loss** until Jim learned he had a debilitating disease. He suffered loss of dreams and aspirations, independence, pride, dignity, and even his facial expressions and normally erect posture. With all these losses came the loss of hope. But, he never lost the sparkle in his eyes, his love of home, family, and friends, or his wonderful sense of humor.*

As Jim's caregiver, I also experienced loss. Jim's outward appearance had changed. His face became blank and no longer showed emotion. He wasn't the strong, athletic man I'd married. Even his personality was different. He was more mellow, patient, and emotional and less feisty than he had been.

I missed his strong arms and big bear hugs. In their place, I held him upright and balanced him in order to get a little squeeze. I missed telling him my problems and hearing his patient counsel. Instead, I donned my game face and pretended everything was fine. I missed my independence. I couldn't leave his side because of his frequent falls. I missed seeing Jim dressed in attractive casual sweaters and trousers. I began to dislike sweat suits—the only outfit I could put on him easily.

I especially missed dancing with him.

****

On our final dance together, we were attending a nephew's wedding. The DJ called for the couple that had been married the longest to come to the dance floor.

"Raise your hand if you have been married more than 40 years," he announced. Four hands.

"Longer than 45 years." A few hands.

"Over 50 years." My hand.

"Come to the dance floor," he called into his microphone.

I heard a gasp of breath when I wheeled Jim to the floor. No one expected a man in a wheelchair to be the finalist. As the slow ballad "Moon River" played, I pushed, pulled, and spun Jim around, immune to the staring eyes. His eyes shown with enjoyment, and he waved his arms above his head in time with the music. I danced in a trancelike state as if we were enclosed in our own cocoon. Murmured oo's and ah's of the crowd didn't interrupt our moments of delight. Jim no longer held me in his strong arms as we danced, but I felt as connected to him as I had ever been. It was magical.

When the music ended, the bride was smiling.

"I told the DJ there was no way to predict what was going to happen at my wedding," she said. "Everyone was so touched by that dance. It's wonderful to see a couple so in love as the two of you. That was special."

Yes, it was special, and we are in love. But, oh how I want Jim back the way he used to be. I still want to jitterbug and glide across the floor like Fred and Ginger.

I thought back to how we first learned Jim was ill. I remember that day in 1988 so clearly. Jim shook his right arm back and forth. "I don't know what's wrong with my right arm. I just can't get it comfortable."

"Well, you've probably pulled a muscle. You've been splitting wood and trimming trees. How do you feel otherwise?"

"Fine. I don't feel sick. My arm just feels strange."

I wasn't too concerned.

At the time, we were busy preparing for two weddings—eight weeks apart. Our oldest son was marrying his college sweetheart in July. Our daughter's wedding to her longtime boyfriend was scheduled eight weeks later in October.

"I want these weddings to hurry up and happen," he said several times.

"Why are you in such a big hurry? Enjoy the ride. This'll be fun."

"I don't know." He rubbed his hand along the back of his neck and looked away. "I just want them to happen soon."

His impatience was unusual. I didn't know he was keeping secrets. He had noticed a slight tremor in his right hand and looked for information in an outdated encyclopedia about Parkinson's disease. His symptoms and the negative description left him fearful he'd be crippled or dead before the weddings took place.

The flurry of activity preparing for two weddings kept me on a demanding tightrope for several months.

"I never knew there was so much to planning a wedding," I confided to my girlfriends. "There are rehearsal dinners to plan, wedding quilts to make, bridal shows to attend, guest lists to hammer out, gowns to stitch, and favors to create. I never leave the house without my checkbook."

I scurried from project to project. It was a busy, exciting time for our household, and Jim and I had visions of happy homes filled with perfect grandchildren.

The DJ hired for Kerry's July wedding kept our guests on the dance floor all evening. "Okay everybody, it's time for the chicken dance." The crowd hustled to the floor and flapped their arms, bent their knees, and hooted with enjoyment.

Everyone was in high spirits, especially Jim's brother, Ed.

"Will you look at Ed, Hon?" I said. "He's doing dance maneuvers I've never seen before, and he's having a blast."

"He certainly is. Watch Colette. She's so out of rhythm, the DJ has to close his eyes."

On the day of Shelly's wedding, the weather was perfection, but the bridesmaids' gowns were not. "Can you believe that seamstress dares to sew for people? Her workmanship is atrocious," I complained. "I hope no one will notice."

Shelly looked radiant walking down the aisle with her father, whose smile belied the emotion he was feeling at letting go of his daughter. Everything went off without a hitch until the reception. The party house's toilets stopped working for a while. A quick call to a plumber averted disaster. In the end, Jim and I got through both weddings without going bankrupt and sent our two oldest off to a life of wedded bliss.

After Shelly's wedding, I was putting snapshots into an album. *That's a great picture of Jim and Shelly dancing together. I looked more closely. Something's wrong with this picture, but I can't put my finger on the problem. What is it?*

A cold chill snaked up my back, and I had a nagging sense that I was missing something—an obvious clue. I couldn't explain my feelings about the picture. I just knew there was something different. What was it? The hair stood up on the back of my neck, and I slammed the album shut and pushed it into the back reaches of the cupboard.

There were subtle signs Jim was changing during that year. We were enjoying a day at the lake when I suggested, "Let me teach you to windsurf."

He got on the board and fell off several times.

"You klutz. How come I can stand on the board and you can't? You're more athletic than I am."

His lack of balance should have been a red flag.

Another time he tried to teach me a basketball drill. I could do the drill, but he kept dropping the ball. Then there was the day we went skating in Ottawa. Jim was wearing new figure skates and tripped so many times, he finally changed back to hockey skates.

Firestorms of warning signs were going up all over the place, but I was blind.

Three weeks after Shelly's wedding, Jim said, "I'm going to make an appointment with a doctor and have my arm checked."

"Good idea." I went about my work, oblivious to his concerns.

"Let me watch you walk" the doctor said. "Can you do these finger exercises? Bend over, and touch your toes."

After assessing Jim, the doctor said, "Well, you have Parkinson's disease, and there isn't much we can do about that."

End of discussion.

When Jim came home, he choked, "I've been to a neurologist. I have Parkinson's disease. I've been suspicious."

"Well, Jim. Your hand will probably have a little tremor, but otherwise you seem fine."

Little did I know from that diagnosis forward, our lives would forever change.

"What made you think you had a neurological disorder in the first place?"

"At school, I've been having trouble writing in a straight line on the blackboard. My penmanship is changing. I start writing and then my letters get smaller and smaller, and I can't control them. Also, I've been tripping a lot in class. I knew something was wrong, and the worst part was not knowing what."

He began to cry softly and slumped on the edge of the bed. I crouched next to him.

"I'll never go to that damned doctor again. He didn't explain what I could expect in the years ahead. He didn't discuss any new medications on the market. He didn't talk to me about the newest research—just said there wasn't much he could do."

"The first thing we need to do is find another neurologist—one who knows how to treat a person," I replied. "Then we have to find out about the disease. There must be some medicine you can take, or there may be a cure."

1988 was a transition year, and Jim's diagnosis wasn't the only alteration in our lives.

I left teaching that year and worked for Tandy Corporation selling computers. After a few months at Tandy, a part-time job offer came my way, and I jumped at it—teaching computer applications for IBM and the New York State Education Department. I traveled to various states teaching strategies for integrating computers into classroom lessons. In the process, I became friends with many talented teachers and felt blessed to be well paid for doing something I loved. While I was traveling, Jim kept busy at work and home and cooked complete meals for himself. One day, he made a new recipe for barley pilaf. When I returned, he relayed the story of his cooking disaster.

"While you were away, I made the best barley pilaf recipe. I ate it for dinner three nights straight. Then, McCrackens invited me for dinner.

The barley began to work, and my stomach was churning and gurgling so much I couldn't stand the pain. I was so uncomfortable, I thought I'd explode. Finally, I excused myself from the table and went into the garage to blast off."

Jim chuckled so hard, he had trouble finishing his story.

"I let go with two huge blasts and then heard a whimper behind me. Their dog was in the garage. That poor dog's ears went back, his tail went down, and he slithered into the corner."

Tears of laughter rolled down my cheeks as I pictured the whole scene.

"It's a wonder you didn't kill the dog. What the heck were you thinking anyway? Of all things, barley pilaf three nights in a row."

Moments like these kept us from worrying too much, and we both carried on as if nothing were amiss. But by mid 1989, Jim was feeling more stressed about his symptoms. Although his tremor was mild, he thought it was glaring. He began to keep his hand in his pocket. His colleagues were unaware of these changes; his students didn't seem to notice; Jim felt everyone was staring at him.

"I can't keep teaching like this. I'm going to resign in June. I'll meet with the superintendent and ask to use sick time until the end of September when I turn 55. I'd hate to start the school year with the students and have them switch to a new teacher after a month."

"You know, you have enough sick time. You could stay out sick all next year if you want to."

"I know I could, but the district has always been good to me, and that wouldn't be fair."

His resignation was accepted, but Jim wasn't mentally prepared for retirement. He felt robbed of that final year of wrapping things up.

At the teachers' retirement party in June, his blue eyes seemed dull—the sparkle was gone—when he accepted the Outstanding Teacher Award. It was a bittersweet moment, given his ambivalence about leaving teaching and his well-concealed knowledge of his physical condition.

"The only good thing about retiring is that I'll receive a $20,000 severance package," he told me the next day.

"You've always wanted a fishing boat. Take some of the money and buy one. You deserve it."

"No."

I'd seen that obstinate expression before. It usually meant I would have trouble convincing him otherwise.

"We should save the money. I have Parkinson's and probably won't be able to use the boat very long. Then I'll just have to sell it."

"So what? At least you'll have a year or two to enjoy something you've always wanted."

At last I convinced him, and he purchased a Tracker bass boat.

"Now that you have a boat, I guess we need someplace to store it," I said.

"Good idea. We'll buy a kit for a small barn."

Jim laid a cement foundation and was ready to start the walls when a brilliant idea flashed in my brain.

"How about having an Amish barn-raising party? We'll ask friends, relatives, and neighbors to donate whatever time or skill they can to help us with the barn."

Some people donated a day, some a few hours, and some a whole weekend. A few Tupper Lake relatives, including Marie's daughter, Susan, Sonny and his son, Dana, arrived to participate. Susan strapped a carpenter's belt on her waist, climbed a ladder, and helped shingle the roof. At dinnertime, I donned a long floral prairie dress and bonnet, set up picnic tables and served chicken dinner.

"God, that was the most fun I've had in a long time," Susan said. "What a great idea. It was a fantastic day."

By the end of the weekend, the barn was assembled.

In spite of fun times, during the first year after diagnosis, Jim was often depressed and rarely talked about his fears or feelings. I could see a change in his personality. He was quiet and in his own world. He isolated himself from the family and took naps in the afternoon (very unusual for Jim). For my part, I stuck my head in the sand and approached the situation as if Jim were the same person and his disease wouldn't affect our lives. I encouraged him to participate in his usual activities, including downhill skiing.

In the winter of 1989, I said, "I've got to work while Kim's on February break. Why don't the two of you go to Tupper Lake for a weekend of skiing? You can stay with Mary and Sonny, and she'll probably ski with you."

At dinner, after a day on the slopes, Jim mentioned that he felt out of control while skiing.

"Last week a man with Parkinson's disease lost control on the hill, crashed into a tree, and died," Mary said. "He never should have been skiing."

Jim fiddled with his food while she relayed the story. Mentally, he vowed to give up downhill skiing altogether. We hadn't told our extended family members about his diagnosis. I couldn't say the words Parkinson's disease without crying. Each of us, in our own way, was hiding from reality. I was pretending my husband wasn't ill, and he was pretending he wasn't depressed. When Jim returned home and recounted the story of the skier who died, I knew I had to inform family members.

I called my sister, Janet, and choked out my words, alternating between weeping and gasping for breath.

"What's wrong? What's wrong," Janet screamed into the phone.

I blurted out, "Jim has Parkinson's disease."

The same scenario took place with Mary, my brother, Armand, and my parents.

My siblings were shaken; no one had suspected a thing.

A few nights later, we were watching TV when I heard muffled crying coming from Jim's direction. "What's the matter, Hon?"

"I am trying to deal with my mortality." At that moment, he seemed so fragile.

My whole body shuddered—unable to speak. I hadn't realized the depths of Jim's depression, nor had I entertained the idea he thought his death was imminent. Hidden within his words was the question, "Will you still love me?"

"Honey, what are you talking about? Why do you think you're going to die now? You have many, many years ahead of you." I put my arms around him and felt the trembling in his body. "We're going to work through this together." His shoulders gradually relaxed, and he tried hard to turn his attention to the television.

We made an appointment with a different neurologist—one who was more compassionate. His calm reassurance put us at ease. "You're at the very early stages of this disease and there are new treatments on the market. You've got many good years ahead of you." He explained the most recent research and gave us several books.

We read books and newsletters about the disease and checked the Internet for new strategies. We attended symposiums and made an appointment to visit the Center for Disability.

We stared out at nothing while we waited for the counselor. A large, young man wheeled into the reception room and invited us into his office. As if he saw the question in our eyes, he began, "I've been in this wheelchair for ten years. I was injured in a freak hunting accident. There are many people in the world with disabilities. It doesn't mean you can't live a full and happy life. Eventually, you'll come to a place of acceptance."

The fear of what lay ahead gripped me. *I can't even picture Jim confined to a wheelchair. I don't know if either of us will ever get to a place of acceptance.*

On the way home, Jim said, "I didn't want to tell you, but I've been contemplating suicide. I finally realized that wouldn't have been fair to you or the children." He turned away from me.

How could I have missed it? Why am I not more in touch?

During the following months, Jim's depression waned but was replaced by denial and anger. One Sunday, our priest announced, "Today is our healing mass. I'll come down the aisle to bless anyone who has an illness or concern. Please stand if you want me to bless you."

"Would you like to stand up?" I whispered

"I'm not sick."

I realized in a flash just how deep his denial was and how angry with God he felt. On the way home, he said, "If there were a God, he wouldn't let terrible things like Parkinson's disease exist." I didn't have an answer for that. Even though he mellowed a great deal during his final years, he never again attended church.

We had reached another turning point by 1990. We could pay all of the bills each month. Shelly and Kerry were married and on their own. Tracy was living and working in Baltimore. Kim was graduating from high school and thinking herself too sophisticated and intelligent for her surroundings.

Life was about to change drastically again.

We planned (with less argument from Jim this time) a three-week trip to Ireland, Wales, and England.

"We'll leave for Ireland the week after we drive Kim to college. This is going to be great, Jim. For the first time, it will be just the two of us—like another honeymoon."

In the summer of 1990, Tracy quit his job in Baltimore and moved back home. He was still searching for a career path. In July, Shelly left her husband and moved home. In late August, we headed to Albany to bring Kim to college.

"I'll leave you in Oneida, Hon, to visit Mom and Dad for a few hours. I've got a little work for the State Education Department while I'm in Albany. I should be back in Oneida about four or five. We'll have dinner with Mom and Dad and then head home."

"Sounds like a plan," he said.

When I returned from Albany and pulled into the driveway, Jim bolted from my parent's home and said, "Guess what. Your mother's leaving your father and moving in with us."

Oh, my word. What happened? One person is moving out and three moving in.

"Mom, you're more than welcome to live with us and stay as long as you like, but you do understand we're leaving for Europe next week? The trip is all paid for so I can't very well cancel now."

"That's all right with me. I'll be fine there, and I understand about your trip," she assured me.

"Did you tell Dad what you're doing?"

"No. I'm not going to tell him."

"Well, I am." I went into their house.

"Dad, Mom is moving in with us for a while. I don't know for how long or why, but that's the story."

"Good. Maybe I'll have some peace and quiet," he said.

All the bedrooms were full again. Each day, my mother announced, "If your father calls, I won't talk to him, and if he shows up at your door, I'm not going home with him."

"Don't worry about it, Mom. If Dad calls, I'll talk to him."

My heart was heavy when we left for Ireland. *What would my Mom do all day? Both kids are working. She doesn't have a car. What if she gets sick while we're gone? I've left her with a list of phone numbers for our friends and neighbors in case of an emergency, but will she call them?*

My father didn't call or come after my mother.

She stayed for three weeks, and then asked Tracy to drive her home.

"What ever happened to that empty nest plan of ours?" Jim asked.

"What are you going to do? They're our babies, and we need to help them as much as we can," I said.

During the first year after Jim's initial diagnosis, his symptoms were mild, and he didn't take medicine. Two years later, his doctor prescribed three L-dopa tablets a day. Jim found he could manage quite well on one tablet a day. At first, L-Dopa was like a miracle drug.

"I can't believe it. I feel as good as new," he said.

His excitement was short lived. The medicine progressively lost its beneficial effects. Soon he increased the number of times per day and the number of pills each time. When L-dopa wasn't enough, his doctor prescribed medications that act as agonists and help the L-dopa work. Eventually, he was taking pills every three hours. Even with that, there were very few hours a day when he was functioning well. Few people, including me until I was involved, have knowledge about Parkinson's disease. That fact was made painfully clear when Rush Limbaugh trashed a political ad featuring Michael J. Fox.

"He is exaggerating the effects of the disease," Rush said. "He's moving all around and shaking, and it's purely an act. It's the only time I have seen Michael J. Fox portray any of these symptoms. This is shameless of Michael J. Fox. He either didn't take his medication, or he is acting."v

"That man must be an idiot," I complained to Jim. "He constantly reinforces my belief that he shoots off his mouth on subjects about which he knows nothing. The problem is that some people believe him."

More than likely Michael had taken the same dose of medicine on the day the ad was filmed, as he would have on any other day of the year. The medicinal regimen for Parkinson's disease is a balancing act. Nothing stops the progress of the disease. If you don't take enough medicine, you can't function. If you take too much, you get dyskinesia (characterized by involuntary jerky movements similar to a tic or spasm).

We also soon became well acquainted with bradykinesia (characterized by slowness in one's ability to start or continue a movement). Jim would start walking smoothly down our hall on his way to take a shower and halfway there freeze, unable to go any further. Or he would start through a doorway and stop part way through, unable to continue the forward motion. At times like that, I'd hold onto his waist and call out *left, right, left, right*. Sometimes that got him moving forward, but not always. At other times, I simply held onto him until the message passed through his brain.

It was all a matter of picking our poison. Did he want to be frozen or thrashing about? The medicine didn't act the same way every day or every hour of the day. Some days the regimen worked well, and Jim was able to function. Other days, after taking the very same dosage, all bets were off. Stressful situations also caused bradykinesia or dyskinesia. There was no way for us to plan the day's activities. We never knew whether or not the medicine was going to kick in when needed and how long its beneficial effects would last.

Certain foods and the amount of physical activity affected how well Jim's medicine worked. Too much protein caused an adverse reaction SOMETIMES. The word sometimes is critical because the situation changed frequently. No matter how good we performed this tightrope act (and we were pretty good), we could never predict the outcome.

As a couple, we learned to become flexible in our plans. When invited to any event, I responded, "We'll try to make it, but I can't promise." That was the best I could do. Most people understood.

One thing I knew for certain was that Michael definitely wasn't play-acting for his audience. In the end, Rush received so much bad press that his remarks helped increase donations.

Through it all, we remained committed to one another. One afternoon as Jim drove home from the store, he called me from his cell phone. He sounded very emotional. "Hurry up and turn on the radio to Legends 101."

I rushed to turn on the radio station and heard, "Your soft assuring ways, the rock I lean on. You saw me through my darkest days when all hope had gone. You're still the only one I'll ever hold near. And I still love you, after all these years."[vi]

When he entered the kitchen, he closed me in his arms, and I knew we both felt every word of the song.

Jim's Parkinson's was progressing but had not yet taken complete control. He was still in fair condition. We were on the hunt for a new drug or surgery in 1994 when we heard about a surgery called a pallidotomy. At a meeting, we listened to a speaker who had just returned from having the surgery at Loma Linda hospital in California.

"This surgery is the best thing that could have happened to me. My symptoms are almost gone, and I feel great. The doctor in California was amazing. I recommend that everyone in this room look into having a pallidotomy."

"We'd better do a little more research," I suggested. "You aren't that bad yet, and I don't want to take any chances."

After checking more thoroughly, we decided to keep our options open for later consideration. Neither of us liked the idea that the surgery would destroy a small section of his brain. A month later, a letter arrived from the speaker. "DO NOT under any circumstances have a pallidotomy. I am in worse condition than ever. I think the doctor is a fraud and the surgery worthless."

My hand went to my heart. "Thank God we hesitated."

After Jim retired, he joined a group of colleagues for a golfing holiday. When he returned, he said, "I was pretty quiet on the ride home. The other guys in the car were talking about the books they read when they were growing up or the operas their parents listened to on the radio."

I could see the sorrow in his eyes when he told me about the conversations. He still felt he hadn't kicked the sand of his upbringing from his feet.

"All I could have told them was about my mother's off-color ditties. In our house, we didn't read or listen to operas. I was lucky to get through high school."

"Don't talk like that. You've done amazingly well and should be proud. Look at all you've accomplished. I've never been awarded Teacher of the Year."

Our lives were changing faster than our comprehension to accept the inevitable.

On the morning of April 1, 1994, I checked our calendar. A handwritten note was penciled in. Mary and Sonny. Arriving 2 p.m.

The clatter of dishes and smell of roast pork filled our kitchen upon their arrival. We chatted over a glass of wine.

"How's Mom," Jim asked.

"Not good. She's still in the hospital. Pneumonia, I think. Mom was always heavy. You wouldn't believe how thin she is now. No more than 130 pounds. For the last six months, she's barely eaten anything," responded Sonny.

"The last time she was in the hospital, I visited her," Jim said. "She was unbelievable. She hollered 'Get me a nurse, and not that one from Germany. She's not even a nurse.' You could hear her all the way down the hall. I kept saying, Mom, be quiet. Your roommate is trying to sleep. Mom said. 'I don't give a damn.' She was so bad that the woman in the next bed begged her husband and the staff to move her to another room. I was mortified."

Sonny and Mary snickered.

"Yep, that's Mom—could care less about anyone else."

The day wore on over dinner and the comfortable conversation that only happens between longtime family and friends.

6 p.m.—the phone rang.

"It's for you, Sonny. It's Dana."

"Yes, yes. When?" Bringing his hand to his temple, he cried softly. "Thank God. Thank God. Okay. I'll talk things over with everyone and call you later."

"Mom died this afternoon." Sonny's chin trembled and his head bent forward. "I've been praying every day that she would go soon. I didn't want to put her in a home."

The final physical link to their childhood was severed. Not so the emotional link.

We sat quietly for a few minutes—each of us harboring our own thoughts and memories.

"As you always say, Sonny," Jim said. "It was just her time."

"I know, I know. I'd better call everyone. They'll need time to make arrangements to get home." He dialed Marie.

"Yes, today. Pneumonia. Yes. Roy and Ed were with her. Later this week. We're at Jim's. I'll call again as soon as I know. Probably not before Friday. No, no. She didn't know. Just went to sleep."

Four more times he repeated the call.

"Why don't we look through my photo albums and pull out any pictures you might want to use," I suggested.

I soon realized that pictures reveal so little of a person. Who was she as a person? What were her dreams? Was she happy with her life? In my head, I composed her obituary.

Gladys Boucher Savard, born in Tupper Lake, 1904. Oldest of six children born to Randolph and Agnes (Henley) Boucher. Survived by her children Marie, Sonny, Dick, Jim, Evelyn, Ed, Roy, and Don Savard. Moved to Barchois Canada in 1906 and returned to Tupper Lake in 1921. Predeceased by a son, Bobby, and her husband, Leon Savard, from Brandon, NY.

"An obituary doesn't reveal much," I muttered to no one in particular. "How can anyone sum up a life in a few paragraphs?"

"Here's a picture of you with your mom, Sonny," Mary said. "You must have been about three then. Poor Gladys—dressed in an old cotton housedress with her hair pulled straight back." Mary stroked the book's pages. "Gosh, your family was poor. She was fairly old before she could afford to buy anything nice."

Guilt spread through me. I had never really liked his mother.

"You know," Sonny said. "Mom never talked much about her childhood. We don't even have any pictures from when she was young. The only thing I know is that she only went to third grade. She told me that she walked a mile to and from school every day even in the brutal Canadian winters. After third grade, she had to stay home and take care of her siblings. That's all she ever did—take care of children."

"When you think about it, Mom had a hard life," Jim said. "So many kids, the depression, a husband who ran around on her and didn't work. Dad was always putting her down, making fun of her, and slapping her around."

The quiet of evening descended. We gathered the pictures together and straightened the kitchen. "I think we'd better turn in. We've got a busy few days ahead of us."

After a five-hour drive, we immediately began preparations for the funeral. The church needed to be contacted, the obituary written and posted, our flowers ordered, and more phone calls made.

One by one, Jim's siblings arrived and we sorted through Gladys's belongings. In her trunk, I found a beautifully framed picture of Leon.

"He looks so handsome in this picture," I commented. "I never saw him like that. He was always so skinny and frail looking when I knew him. If it's all right, I'll keep the picture?"

"Yeah, that's when he was around twenty. He was strong from working in the woods, and he was an amateur boxer at one time. Do you know when he was young he wore monogrammed silk scarves and spats?

Not only that, he drove his own car at sixteen. I never figured out how he did that. My grandmother and grandfather were only cooks in lumber camps. They must have spoiled my father rotten."

In Gladys's wallet, we found a picture of a nurse holding a baby. Part of the picture had been cut out.

"Who's this?" I asked.

No one knew.

Over the next few days, Jim's family filled their time together hashing over their upbringing and, surprisingly, laughing a lot. The stories, both good and bad, were retold.

"Do you remember our little apartment on Emma Street?" Marie asked. "I'll never forget the night Dad was out with a girlfriend, and Mom decided to look for him. I was only six, and Sonny and Dick were just toddlers. Mom left me in charge of them. I was so scared. Finally, I left you two boys alone for a short while and went to find Mom. I got as far as the corner but was so afraid of the dark that I soon scrambled home and shut the door."

Sonny, always the storyteller, didn't want to be outdone.

"The main thing I recall from Water Street was the time Dad thought someone was stealing his wood. He bore a hole in a log, filled it with gunpowder, and plugged the hole. When the neighbor placed the stolen wood in his stove, it blew the cap off his chimney. Dad went next door and told the man his little experiment proved who was stealing our wood and don't ever do it again."

Laugh lines crinkled on Jim's face, even though he'd heard the same story a dozen times.

"I'll never forget the day we moved from Water Street," Marie said. "I was in school. It was about 1940, so I was only thirteen at the time. They never told me they were moving, and when I came home to an empty house, I was frantic. A neighbor told me that they moved to Webb Row. What parent does that?"

"The same kind of parents who leaves you in charge of six children while they go to Canada for a month-long vacation," Jim suggested. "You were only seventeen. We did have a lot of fun while they were gone, though, didn't we?"

Dick snickered at the stories and then suddenly got quiet. He stared at the floor, and a tear slid down his cheek.

"The old man beat Mom a lot," Dick said. "I remember the day when I was twelve, and Dad was beating on her. I jumped on Dad to make him stop. He punched me hard in the center of my back and my chest. I didn't cry. I acted as if I hadn't noticed. That made Dad furious, but I wasn't going to let Dad see me cry. I went to my room to cry where no one would see."

"Why was your father so mean, Dick?" I asked.

"He was crazy—that's all—just plain crazy."

The truth of what they each shared gave me a glimpse into a history about which I had previously only guessed. Again, I wondered how they all turned out so well. Was it because of Gladys or in spite of her? Their father was a tyrant and their mother was weak. Maybe it was the balance between the two parents. I didn't know the answer.

At the funeral mass, Jim leaned his head against the back of the pew in front of him. His shoulders shook, and I patted his back. I knew he loved his mother in his own way, even though he didn't always like her behavior.

Marie whispered to me, "I don't feel anything. I don't miss her, and I don't feel sorry that she's gone. I know I should, but I don't."

I didn't know how to respond. I sensed she knew she was wrong to feel the way she did, but she said it anyway.

We said goodbye to family members and returned home to our normal routine until the next crisis in 1995.

Jim was dressing to go out. "When I bend over, I feel fat," he complained.

"You have a lot of other issues, Hon, but being fat is not one of them. Stop worrying."

It was another sign of trouble on the horizon that I missed. It manifested itself in mid-March of 1996.

My two sisters and I flew from the Syracuse airport to Utah for our annual ski trip. Jim and Sonny flew from Syracuse to Florida for a visit with Marie and to golf. We planned to reconnect in Syracuse.

On their third day in Florida, Jim said. "I don't feel very well today. What do you say we skip golfing and just visit with Marie and Bob?"

"Maybe you have a 24-hour bug," suggested Sonny. "It's fine with me if we take a day off." Jim slept most of the day.

They golfed the next day, and at the end of the week, Marie drove her brothers to the airport for their flight home. They hugged their sister goodbye and started down the plane's ramp.

"I feel terrible," Jim said. "I don't think I'd better get on this plane."

Marie had the habit of watching until the plane and her guests were airborne. When she spied Jim and Sonny exiting the plane and saw Jim's condition, she drove them to the nearest hospital.

Meanwhile, my sisters and I returned from Utah to the Syracuse airport, unaware of the events taking place in Florida. We searched the airport. "I don't see the guys anywhere. Maybe their plane is late, although it's not listed as delayed," I said.

After an hour's wait, I went to the reservation desk.

"Excuse me. Do you know if the flight from Orlando had a problem? We were supposed to meet Jim and Sonny Savard here at 4:30, and we can't find them."

"Oh, yes. The plane arrived, but the Savards weren't on it. One of the men got sick and was taken to a hospital."

My pulse quickened, and I hurried to my sisters. "They're not on the plane. One of them is in the hospital. I don't know how to find them. What's Marie's number?"

My hands shook as I dialed Marie. No answer.

"Jim knows Shelly's number. I'll call her," I said.

"Have you heard from your father? We're at the Syracuse airport, and he didn't come in on the plane. Either your Dad or Sonny is in a hospital in Florida. I thought maybe they called you. I'm trying to find out where they are."

"No, Mom. No one has called me."

I hung up without further explanation.

"Hurry up," I said and grabbed my luggage. "I'm going to drive you two to Oneida. We can stay there while I dial every hospital near Orlando. If Jim's in the hospital, I'm heading back to Syracuse and taking the first plane to Florida. You two can stay at Mom's and have Ronnie pick you up tomorrow."

Soon after we arrived in Oneida, Shelly called. "Mom, I called every hospital in Orlando until I found Dad. He's pretty sick, and doctors are preparing him for surgery. Here's the number for the emergency room."

The news wasn't good.

"Jim passed out while they were taking stomach x-rays," Marie said. "It doesn't look good, Sue. He has a mass in his abdomen, and they think it's cancer."

"I'm heading for the Syracuse airport right now. I'll call as soon as I get a flight. Can you pick me up?"

It was Easter vacation. The only available flight left Syracuse at 10 p.m. and cost $500 one-way. My luggage contained long johns, ski pants, jacket, neck gaiters, and winter sweaters. On arrival, Marie drove me directly to the hospital. Jim's surgery was over, and doctors were assessing his situation.

"I got here as fast as I could, Hon."

He raised his head. His eyes were wide, and his chin quivered. Then his head dropped back against the pillows. For the next four days, I slept at the hospital. He was too ill to swallow his Parkinson's medications, and too stiff and weak to push a nurse's call button.

Two days later, a nurse came into the room. "He'll be going home tomorrow."

Over my dead body. He is too ill to move; he is too stiff to move; we are miles from home.

The tissue was sent to several labs for analysis before a report was sent back.

"The patient had a stromal tumor—a rare type of gastric intestinal tumor. It was attached to his small intestine by way of a thimble shaped growth. At this point, it is not cancerous but could return as cancer at a later date."

I nodded and thanked the doctor, but I had concerns. The tumor had burst, causing internal bleeding that showed up as a mass on the X-ray.

What if the blood contained cancerous cells? Why hadn't I paid attention to him when he said he felt fat? We wouldn't be in this mess if I had just listened to him.

I tried to reason with myself. *If every time I felt fat I ran to the doctor, I would be there every other day. How would I have known he had a tumor? I'm not a doctor.*

I still felt guilty.

Three more days passed before he was discharged. We stayed with Marie for five days, and she took me shopping for summer clothes since ski pants and long johns and Florida don't mix in March.

For the next six years, we ignored his cancer. After all, it had not been cancer and might not return. Our more immediate struggle was his worsening Parkinson's disease, which couldn't be ignored. It was in our face twenty-four hours a day.

In spite of the constant turbulence in our lives, we also had positive moments. In 2000, Jim received word that Luke had nominated him for the Tupper Lake Hall of Fame.

"Should we go to the ceremony?" he asked.

"Of course, we're going. It isn't every day you get such an honor. I wouldn't miss it."

During the ceremony, the high school Principal read the following:

During high school, Jim had been named to Northern Athletic Conference All Star Team for football. He finished 1st and 2nd in the sectional championship for pole vaulting. He set an individual scoring record of 43 in a basketball game against Massena and helped lead his basketball team to two league championships.

Jim's eyes brightened at recalling those happy memories. He was humbled and pleased to be honored. My brows wrinkled as he walked across the gym floor to receive his plaque. I sat motionless, hoping he wouldn't stumble. He made it through the ceremony and party without any major mishaps.

When we returned home, I pledged to myself: *We will not stay in our house until we are in a crisis.*

His condition had deteriorated. He fell more often; he had trouble getting in and out of chairs; he was having difficulty maintaining our two-story colonial home. We had to move. *How will I approach this subject?*

"Hon, we have to think about moving. This house is becoming too difficult for us to maintain."

His eyes narrowed and he muttered objections.

"We can't move. Where will we go? It's too expensive to build a house. It's too much work to move. We won't get enough for our current house. There are too many memories here."

I agreed, but I knew it was the right decision. He hemmed and hawed when we looked at available lots. Nothing for sale suited either of us until, on one drive, we spotted a lot we liked that wasn't for sale.

Maybe the owner can be convinced to sell.

I knocked on the door of the landowner's home. "Would you consider selling a lot? We'd like to build a ranch home, and we love the lot at the end of your property."

"Sure. I'll sell a lot if you'll pay the asking price."

What could we do but pay? I purchased an architect's program and began to design a one-story house that would meet our needs: wider doors and hallways, a handicap shower, higher toilets, and a smooth flow of traffic. No grab bars or ramps yet.

We visited model homes, looked at plans, and read a home construction book. I circled a statement in the book. "If it's not in the contract, don't expect it to be done."

With that in mind, I listed every possible item I could think of in the contract.

All holes for pipes or electrical conveyances will be drilled or cut—not punched out with a hatchet or hammer (as the builders had done in our previous home).

Insulation will be stapled at least every six inches.

And so it went.

The builder made fun of my list.

"I'm trying to avoid the poor workmanship we experienced on our last house."

Our mood was bleak on our last goodbye to our property. Our home had been our shelter and held so many precious memories. We'd planted every tree and shrub, built the boat barn, carved out flowerbeds, and added an enclosed porch. Before turning over the keys, we walked through our woods for the final time. The large evergreens seemed to gather us in their arms, giving us both an overwhelming feeling of tranquility and peace. My throat was dry with sadness. I could leave the house easier than the land. I thought back to the day that Mr. Lydig watched as Jim painted the ceilings in our first home. Now I understood. He had felt violated when he saw Jim changing his cherished house.

The remembrances of good times would remain with us, but we had to accept it was time to move on. We moved into a rental house, finalized the architect's plans, and received approval for a subdivision. From the apartment, Jim drove several times a day to the building site to watch the progress, check on the subcontractors, and hassle the builder.

When the electricians or plumbers saw him coming, they held up their saw or drill. "We're following the contract." They laughed.

Moving day - June 22, 2002. "Honey, I love this house," I gushed. "It's open and bright and comfortable."

From the large windows in our sunroom, Jim watched the turkeys, deer, and fox roam around our back lot. "I love it too, Sue."

We unpacked our belongings and settled into making it ours. At the time, Jim could still drive, mow the lawn, cook meals, take care of his personal needs, and do basic tasks around the house.

He returned to singing with his chorus. On the night of the annual spring concert, Jim paced back and forth and cracked his knuckles.

"You don't have to stand on the risers," I said. "You might be more comfortable in a chair. We've seen plenty of other men do that."

"No," I can stand. My Ex-Marine was not giving in.

I watched the show and tried to rein in my tears. Jim's face was screwed into a pained expression, and the sparkle in his eyes was gone. His terror of falling was written on his face. He was using every bit of willpower to stand upright on the risers. I knew it would be his last night with the chorus.

Later that summer, at Jim's high school reunion, the evening began on an upbeat note. Jim shook hands and teased and joked with his former schoolmates. Normally summer evenings in the Adirondacks are cool, but that evening was stifling, and there was no air conditioning in the building. A major attack of dyskinesia hit, and his body jerked and spasmed. He didn't realize he had sweat entirely through his suit jacket. His former girlfriend was there. He didn't want her to see him.

He grabbed my hand. "Sue, I've got to leave."

We slipped out the door and rushed back to the comfort of Sonny's front porch swing. Jim's body gradually stopped twitching, but we had missed most of the party and all of the dancing. The old swing creaked as we slowly rocked it back and forth.

"Was Pigears there?" Sonny asked.

"I didn't see him. I saw Jughead, though. How does that story go, anyway?" Jim asked.

"One day, there was a substitute in the social studies class."

She said, "When I call your name, I want each person to stand and say your name."

When she got to Donald Harris, he stood up and said, "Jughead."

"What's your real name, young man?"

"Jughead."

"If you say that name again, I'll send you to the office."

He said it a third time. "Go to the office immediately."

Jughead said, "C'mon Pigears, she won't believe you either."

"The kids both caught the dickens from the principal."

We laughed at the story and relished hearing it once again. After the stress of the reunion, it was good see my husband laugh.

CHAPTER 13 - I WAS LOST AND NOW I'M FOUND

Rumors had been whispered from time to time about an out-of-wedlock child, but no one paid attention until a year and a half after Gladys's death.

Deep frown furrows creased Jim's forehead. He hung up the phone. "How come I didn't know about this?"

"What's that?"

"It seems I have another brother. My sister, Marie, just told me that Mom had a baby boy before she married my father and gave him up for adoption. Now that Mom's passed away, she's going to try to find him."

"Gosh, I didn't know about that one either," I said. "I wonder how that's going to go over with your siblings. It could be dicey."

It all seemed surreal. The year 1994 had brought major changes to Jim's family. His mother and his brother, Ed, had died and, with that call, he'd gained a brother.

A few days later, Marie called again. "I found him. It's really strange how this all came about. Before Mom died, she wrote Dick and Theresa about her son and enclosed a letter and picture he had sent her many years ago. After her funeral, Dick gave me all the information he had, and I did an Internet search. I found Paul in Houston, Texas."

"Yuck. Not Texas," Jim sputtered. "He's probably a Republican. I'll bet he even voted for George Bush."

"If that's the case, he can't be a true member of the Savard Democrats," I quipped.

Soon Paul arranged to visit Tupper Lake to claim his place in the family.

With the warm sun glinting on our windshield, we drove to the reunion and discussed the situation. Will everyone in the family welcome him? Will he feel comfortable with his new siblings?

We needn't have worried. Paul Joseph Erhart was sitting in a beach chair and wearing a Hawaiian shirt. His feet were crossed at the ankles and his hands folded over his ample stomach. A slew of newfound relatives surrounded him.

Jim walked across the picnic grounds, held out his hand and said, "I'm your brother, Jim. Glad to meet you."

There was no denying Paul's birth mother.

"Gosh," I whispered. "He looks more like your mother than the rest of you. He's big boned and heavy, and watch the way he walks. I think if we put a blonde wig, lipstick, and big earrings on him, he'd pass for your mother."

Jim laughed. "You're right. He does look like Mom."

After lunch, we all sat around a picnic table.

"Were you surprised when Marie called you?" asked Sonny.

"I was dumbfounded," he answered. "I've been waiting all my life for that call."

Paul breathed deeply and looked down at his hands. "When I was in the Navy, I visited the orphanage in Lackawanna where I was born and asked the nuns to tell me my mother's name. At first they refused, but then a nun must have felt sorry for me, and she told me my mother was Gladys Boucher from Tupper Lake. I wrote Mom and sent her a picture of myself in my Navy uniform. Eventually, she wrote back and said it would upset her life too much to have me come to Tupper Lake. I respected her decision, but I was sure disappointed."

As the picnic wound down, relatives said goodbye. We went back at Mary and Sonny's house, and Marie continued to fill in the missing pieces.

"From what I've learned, Mom brought you back to Tupper Lake by train. She didn't want to give you up, but my grandfather couldn't afford to feed another child. He sent her back to Lackawanna to put you up for adoption."

"Paul, I've put in a video of Gladys at her 80th birthday party. I thought you'd like to watch it," Mary said and pressed Play.

Tears dotted Paul's cheeks when he saw his mother for the first time. It was the fulfillment of his dream to have a family to call his own.

When he continued to relay his background, we were all astounded at how similar his life had been to that of his siblings. He, too, had been abused. Yet, he didn't wallow in self-pity. He described his life in a matter-of-fact, unemotional manner—as if he were telling a tale he had often told, but one that could no longer hurt him.

"You know, Paul," Don interrupted, "when I was little I had blond hair. I hated that I didn't look like any of my brothers. One day I asked Mom if I were adopted. She got all upset and started crying. She said, 'why do you ask such trash?' I didn't understand what was wrong. Now I know. She must have still felt guilty."

Paul tilted his head to Don as if thanking him for sharing that story.

"I was adopted at age four by an abusive family. My mother was mean, and my father was weak. If I asked for food, my mother burned my hands on the stove. When my adoptive parents went to a movie, they locked me in a closet. My life was hell, and when my mother gave birth to my brother, Joe, it got worse. One time, I asked my father why he let her treat me so. Dad said, 'I just couldn't fight her.' "

"Paul, your story brings back so many memories," Marie said. "When I was about ten, my mother locked me in the closet. I don't know why she was so angry with me, but I do remember being terrified that the rats would get in the closet with me. I wanted to run away, but I didn't know where to go."

"Well, I did run away at fifteen and supported myself any way I could. I washed dishes in restaurants and took on menial jobs just to survive. By age seventeen, I decided to enlist in the Navy, but I needed my parents' signature. I went back home and asked my mother to sign for me. At first she refused, but my father convinced her to sign the paperwork. She signed me up for six years instead of three. I was trained as a cook in the Navy."

"You're my third brother who's served in the Navy," Jim said. "We Marines called you swabbies our taxi service."

"I hate to say this, but your life wouldn't have been any better with Leon as a father," I said. "He was miserable to his own children. Can you imagine how he would have treated a stepchild?"

Over the next few days, our conversations went from music, to politics, to antiquing, and we were amazed at Paul's breadth of knowledge.

From that week on, Paul kept in close touch with us. His phone calls to Jim usually involved a political discussion.

"Tell me," Jim said, "do the Texans love George?"

"Not the ones I talk to. A lot of them are embarrassed by George."

If I answered the phone, I never missed an opportunity to get Paul riled. "I can't talk very long," I lied. "I'm hosting a house party to raise money for George's re-election campaign."

That generally caused him to blubber a few expletives and then chuckle.

For Christmas, I sent Jim's brother a photo album with pictures of Gladys and each of his siblings with their families.

"That's the most wonderful gift I've ever received," he cried. "Now I can show off my family."

CHAPTER 14 - HE CHOSE LIFE

"I don't want to live like this."

Jim was discouraged and began to look into new treatments. By 2004, a surgery called a DBS (deep brain stimulation) was no longer experimental, and our insurance would cover the procedure. Jim was interested.

Kim was against it. "The procedure is too risky, Mom. Dad shouldn't have it. He's doing okay without taking such a risk."

"At this point, Kim, we're just looking into it. Your father hasn't made any decision yet."

We scheduled an appointment with Jim's neurologist.

"I think you may be a good candidate for the procedure," his doctor said. "You'll have to go through a rigorous vetting process. Not only will doctors check your physical condition, they'll also give you a battery of psychological tests."

After much Internet research, we realized there were risks, but there was also the potential for relief of symptoms.

"I have to take a chance and do something, Sue. I don't want to keep living the way I am."

Considering everything, Jim was in remarkably good shape—always physically active, never a drinker, gave up smoking, weight under control, mentally sharp, and no signs of dementia. He was accepted for the surgery.

DBS involved three surgeries, a team of doctors, and a great deal of risk. Jim's hopes were high.

"Let's go over the procedure, Mr. Savard," the doctor said. "We'll give you a shot to deaden the skin on your forehead and then screw a halo into your head. Once you're in surgery, the halo will be attached to the operating table to prevent your head from moving. You won't feel anything because the brain has no sensation of pain."

Jim's face was expressionless, and he shook his head that he understood. After the halo was attached, he said, "I don't feel anything—no pain at all."

He was awake throughout the entire process. In the first surgery, surgeons placed electrodes into the deepest recesses of his brain (the subthalamic nucleus). To insure the correct placement, Jim responded to the surgeon's commands.

"Lift your right leg. Move your left arm. Point with your right index finger."

The surgery lasted four hours. In the recovery room, his body bounced from dyskinesia as if he were on a trampoline. We were uncomfortable watching his gyrations, but he didn't seem to notice. Hunger was his biggest concern. He hadn't eaten in twenty-four hours.

"Please, Sue. I'm hungry. Go to McDonalds and get me a hamburger and fries. I can't wait any longer. Please."

"I'm sorry. The doctors said you can't eat for a while yet. I can't help you."

The following day, he came home to await the second surgery, a month away. The electrodes weren't activated, but he seemed better. He could cross one leg over the other smoothly. His face was less set. He reached up and scratched his head with one swift movement. I didn't understand why. Was it a placebo effect? Was it because of the temporary disturbance of his brain?

Still, I was afraid of being too far away from him in our house. If he called me, I wouldn't hear him. Betty supplied me with a gym whistle.

"Look at what I've got," he chuckled to friends and held up his whistle. "All I have to do is blow this, and she comes running. If I had only thought about using a whistle when we were first married, my life would have been heaven."

One month, two months passed—still no second surgery.

I called the doctor's office.

"I'm sorry, Mrs. Savard. There are scheduling problems among all the doctors involved. We'll call you as soon as we get it worked out."

Finally, the second surgery was on our calendar.

On the way to the hospital, Jim sighed deep down in his throat, "I don't think this surgery is going to go very well. I'm apprehensive. I don't want to go through with it."

"But why?"

"For the first surgery, I didn't know what to expect. Now I know, and I don't want to face it again."

"I don't blame you one bit. But, if you don't do the second surgery, the first surgery was useless."

He nodded in agreement, but I could tell he had misgivings.

Our children and I gave him a kiss and a high-five, and began the long wait in the lounge. It seemed an eternity until the doctor called. "We're wrapping things up, and everything looks good."

Another hour went by. I paced back and forth while waiting for further word. I jumped from my seat when the call came. "Has Jim ever had heart trouble?"

"No. That's one good thing. He has a strong heart."

Again we waited. Two hours later, the call came.

"Your husband's in the recovery room, Mrs. Savard.

I hurried to his room and couldn't believe my eyes. No dyskinesia—in fact, no movement at all. He was immobile.

"What's wrong? He can't move. This isn't how he was after the first surgery."

"I'm not sure what's wrong," the doctor said. "I think he's had a heart attack. He has elevated chemical levels in his blood."

All evening, doctors paraded in and out of the room assessing his situation and ordering every imaginable heart test. No other signs of a heart attack showed, but still, no movement.

At eleven-thirty p.m., I spoke to his doctor for the final time before heading home.

"I don't care what you think about a heart attack. Jim's had a stroke."

Why did I say that? I don't know. Jim's condition was just different from any person I'd ever seen after a heart attack

By the next day, his doctors agreed with me.

For several days, I slept in his room. He was unable to sit up, feed himself, speak, walk or move. He couldn't push the call button; he needed me by his side.

The surgeon explained: "He had a stroke on the surface of the right side of the brain. If you think of a berry pie, his stroke is on the crust—not in the filling."

I'm not sure that made me feel better.

After three days, Jim could speak, and I returned home to sleep. Each morning when I arrived, he was visibly terrified and relayed events that he was convinced were true.

"People are having sex in the halls."

"See that night nurse. She's doing tricks all night to make extra money."

"The nurses don't like me. They're laughing at me."

"Oh, Jim, I'm sure they like you. Maybe they're just telling stories."

"You never believe me, Sue. Last night, three black men jumped me and tried to force sex on me."

"If you're so afraid at night, I'll stay with you."

"No. I'm too weak. I can't protect you from them."

I pulled his doctor aside. "I don't know what's going on with my husband. He tells me the most outlandish stories when I come in to visit. Why is he so mixed up?"

"Your husband is hallucinating, is paranoid and delusional. To him the things he's seeing and hearing are real, and there is no way to change his mind. We're in hopes these incidences will go away as he heals from the stroke."

His wild imagination continued.

"Last night, people took the rods out of my head, and a college professor stood right there and let them do it."

"Sweetheart, I'm sure no one is taking the rods out of your head. They're still there, but they haven't been activated yet."

"Why don't you believe me? You always think I'm crazy."

I couldn't understand where he was getting those ideas—especially the one about the college professor. After thinking about it, I remembered the brain surgeon always wore a bow tie. Jim was remembering Dr. Crandall, his favorite college professor, who also wore bow ties.

Mary called. "How are things going?"

"You wouldn't believe it. He's out of his mind, and he's imagining all kinds of crazy things. If he doesn't straighten out soon, I'm going to shoot myself."

"Don't talk like that. You scare me."

"He's scaring me. What if he doesn't get better?"

When I arrived at the hospital, he was still in his own world.

"There are mice running all over my room. Can't you see them?"

"The nurse keeps putting my urinal on my breakfast table. How is that sanitary?"

"The nurses are skipping my night medicine."

I gave up arguing with him. He was like a newborn whose days and nights are turned around. Often during the night, he was taken for scans and tests. During the day, he slept.

One morning, I got up, dressed, ate breakfast, made the bed, straightened the house, drove thirty minutes, parked the car, went up six floors on the elevator, and entered his room by 7:15 a.m.

"Where the hell have you been?" Jim yelled.

"And good morning to you, too. If it's all right, I went home to get some sleep."

By the time I had a consultation with his doctors, I was at the end of my rope. "This stroke is a huge setback. I can't believe we've chosen for Jim to have the DBS, and now he's in worse shape than ever."

There was nothing anyone could say. Six days after surgery, I noticed a miniscule movement in Jim's big toe and ran to tell the brain surgeon, "His big toe just moved. Is that dyskinesia?"

"No, it means he's showing some signs of improving. With a stroke, even dyskinesia won't move a toe."

I was ecstatic but knew it was only a beginning. When I left his room that evening, the nurse said, "Here's a booklet on strokes that we give all our patients' families. It may help you understand."

One of the first sentences stated: "Some people recover from strokes. They may even be able to feed themselves again."

I threw the book in the trash.

I can't conceive of the possibility that Jim might not recover.

Meanwhile, I called our four children together for a family meeting. "If your father doesn't recover from his stroke, I'll have to place him in a home. I want you to be prepared for that eventuality. I will not be able to care for him."

"Dad can move into our home," Tracy offered.

"I'm touched by your offer, but you both work. Your home isn't built to accommodate someone in your father's condition. If he stays the way he is now, he'll need 24-hour care. The doctors say your father may not get better. But, they don't know him. If anyone can, he can."

The drab room in the acute physical therapy unit where they moved Jim was crowded with two beds, nightstands, wheelchairs, walkers, monitors, and visitor's chairs. He made little progress at first. But by the end of the week, the therapist said, "Your husband walked three steps today holding onto the support bars."

The next day, he took twelve steps, and each day thereafter he improved. He began to speak clearly, and his hallucinations were subsiding. He worked hard with physical, occupational, recreational, and speech therapists. He was desperate to come home. I wasn't certain he would ever come home. One afternoon, in an attempt to get to the bathroom, he fell and hit his head and shoulder on the door jam.

"We have to do something about my husband," I told the nurse. "I'm warning you, he can't be trusted. He will try to escape. You can't keep a Marine down. Is there any way to confine him?"

"We'll order an alarm bed for him immediately. As soon as he moves, an alarm will ring at the nurse's station."

I faced the truth about Jim's impulsivity. From then on, whenever he was in the hospital, I requested an alarm bed.

Jim's regular neurologist eyes registered concern when he visited and saw Jim's condition. "I feel so guilty. I'm the one who recommended this surgery. I can't believe he's in this condition."

"We don't blame you, doctor," I said. "We knew there were risks, but we hoped for the best. DBS surgery sure isn't for the faint of heart. You've got to be one strong S.O.B. to go through with it."

Jim's progress continued. One morning he said, "I'm coming back."

"I'm sure you are," I assured him, but I had doubts.

"If I just could get back to the way I was before this happened, I'd be happy. If I ever get out of this place, I'm going to buy an expensive set of golf clubs."

"Absolutely," I said, never thinking I would have to keep that promise.

A week in rehab went by, and the discharge nurse informed me, "On June 15, your husband will no longer meet our criteria."

"You must be joking. How can you decide that in three weeks he won't meet your criteria? That policy makes no sense to me."

Her answer was vague. I consulted a friend who was the discharge nurse at another hospital. She educated me. "Sue, each procedure or hospital stay is assigned to a group. Based on a number of factors, patients within a particular group are expected to use the same time and resources of a hospital. In your case, acute rehabilitation is considered a 10-14 day hospital stay. In order to extend that time period, a hospital can request an additional length of stay from the insurance company, but has to give periodic updates on a patient's improvement. In some cases, if a hospital can discharge a patient before the anticipated time, it's still paid for the number of days allocated. Other times, a hospital loses money because a patient stays longer than expected."

Each day the young, pleasant, but inexperienced discharge nurse checked on Jim.

"We're planning on discharging your husband soon and want to make certain he'll be getting the care he needs when he gets home," she said. "Now, you have four children who could help. Is that correct?"

"Yes, we do. However, they all live an hour away," I responded. "They have jobs. They have young children. How will they be available if I need help during the day?"

"Don't you have neighbors?"

"Yes. We have great neighbors, but how many times do you think I'm going to call them when I need help in the middle of the night?"

Another morning she suggested, "I have a great idea. Jim could go to a day-care program. That would give you eight hours relief during the day. It's in Rochester and costs $125 a day."

"That's nice. We could afford to do that two or three days a week for a while," I persisted. "How am I supposed to get him dressed and in the car? Have you noticed he can't walk, can't sit up, and it takes two nurses to get him on the bedpan? Also, what am I supposed to do with him the other 16 or 24 hours a day when he isn't in day care? Can we get real about my situation?"

A two-day extension was granted, and then he was sent to another hospital for continued rehab. On the day he was transferred, I was apprehensive.

"It's six p.m.," I reminded the nurse. "Jim hasn't been given his nine, noon or three o'clock medicine. Do you know when they'll get his medicine?"

"Probably about nine this evening, but that doesn't matter," the nurse said.

Oh, my goodness. Jim's in real trouble in this hospital. The staff hasn't a clue about Parkinson's disease, and they don't understand how critical his medicine is to his functioning.

The new physical therapy unit was a nursing home. Most residents were unresponsive and sat in the halls in Geri chairs. He received one hour a day of poor quality group therapy. The rest of the day he was pinned to his alarm chair or bed. His roommate was comatose following three major strokes.

I stayed there as much as possible to walk him, stimulate him mentally, and hassle the staff about his medicine.

"I'm signing my husband out and taking him home," I said after one week.

"He should really stay in the hospital a little longer."

"If he stays in this hospital any longer, he'll die."

The next few weeks were exhausting. During the day, he required constant supervision. At night, his dyskinesia was so bad that he shook our bed. He had violent dreams and kicked or punched me. (At least he claimed it was the dreams.)

I moved into another room and purchased a baby monitor. Sometimes, he chose to sleep on a floor mat. I learned that all home health agencies are not equal. Jim needed to get up by six a.m. to take his medicine, and because his backaches were severe. I called the agency.

"I need an aide at six a.m. to help me get him up and nine p.m. to help me prepare him for bed."

"We can't fill those time slot," the scheduler said.

Most days, the aides didn't show up. Of the forty-two times I was approved for aides, they appeared seven times.

I left a message for the CEO. "I am having difficulty with your service. Your employees don't show up. Could you please call back, and we can discuss my situation."

She never responded.

In spite of the difficulty, I had made the right decision. Once home, Jim was determined to make progress. I tried everything I could think of to help him walk. I cut large foot shapes from construction paper and pasted them down the hallway. He practiced walking from foot to foot while I held onto his waist and called cadence—left, right, left, right.

At times, I gave him the Marine Corps drill sergeant's routine: "Okay Savard, I don't want to see anything but assholes and elbows when you walk."

That statement made us both laugh and eased the tension.

Dressing himself was a problem. He put his shirts on backwards. Yet, each day he improved beyond my wildest dreams. One night after dinner, I put on a Frank Sinatra CD.

"C'mon, Hon. Let's dance," I said and pulled him from his chair.

Facing him, I placed my hands under his elbows to help him balance. His steps were halting and stumbling at first. Then, slowly he began to glide to the music. He moved his arm around my waist, and I rested my head on his shoulder. I closed my eyes and thought back to our first dance at Mary and Sonny's wedding. My Fred Astaire was back.

Unbelievable.

We even tempted the gods and tried a jitterbug. That was asking too much.

But, we weren't done with the DBS yet. Surgery number three still needed to be scheduled to implant the brain pacemaker into Jim's chest, connect the left to right side of the implants in his brain, and run a wire under his skin behind his ear connecting the brain pacemaker. The brain surgeon was concerned.

"I'm not going to proceed until I'm certain there's no danger of a heart attack. He has to be examined by a cardiologist."

On the Internet, I found a condition called stress cardiomyopathy, described as emotional stress that releases chemicals and mimics a heart attack. In my mind, that was a perfect analysis of what had happened to Jim.

"The only sure test is an angiogram," the cardiologist said.

The results were negative, and the doctor wrote a letter: "Mr. Savard sustained a non-heart related event."

All went well with surgery three, but still the pacemaker needed to be calibrated to activate the electrodes. To do so, the doctor's assistant taped a palm-sized computer to Jim's chest. With that, she could read a complete analysis of the electrodes in his brain—the current settings for both the left and right side, the number of hours turned on, the strength of the battery, and innumerable other bits of information. Each small adjustment caused an immediate reaction.

"I'm going to raise the impedance on the right side," the doctor said.

Jim burst into sobs.

"Well, I guess that wasn't quite right, was it?"

The neurologist adjusted another setting. Jim's face twisted like a corkscrew

When will everything be set so that Jim can feel some benefit from the surgeries?

The neurologist, a history buff, looked forward to our visits, and Jim planned a trivia question to stump the doctor. "Who was Lincoln's Secretary of State?"

"Well, let me think about that a minute. I know. William Seward."

Jim laughed. "Darn. I'll trick you next time."

They continued to banter. "So, tell me what you did in Tupper Lake for excitement," the doctor said.

"I haven't lived there for a long time, but when I was a kid, I decided to ride a bike down a ski jump."

"Are you joking? What ever possessed you?"

"I was there with a bunch of friends, and one of them had his bike. We drew straws, and I drew the short straw. Besides, it looked like a good idea at the time. You know how stupid young boys are."

"Whoa." The doctor chuckled. "What happened?"

"About half way down, I got pretty concerned and bailed out."

"Did you get hurt?"

A slow blush crept across Jim's face. "Well, I managed to father three children."

The neurologist was so amused that he repeated the story every chance he had to his colleagues. I'm sure the story sprouted wings and spread even farther.

After six months of weekly visits, the DBS settings were correct. Jim experienced improved mobility. His dyskinesia and tremors were gone. His medicines' effects were more predictable. He didn't freeze going through doorways. His face was less fixed, and his leg cramps disappeared. His balance did not improve.

Once better, Jim wanted to drive his John Deere tractor. I agreed (with trepidation). He was like a little boy with a new toy. Our cousin, Joan, was visiting.

"I've never seen such a big grin on anyone." She laughed. "It looks as if he's saying, 'look at me world. I'm driving my John Deere again.'"

His driving was erratic. He drove down a hill, into a tree, and over a culvert, but I still felt I had to let him have that freedom. Before the summer was over, Jim was driving the car and golfing.

"I assume it's time to order that new set of clubs."

The Ping clubs cost $1,200. They were worth every penny.

A few weeks after a Justice of the Peace married Kim and Jason in 2005, his parents hosted a party at a local country club. Jim was still self-conscious in crowds and could feel when his medicine was done working its magic. I was having a grand time visiting with family and friends when I noticed he had disappeared.

"Where's your father?" I asked Shelly.

"I think Dad left."

I quickly thanked the hostess, rushed out of the room, and ran in my heels down the driveway to catch Jim.

"I had to get out of there while I still could," he said.

He hadn't let me know he was leaving or said goodbye to anyone—just left. On the way home he said, "You seem a little crabby."

I couldn't say what I was feeling. Anger was erupting through my veins. *I'm crabby because I didn't want to leave, but everything has to go by you and your damned disease.*

I kept my comments to myself. I knew none of this was Jim's fault, but sometimes inside I felt resentment. Afterwards, I felt guilty for feeling that way.

Medicines and surgery couldn't counteract Jim's lack of judgment. Mealtimes meant spilled drinks and food. I tried every type of chair—never use one on wheels—and every type of spoon or dish. Nothing worked well. Impulsivity was ever present. His habit of reaching over the top of his beverage glass to retrieve some item usually spelled disaster. At dinner one evening, I could picture the scene playing out as he reached over his water glass for the butter dish. I slid his water glass to the side.

"Will you quit adjusting me?"

"I'm not adjusting you, Honey. I'm just trying to prevent you from hitting your water glass."

"I won't hit it."

Shut up right now, Sue. I didn't.

"You often bump your glass when you are reaching, so I'm trying to prevent a spill."

His lips tightened. "Will you sit down and please stop nagging me?"

At that point, I bumped MY water glass spilling its contents over the table and floor.

Jim's eyes glowed, and he laughed until he cried. Looking upwards at the ceiling, he exclaimed, "There is a God."

Ya gotta love him.

By fall, Jim was anxious to mow. A section of our property was crossed by a wet swale that didn't always dry up. Jim headed for his tractor, and I called, "Stay away from the swale. It's still wet, and you'll get stuck."

"Yeah, yeah," he responded, paying no attention and starting his tractor.

Like a naughty little boy, he entered the house a few minutes later. "Sue, the tractor's stuck in the mud."

"Okay, I'll call our neighbor, Everett, and ask him to tow you out."

That same scene played several more times, and I was losing patience. By mid-July, with the swale still muddy, Jim had not yet learned his lesson.

"Sue, the tractor's stuck."

Words clipped off my teeth. "I don't care if your tractor stays there for the rest of the summer, and the grass gets knee high. I refuse to call Everett again."

"I know, I know," he said. "I should've listened to you, but I was sure it was dry enough."

"We own three acres. You have plenty of grass to mow without mowing near the swale."

For two weeks, the grass grew taller and taller, and the tractor sat mired in mud. Late one afternoon, the doorbell rang. It was Everett.

"Are we having a little problem here? I've noticed your tractor has been in the field for a few weeks."

I couldn't stifle a laugh. "Yes we are, but I refused to call you one more time."

"I brought over my big tractor, just in case," he said and headed for the back field.

Maybe, just maybe, Jim had learned his lesson.

As Jim's condition deteriorated, he began to stoop forward which forced him to go up on his toes causing him to fall. Using a cane was of little help because he fell either forward, backwards, or sideways, and the cane went with him. For both of us, acceptance was a gradual process. I began to talk more freely to others about my husband's condition and stopped expecting him to participate in his usual activities. He was no longer embarrassed when others noticed his condition.

"So, I have a problem. If they don't like it, they can look the other way."

He was never one to give up completely on an activity he loved. He just changed HOW he pursued his passion. He joined a senior chorus whose director was a former colleague. Then he convinced his singing friends to join, and soon formed a subgroup barbershop quartet. He was the director's Pied Piper of music.

Although often quiet, he could give a quick comeback. One afternoon I said, "When I come back in my next life, I'm going to be very beautiful, tall, intelligent, very rich, and have perky boobs, not really big—just perky—beautiful legs, and a small butt."

He chuckled and his blue eyes twinkled as he thought about that image for a bit. Then he responded, "I hope I get ta meet cha."

Jim always needed to feel useful, "What can I do to help with the yard work?"

"How about going out back and pouring a half gallon of blue dye into the pond. Maybe that'll keep the weed production down."

The distance to the pond wasn't great, but as good as running the Boston Marathon for Jim. I went into the kitchen to prepare supper. After a while, I looked out of the back windows. He was nowhere in sight. *I hope he's okay and hasn't fallen into the pond.*

"Sue, I need your help." The call came from the garage.

"Oh, my God, what happened?" I screamed when I saw him. Jim was transformed into a 5'11" blue statue.

"Well, everything was going all right until I started to walk back. I hadn't put the lid on the container tight, and I tripped and fell. Blue dye went everywhere."

He wasn't joking. He had blue teeth, blue tongue, blue hair, blue ears, and blue clothing—even his nostrils were blue.

"Look at you." We both burst out laughing—he showing his beautiful blue teeth. Where was my camera when I needed it?

"Don't touch anything. Stand still while I find out what to do." (What was I thinking telling a person with Parkinson's disease to stand still?)

The bottle's directions stated: "In case of an accident, mix half and half bleach and water."

I mixed the bleach and water and handed it to Jim. "Here. Swish and spit. Whatever you do, don't swallow it."

He stripped and threw the blue clothing into the garbage, and we headed for the shower. From the garage to the shower, Jim left a trail of blue dye on the walls, the floor, the door casings, and the shower curtain. I scrubbed hard with fels-naptha soap until his skin, once again, glistened bright pink.

On Monday night, I entertained my quilting group. "You won't believe what he did this weekend," and relayed the blue dye episode.

The girls said, "We'll just call him the blue smurf from now on, Sue."

We would have been doomed if we hadn't both had a sense of humor, a circle of close friends and a loving family. We cackled often and long at some of the messes we got into and that saved us.

His sister Marie described him perfectly. "I have never seen anyone try so hard and so constantly to keep going. All of us are amazed at him."

Friends sometimes shared stories of their brush with Parkinson's disease. "My Uncle was diagnosed with Parkinson's disease when he was sixty, and he wouldn't do one thing after that. He just sat in a chair."

Jim chose a different response, "I don't have much time left. I have to get it all in."

Or, "My mother had that disease and she stopped doing any of the things she enjoyed."

Jim, on the other hand, would say, "I have Parkinson's disease, but it doesn't have me."

For a time after Jim's diagnosis, I thought he also would give up, but I soon learned differently.

Jim chose life.

CHAPTER 15 - THE CAT WITH TEN LIVES

Between his episodes of hospital stays, we kept socially active. We went to movies, plays, museums, and concerts. We attended hockey and baseball games and our grandchildren's' school and sports events. We had company for dinner and cards and took trips to visit relatives and friends. We talked about little, insignificant things and played a nightly game of cribbage. Jim had bounced back so many times from near-death that I dubbed him the *cat with ten lives*.

For twenty-five years, every Wednesday afternoon at four o'clock, he had bowled in the same league. "I'll be home around six for dinner," he'd say and head out the door. After each surgery, Jim's teammates cheered and clapped when he entered the alley. But, they closed their eyes when he struggled to maintain balance as he weaved down the approach.

He's going to fall for sure. Yet, they knew if he fell, he'd get back up and try again.

Ray, the owner of the local bowling alley, had a love and admiration for my husband that transcended friendship. To make light of the seriousness of Jim's situation, Ray provided comic relief, and Jim looked forward to Ray's teasing and antics. "Are you wired in yet, Savard? What stations can you listen to on those contraptions in your brain?"

Another time Ray brought jumper cables into the alley. "I'm going to jump start you today."

Jim was discouraged that his bowling average had gone from 160 to 120. "It's unbelievable that you can still bowl," I said. "Don't worry about your score. You're an inspiration for everyone around you. Even Dan told me that he'd never seen anyone with your spirit. Your teammates have so much respect for you."

To keep my own equilibrium, I began to take early morning walks while Jim was still in bed. But, the walks were too short, and I was beginning to feel as if I had a tight noose around my neck. If an ambulance, fire truck, or police car sped by while I was away, my heart raced and I could barely breath.

"Why do you need a walk?" Jim asked. "You get plenty of exercise around here taking care of me and the house."

"I just feel better when I walk."

How can I tell him the walk is the only chance I have to relax, get away from the pressures, and get my head together to face another day?

Jim's fainting spells were becoming part of our daily lives. He sometimes fell or sat in his chair totally unresponsive, dazed, drooling, and unable to focus. A spell could last a minute or five minutes—there was no predicting the onset or length of each episode. Then, just as suddenly, the dizziness would pass. His doctors had no answer but suggested, "It may be autonomic dysfunction—his brain can no longer control his blood pressure."

One morning, Jim had such a spell. He was sitting at the breakfast table, staring straight ahead and pokerfaced. I knew that look. I put my arm around his waist to keep him from falling to the floor.

"Jim, Jim, can you hear me?" I said. No answer.

"Tell me your name." Silence.

I gently slapped his face. No reaction.

I was frightened and dialed 911.

"My husband has had a fainting spell—it may be a stroke. I can't tell. I can't get any response from him."

I held the phone to my ear and kept trying to get a reaction, but Jim continued to stare straight ahead.

"It must be a stroke. He's not acknowledging anything I do."

"I'll stay on the line, Miss, until we decide whether or not I should call an ambulance," the dispatcher said.

Just as suddenly, Jim looked at me with clear eyes.

"Hon, you scared me," I said. "Why haven't you been answering me?"

"Because," he grumbled, "you ask too God damned many questions."

I smiled, made the sign of the cross, and told the dispatcher, "I think he's his old self again, and we won't need an ambulance after all."

Jim's observation abilities had also changed. Before the onset of the Parkinson's, he noticed everything in and around our property. He'd come home from school and say, "Who was here today? There are different tire tracks in the driveway."

Now, he was the opposite. At mealtime, he'd place food on his dish, tip the dish slightly as he walked across the floor, spill half of it on the floor, and walk through it. As I cleaned up the mess, he looked shocked that there was food on the floor. I began to fill his dish to prevent spillage. Jim didn't like that. He wanted to help by taking care of himself. I repeatedly asked him not to take his dishes to the sink after dinner, but he persisted. I tried to control my temper, but one day after he fell, spilled his food, and broke the dishes, I exploded.

"Please don't clear the table," I screamed. "How is this helpful? Now I have to try to get you up off the floor, clean up the food, and the broken dishes. Can you tell me how this helps me?"

Whenever I lost my temper, I felt ashamed. I knew I should be more understanding and never lose my patience. Now I know. I was asking the impossible of myself. The day-to-day challenges were overwhelming. I had to learn to forgive myself for being human.

One Sunday morning, Jim had showered and put his robe on over his naked body. I was dressed for church. I smelled the scent of hickory-smoked bacon drifting down the hallway. He was cooking his own breakfast. I stopped a few feet from him to say goodbye and remind him to be careful around the stove. A fainting spell struck. Everything was happening in slow motion. My breath caught in my throat. I could see a catastrophe beginning to start but couldn't move fast enough to prevent it. Jim began to fall backward onto the floor; his arm hit the pan as he tried to steady himself; his robe spread open when he landed. The pan of half-cooked bacon and bacon grease landed on his arms, his legs, and his exposed groin. His body was between the stove and refrigerator. He lay half conscious but didn't say a word. He was in shock. For a brief second, I was so stunned that I was immobile. Then I sprang into action and, slipping in the bacon grease, hurried to the refrigerator to get ice. Huge blisters immediately appeared over his body. I was crying and placing ice bags on his burns. He was still utterly silent. Once I could pull him upright, I maneuvered him to a chair. He left the robe open to let air circulate and held the ice packs on his burns. That night we put gauze and salve over his injuries.

The next day, we covered his blisters in bandages, and he went golfing. He refused to let something like third degree burns interfere with his plans.

By the summer of 2006, I was increasingly uneasy about his driving. *How will I ever tell him that he can no longer drive?* The problem came to a head in July. We were returning from a fishing trip to the Adirondacks. His bass boat was hitched to the back of the car, and I was driving.

"Let's swing around to Auburn and stop at the Bass Pro Shop," Jim said. "I want to look at fishing gear."

At the store, he climbed into an electric cart and drove in the direction of the sporting goods department.

"I'm going to look at a few things over here," I said. "I'll catch up with you in a minute."

I walked towards the shoe department. When I finished and headed for the sporting goods department, I didn't see him. Then I noticed several clerks scurrying around frantically. Jim was sprawled on the floor at the bottom of the stairs, and the cart was tipped over on its side.

I flew down the stairs and bent over him. "Are you okay, Hon?"

"Are you all right, sir?" several clerks asked.

"Yes, yes. I'm fine," he said. He seemed embarrassed and puzzled as to how he got there.

He had driven the electric cart DOWN a set of stairs.

I was flustered. Why hadn't he used the ramp?

The clerks checked their *embarrassed drop-in customer* over, filled out an accident report, righted the cart, and helped him into it. He bought a fishing rod.

Back in our car, I asked. "Whatever happened in there?"

"Well, I was wearing my transition lens glasses, and they were still dark when I got in the store. Besides, that store is kinda dark. I never saw the wheelchair ramp and just headed for the sporting goods section. I didn't even see the stairs. And, don't you go telling your friends about this one. You're always telling stories on me."

"All right, all right," I promised. "I won't say a word."

The store's headquarters called the next day to make certain he was okay, and to feel him out about a possible lawsuit.

"Yes. I'm fine," Jim said. "I just never saw the stairs."

It was time to break the news. "I hate to say this, Hon, but it isn't safe for you to drive any longer."

"I'm okay to drive. You never trust me." He sounded so hurt.

"Jim, your reaction time just isn't what it used to be, and you don't notice your surroundings any more. How will you feel if you cause an accident and injure someone? You'll never forgive yourself. We just can't take a chance."

It was my husband's final loss of independence.

As his caregiver, I was constantly amazed and in awe of his determination. At the same time, I often fought to keep my own feelings and needs in check because I was facing an equally large challenge, and I didn't know if I was up to the task.

In addition to my constant stress and Jim's frequent crises, we had money concerns. Between Medicare and our health insurance, hospital stays and surgeries were covered. His prescriptions, sometimes running in the thousands of dollars, cost us only $5 each time. Still, I found it necessary to hire help whenever I wanted to leave. I couldn't trust Jim. He needed constant supervision. In the back of my mind, I knew it would only get worse. *What if I have to place him in a home?*

New crises continued to happen. In January 2007, while on a trip, Jim fell and injured his back. We returned home and consulted a back specialist who diagnosed two compressed vertebrae. "I can repair your back with a procedure called kyphoplasty. I'll make a small incision in your back and insert and inflate a balloon to spread the vertebrae apart.

Then I'll inject a cement-like substance between the vertebrae to relieve the pressure."

It sounded so simple.

Jim was on a drug called Azilect, recently prescribed to help his Parkinson's condition. A side effect was that no painkillers could be used unless a person was off the drug for two weeks. He was in the hospital cubicle, prepped and ready for surgery when the anesthesiologist arrived.

"My husband is on a new drug called Azilect. According to his doctor, he can't have any pain killers?" The anesthesiologist's eyes popped open, and a look of concern crossed his face.

"Just check it out before you give him something he shouldn't have," I suggested.

The doctor left to confirm my statement.

A second anesthesiologist flaunted into the cubicle. He looked at me with disdain. "That's ridiculous. There is no such thing as a drug which precludes using any pain killers."

"Well, that's what our neurologist said. I didn't think you would be using painkillers since the surgery sounded fairly easy, but I wanted you to be aware of that fact."

His nostrils flared; he pulled himself to his full 6'2" height; he stuck out his chin. "No doctor, who isn't present and doesn't know what we are doing, is going to tell ME what we can and can't do."

"All I can say is that you need to be aware of this drug and not give Jim anything that will cause problems."

He stormed out. Orderlies wheeled Jim into the operating room. Once there, he listened to three anesthesiologists arguing about whether or not to proceed. The surgeon, the same one who had performed the DBS surgery, listened to the three and said, "Cancel the surgery until he's off this drug for two weeks."

Jim dressed; we went to breakfast; we went home. A call to his neurologist confirmed my facts. "You did the correct thing."

"You know doctor, after this scare, I think I won't give Jim Azilect anymore. It did seem to be helping him, but he requires too many emergency surgeries. I can't take the chance."

"I agree, although it's too bad."

Oh, how I nagged Jim. As hard as I tried to bite my tongue, I just couldn't stop myself. When he got disgusted with me, I said, "I'm trying to protect you from yourself. You just don't seem to have good judgment any more."

"Why? What do you mean by that?"

"For example, you walk across the kitchen carrying a butcher knife in your hand."

"I don't see that as a problem," he responded.

"That's just my point. You should see that as a problem. You fall all the time without any warning. You could stab yourself to death."

I repeated in my head: *He can't help it. He can't help it. He can't help it.* Then, I decided I couldn't always help it if I nagged him.

That spring, I took up golf, which involved more than just hitting the ball. After helping Jim get dressed and in the car, I loaded both sets of clubs, drove to the course, unloaded Jim and our clubs, and drove the golf cart. I helped him get out of the cart and up to the tee. Then, I put the tee in the ground and the golf ball on top. I stood behind to catch him if he started to fall. Once he got his balance and zeroed in on the golf ball, he amazed me with a long straight shot. We played what we called, *No Stress Golf.* We no longer kept score, didn't worry about how many extra swings a shot took, moved the ball to a better spot if it landed in the deep grass, and giggled our way through nine holes. We chatted about how lucky we were to be outside enjoying a morning together.

Still, we never knew when the next calamity would happen. It occurred in May of 2007 when we were prepared to attend a relative's wedding in Tennessee. Jim's legs had been swollen for several days. I was alarmed. On the morning of departure, our luggage was in the car and our cooler filled with snacks and drinks, but he didn't act right.

"I don't think we'd better go to this wedding."

"I can make it."

"We're not going. I'm taking you to the emergency room instead. We can't take a chance on being away from your doctors."

A new doctor was assigned to our case. He ordered a CAT scan.

"Your husband has internal bleeding and renal failure," the doctor said.

I was ready for a nervous breakdown. With shaking hands, I dialed Shelly. "I can't take much more of this," I cried. "His hospital visits are frequent, and his needs are great. I can't deal any more. I'm not a doctor. What if I miss the signs and don't get him to a hospital in time?"

"I don't blame you, Mom." I could hear the strain in her voice. "I don't know how you've stood it this long."

After a while, I calmed down and off the top of my head answered the doctor's questions regarding all of Jim's health issues, his surgeries, when they occurred, and the medicines he was taking.

"Mom," Kim said later that day, "you have to get all of this in a book. If something happens to you, Dad's in trouble. None of us knows all of this information."

In the next few days, she and I prepared a booklet. It contained a list of contacts, medications, doctors, previous surgeries, and copies of health care proxy, power of attorney, do not resuscitate form, and insurance cards. This new *Bible* became my constant companion.

Jim's new doctor tried to absorb all of the complex information in a short time.

"Does your husband experience hallucinations?" he asked.

"Sometimes he hallucinates." (Why wasn't I more specific?)

Jim's hallucinations were in the form of violent dreams causing him to kick or hit me during the night. His dreams didn't occur every night and always took place in Tupper Lake even if they involved people from Brockport.

"Your husband is overmedicated," the doctor insisted. "You have to take him off so many medications."

"I'm sure he isn't overmedicated. We keep in close touch with his neurologist. Without these medicines, he can't move." Once home, I called Jim's neurologist.

"I have some patients who overmedicate themselves. Your husband isn't one of them."

Still, the primary care doctor pressed the issue and insisted the side effects were as bad as the disease. "You have to reduce his medicines."

The topic came to a head one morning when I arrived early to visit Jim. The nurse met me at the check-in station. "Your husband was so agitated during the night that we had to place him in a Geri chair near my station. He was hollering he's a citizen and has rights. We sent a counselor in to speak with him."

"What did the counselor say?" I asked.

"The counselor said there is nothing wrong with him. He's angry because he wants to use the bathroom instead of a bedpan."

"Can't say I blame him," I responded.

I sat down, took Jim's hands in mine and said, "Honey, the nurses have to make certain you don't get hurt. Right now you're weak from being in bed so long. Until you get your strength back, you have to listen to them and use the bedpan. I know you don't like that, but you have to comply."

"All right. If you're asking this of me, I'll do it."

"Maybe you should give him something to calm him down," I said to the nurse.

BAD DECISION. They prescribed Haldol—an antipsychotic drug. The drug had the opposite effect and sent my husband on an LSD trip.

For the next eight hours, Jim believed he was flying an airplane. He was gripping an imaginary steering wheel and moving side to side as if flying. His eyes were buggy. He was sweating, screaming, and scared. "I can't land this plane. Kay is sitting on my shoulders, and Lloyd is in that chair. They won't talk to me. Why are they ignoring me? Why don't they answer me? What's wrong with you? Can't you see them?"

I called Kerry who left work and rushed to the hospital. Jim continued to try to land the plane until the drug wore off. After that, Haldol was on the list of medicines to which Jim was allergic.

"Mom, how long can you keep this up?" Kerry asked. "It may be time to place Dad."

My answer was always the same. "I'll know when the time is right."

Again the doctor said, "He's overmedicated. He's agitated and hallucinating. There are terrible side effects to all the drugs he's taking. You have to reduce his drugs."

"He does not normally hallucinate. If he is taken off the drugs, he will be stiff as a board, unable to move, and confined to a bed. He is not overmedicated."

The doctor countered, "You are wrong, and if I think you are wrong, it is my duty to tell you."

I pulled myself to my full 5'6" height and got inches from his face. "When I think YOU are wrong, I will tell YOU. AND, YOU are wrong."

After several days, the abdominal blood and renal failure problems somehow righted themselves. I was headed to the car to drive Jim home when the doctor stopped me.

"You're very stressed. Go home, have a glass of wine, and put your feet up."

"You're right. I am stressed, but as you see, I am taking my stress home with me."

When the doctor became more familiar with his new patient, he was in awe of him. He'd pat Jim's shoulder and say, "You're quite a fighter, aren't you? I've never seen anyone with your determination."

The usual round of home visits began. A day or two after his discharge, a social worker visited to assesses Jim's needs. Another few days after that, a visiting nurse arrived to take vital signs and put the information into a computer. Eventually physical and occupational therapists were assigned and home health aides allocated for two hours a day for twenty days. All of this lag time in assessing and assigning meant that I was alone with Jim and trying to keep things under control.

"What about people who don't have a willing or able caregiver to tend to their needs? What do they do?" I asked a home health aide.

"They suffer. Our system in this country is terrible."

A wheelchair supplied by Medicare arrived—a heavy, bulky wheelchair. It took all of my strength to lift it into the car. I called the Medicare office to request a lighter chair.

"Can your husband move the wheels to get around?" asked the receptionist.

"Yes," I said, "but I can't lift it into the car when I have to take him to the doctors."

"Unfortunately, that doesn't matter. The regulations stipulate that if the patient can move the wheels, then he/she cannot have a lighter wheelchair."

"Then please pick up the chair. It's useless to us." We purchased our own portable, easy-to-lift chair.

Shelly called one afternoon. "Mom, I'm going to come out once a week to stay with Dad and give you a break."

"That's not necessary. You're busy with the kids."

"I want to do this. What day is good?"

"Okay. Tuesdays work best for me."

Every Tuesday Shelly arrived and the two played Wii bowling, did crossword puzzles, or cooked supper together. She got the true flavor of Jim's stubbornness. "Let's make meatloaf for supper, Dad."

Together they mixed the meatloaf, shaped it, and Shelly put it in a round Pyrex dish.

"You can't use that Pyrex dish," Jim said and stumbled his way to the cupboard. "It has to go in a bread loaf pan."

"No, it doesn't. Mom doesn't always use a bread pan. This round one will be fine."

He wasn't to be dissuaded. "It's right up here over the refrigerator, and he swayed side to side trying to reach."

It was useless to argue. Shelly held onto him while he pulled a loaf pan from the cupboard.

We made adjustments as the need arose: purchased a lift chair; he slept in his chair; changed to a walker with brakes and a seat; purchased an electric wheelchair (just in case); ordered a medical alert system; protected his legs from cuts and bruises with soccer shin guards; hired more help.

It was time for me to make adjustments in my life. Articles I had read warned: "A caregiver must take care of himself/herself in order to be around to be a caregiver."

I placed Jim for five to ten days in a respite facility once a year.

"I don't want you to go away and leave me." His voice strangled on the words.

He felt abandoned by me and betrayed by his body. But, I stood my ground. "Sweetheart, I have to get a break from time to time. If I don't, I can't keep up this pace. I'm sorry, but that's the way it has to be. I'll arrange for friends and family to take you to dinner, to chorus, or a movie so you won't be stuck every day."

After a second cancerous tumor attached to his bladder was discovered in 2007, it was successfully removed. His silver hair had thinned, and he seemed smaller and weaker each day. He'd lost his strength, his flexibility, and his ability to take care of himself. But, his stubbornness and strength of character never left him. He was in for a month-long hospital stay.

He weighed 148 pounds when discharged. It took months for him to gain the weight back, but by spring, Jim and his John Deere were like peanut butter and jelly—stuck together. He'd don his straw hat, fill the tank with gas, and head for the back forty for a few hours of peaceful mowing. One afternoon, I looked out the front and side windows to check his progress. No Jim. I looked out the back windows. No Jim. I headed for the back door.

I found him hanging onto a railing, chest heaving in and out, gasping for breath.

"What's wrong?"

He choked out his words, "I drove (gasp) the tractor (gasp) into the pond."

"You did WHAT?"

He rested his head against the railing. "Well, I put the tractor on cruise control (gasp), and I got too close to the edge of the pond (gasp) and couldn't remember (gasp) how to release the cruise. It's in the pond."

"Oh my God. Here, let me help you into the house. Then I'll deal with the tractor. You're exhausted from walking all that way."

I settled Jim and walked to the pond. The tractor wasn't submerged but teetering on the very edge. I turned again to our good neighbor.

"Everett, could you please come over with your tractor and chains? There's no rush. Whenever you have a minute. Our tractor is almost in the pond."

"I'll be right over." I could hear the smile in his voice.

What would we have done without Everett?

Loss upon loss was heaped upon us. It was May 11, 2008 when our whole family gathered to celebrate a scrumptious Mother's Day luncheon at Kim's 1820 farmhouse. After lunch, grandchildren headed outside to run off some energy and enjoy freedom from hovering adults.

Kerry and Vicki were discussing their upcoming white water trip to West Virginia. Kerry was quiet and shaking his head as he paced around the kitchen.

"Oh, stop being such a Susie (her favorite teasing name for him). It'll be a blast," Vicki said.

"I don't know, Vicki. I'd just as soon go on a golfing trip."

"We go on a golfing trip every year. I want to do something different. Besides, the trip is already paid for.

We hugged as they prepared to head home.

"Have a good time, but be careful," I said.

They left for their trip with friends on May 14. Around one o'clock on Saturday afternoon, I thought about them.

I'd like to call and check, but they're probably busy. I wonder if they're heading home today or tomorrow.

At 8:30 Sunday morning, our phone rang.

"Hello."

"Mom." His voice sounded strange—as if he were fighting back tears.

"Hey, Kerry, how's your trip going?"

"Mom." Crackle. Crackle. "You'd better sit down."

"Kerry, we're breaking up." Crackle. Crackle. "What's wrong? Is someone hurt?"

The line went dead.

"Jim, something's wrong. That was Kerry. There's a problem, but the line went dead."

Jim looked at me with anxious eyes as I fumbled with the phone, trying not to panic.

I dialed Kerry several times but couldn't get a connection. Tapping a pencil, I sat next to the phone waiting for his call.

Ring. Ring. I grabbed the phone. "Mom, you'd better sit down."

"Kerry, what's wrong?"

"She's dead, Mom. She's dead."

"No, no. Not Vicki," I screamed. "Oh my God, Kerry, I can't even believe this. What happened? Where are you? Dad and I will drive down to be with you. I don't want you alone.

"No Mom," tears caught in his voice. "Our friends are with me. I'll call you later. I have to go to the morgue today." The line went dead.

Jim and I hugged, unable to talk—trying to let this new crisis sink in.

"Poor Kerry. I can't believe the horror he must be going through," Jim said as tears ran down his cheeks. Both of us felt helpless. We didn't know what to do.

For the next few days, I was crying uncontrollably. "I know we've got to be strong for Kerry, but I'll never get through the funeral. I'm going to need Valium or something. The last few times I went to a funeral, I hyperventilated. I don't want to pass out at her service."

Once the doctor saw my condition, he gave me a prescription. The two pills I took were enough to get me through the next few days. We were shaken to our core—unable to believe our healthy daughter-in-law of twenty years had drowned. The next weeks were a blur. I had to push forward. We did our best to support Kerry and hold ourselves together through the wake, the funeral, and the weeks that followed, but it all seemed surreal.

"Kerry, you've got to go for counseling. You've been through an ordeal we can't even imagine."

"I know. I know, Mom."

I felt so inadequate and didn't know how to help him. His grief was all consuming, and I prayed that he would heal—not forget—just heal.

For the next few months, Kerry sought professional counseling. It helped to take the edge off, but he was still on a roller coaster of emotions—from denial, to guilt, to anger. He exhibited all the signs of post-traumatic stress disorder. He had flashbacks and relived the events over and over. He couldn't sleep or concentrate. He spent money wildly, as if there were no end to it. He didn't care about anything. His hope for his future had died with Vicki. He tried to hide his sadness from us. He knew we were dealing with Jim's declining health. Tracy stayed by his side as much as possible, even sleeping at his house so Kerry wouldn't be alone.

In spite of all this, Kerry showed more strength than I could have imagined him possessing. Like trying to put the pieces of a shattered glass back together, he began to rebuild his life by making new friends, changing jobs, and selling their home. I knew the weekend of her death would be a shadowy giant haunting him, and I sensed Vicki, the woman he called his *beautiful blue eyes* would always share a corner of his heart.

Gradually, Jim and I settled back into our normal routine of pills, physical therapy, and involvement with family and friends.

August 2008: Mary called to tell us Paul was in the hospital. He'd had gall bladder surgery and was due to be discharged the next day.

"Thanks for telling us," I said. "We'll call him after dinner."

Jim dialed the hospital's number and asked to speak to his brother. Paul's voice was garbled—unintelligible.

"This is Jim. Your brother, Jim. Jim, Paul. You remember me." Jim's eyebrows knitted together. "Something's the matter. He doesn't seem to know me, and I can't understand him."

"Well, maybe he just woke up or maybe he's drugged. Say goodbye, and tell him we'll call in the morning."

Later that evening, Mary called again. "Sue, you won't believe it. Paul died this evening. He was doing so well, and all of a sudden he took a turn for the worse. They think it was septic shock."

I slowly placed the phone back into its cradle and closed my eyes. The twisted lump in my throat garbled my words. "That - that was Mary. I leaned my head into Jim's shoulder. "Your brother Paul died tonight." We remained motionless, letting the unexpected news sink into our brains.

We had only known of Paul for a few years, but he had seemed so much a part of our family. After all his years of being lost, he had come home to his rightful family.

Again in December 2008, Jim was rushed to the hospital at midnight with abdominal pains. With each of these episodes, a different team of doctors treated him. I opened my *Bible* and went over his problems.

"He can't have blood thinners because of the type of cancer he has. Thinners cause abdominal bleeding. He can't have MRI's of his head because he has electrodes implanted in his brain. He can't have EKG's because he has a brain pacemaker in his chest that will cause an inaccurate reading."

On and on it went. I felt I was trying to juggle balls in the air in an attempt to keep my husband alive. I received kudos from the medical team about my knowledge, but what if I missed something. Jim was out of options for surgery. His abdomen showed hundreds of spots of cancer, and every one of those spots had potential to grow and attach itself to an organ.

He returned home Christmas Eve day. "Maybe we should cancel our Christmas Eve party," I suggested.

Jim wouldn't consider canceling and carried on and participated in our usual silly games and songs. After dinner, we left him seated in the living room while we cleaned up the dishes.

"I want to be where the action is," he yelled. He started to get up from his chair and stumble his way into the kitchen.

Nolan, our two-year old grandson, pulled himself to his full height, stuck out his chest, and hollered, "Poppy's movin."

Only then did I realize I had been neglecting Jim and ran to help him transfer. None of us could believe such a young child was so aware of his Poppy's needs. Nolan got so much attention over his warning, he became my best caregiver, and we counted on him after that evening to keep an eye on Jim's movements.

By late spring, Jim was anxious to fish. The weather had warmed, the air was crisp, and the sun was out—perfect for fishing. Jim, his friend Sal Sciremamanno, and I planned a relaxing day at Braddock's Bay.

The phone rang. "Mom, I hate to ask you, but my nanny is sick. I need a sitter. I have an important meeting that I can't skip. Could you possibly help me out?"

"I was going fishing with Dad and Sal, but I suppose they could go without me."

I explained the situation to Sal.

"That's no problem. I can take him by myself."

"Are you sure?" I whispered. "You have to keep an eye on him, you know."

"Don't worry. We'll be fine."

I wasn't so sure.

"Have you got everything—snacks, rods, tackle box, sunscreen, pills?" I asked.

"Quit worrying. We're all set," Jim said.

They hooked up the boat, loaded their gear in the car, and headed out with visions of catching the almighty one.

Once at the launch site, Sal said, "Jim, let's make a plan. I'll help you out of the car and have you sit on the dock. You hold onto the bowline while I back the boat up until it floats. I'll tie the boat to the cleats, help you into the boat, and then park the car and trailer. Just wait here in the boat, and when I get back, we'll head out."

Jim listened and nodded his head.

When Sal got out of the car, he heard a motor running. *Someone must be coming in off the lake.* He hurried to the launch.

Jim was driving away in the boat.

Sal waded into the water and shouted over the noise of the motor. "Jim, Jim, you said you were going to wait. How am I going to get in?"

Jim gunned the boat backwards towards shore and drove it up on the ramp. Sal winced, certain that Jim had ripped up the propellers. He strained to climb over the back of the boat and then noticed the tackle box and its contents spilled all over the floor.

Once he was settled and the gear reorganized, they headed farther out into the bay. Three casts and Jim wanted to move to a new location. A few more casts, and Jim needed help to change his lures. Every few casts, Jim sought a different lure or a new spot. If Sal thought he was going to do any fishing himself, he soon gave up on that idea.

Oh well, it's a day out of the house and a day on the water. But, how am I going to get him out of the boat? Will he stay put? If he falls in the water and, with my back acting up, I'm not sure I can get him out.

After several hours of moving location, changing lures, and no action, Jim said, "What do you say we head back?"

"Okay. Now let's review the procedure," Sal said. "I'll pull up next to the dock. I'll tie up the boat and then help you out. You can sit on the dock, and I'll give you the lines to hold. I'll back up the trailer and hook up the boat. All you have to do is sit on the dock—just sit. Don't get up or try to move—just sit. You realize I'm not worried about you. If you get hurt, I'm worried your wife will kill me for not looking after you."

This time Jim followed the instructions.

Next crisis: June 2009. We were at Jim's dermatologist. "My husband has an infected sore on his head. It's right near the wires under his skin so be careful."

"Good heavens, there's the wire. I never expected to see it so close. You're right. It's infected. Luckily I didn't cut the wire."

We assumed that was the end of our problems and headed for Pennsylvania to spend a few relaxing days with Shelly's family. It was a warm, sunny day, and spring flowers were in bloom. We drove through the mountains and discussed taking a side trip to Gettysburg or Washington, D.C. On our second day in Pennsylvania, I noticed red lines radiating around Jim's brain pacemaker. I was troubled and called our neurologist.

"You better bring him into an emergency department," his assistant said. "It's probably nothing, but I'd rather be on the safe side."

"Well, we're in Pennsylvania, but I can leave immediately and be at Strong in six hours."

"That won't work. We don't have a DBS specialist on staff right now. You're closest to Johns Hopkins hospital. Head there, and I'll call ahead so they'll be expecting you."

My heart dropped all the way to my shoes. I hated to tell Jim he had to spend another minute in a hospital, and an unfamiliar one at that. He was silent when I told him and thoughtful on the hour's drive. The imposing hospital occupied acres of land, and I was tense and gripping the steering wheel till my knuckles turned white. After construction detours, missed turns, and three trips around the building trying to find the parking lot, I lost my temper.

"God damn it. I can see the hospital right there, but I can't find the way into the parking lot."

"Calm down, Sue. We'll find it."

After a few more tries, I located the correct parking lot, loaded Jim into his wheelchair, and pushed him into the emergency department.

The pale green walls, containers of dirty linens, stainless steel everything, painted lines to the elevators, antiseptic smells, and white-coated staff scurrying from room to room seemed all too familiar. The doctors were waiting. I opened my *Bible* and went through the list of illnesses, surgeries, and medicines. Jim lay on the bed with his arms crossed over his stomach as he waited for the team of specialists to begin examinations and tests.

I held his hand, and we watched the activity around our cubicle. A teen-aged heavy-set girl was wheeled into the adjoining partition. She screamed and screamed and screamed until my head throbbed. "She must be in terrible pain," Jim said.

Then we heard the nurse. "Calm down Twana. We haven't done anything yet. We haven't even taken your temperature." She screamed louder.

After fifteen minutes, the nurses moved Twana to a private area down the hall.

The brain surgeon came in. He was short and cute, with thick, curly white hair and a boyish face. He delivered the unexpected news.

"I'm afraid your husband is in critical condition. All of Jim's hardware from the DBS surgery has to be removed. He has a staff infection heading for his brain. If it gets to his brain, there's little we can do."

My own brain couldn't process what I was hearing. Unshed tears burned in my eyes, and I was near the breaking point. My shoulders tensed with rage. "But doctor," I pleaded, "this can't be. The electrodes have been our best friends. They help Jim so much. Please, can't you just give him massive doses of antibiotics?"

"That never works. Once staff infection gets into a person's body, it attaches itself to anything artificial, and we won't be able to stop it. We've bumped other surgeries to make room for your husband. After the infection clears up, Jim can have the DBS replaced."

Jim sat bolt upright. That had gotten his attention. His eyes widened. "I'll never go through that surgery again."

For a few minutes, I held the pen in my hand and stared at the paperwork. I had no choice but to sign. The staff called for a transport assistant. After ten minutes of waiting, the doctor said, "Help me get your husband into a wheelchair." Together we maneuvered Jim into a wheelchair, piled his bag of clothing on his lap, and hurried towards an elevator.

The elevator stopped on the basement level and the doctor, his lab coat flying open, began running while pushing Jim's wheelchair through the bowels of the hospital. Had I not been so frightened for Jim, I would have been amused. I had never seen a surgeon take personal responsibility for transporting a patient, but he was on a mission to get Jim to the operating room for his allotted time slot.

Once again, I sat in stunned silence in the waiting room, feeling as if I were losing the battle to keep Jim alive. *Will these nightmare crises never end?* How could I have missed the infection? For five years, we had relied on the electrodes to help Jim function. I knew tremors, bradykinesia, and dyskinesia would return as our housemates.

I called our children, said a few prayers, waited for Jim to return from surgery, consulted with the doctor, and left for a hotel. A room on the sixth floor of the Ramada Hotel in downtown Baltimore became my home for the next five days. It was like the many hotels I'd stayed in while on business trips—brown floral bedspread, landscape picture over the bed, bed stand with lamp and digital clock, uncomfortable armchair. The pain across my shoulders from tight neck muscles made it impossible to sleep. I worried about Jim all night.

Each day, I ate breakfast in a greasy spoon and rode a subway to the hospital. We made small talk when I visited, never delving into the bigger issue of death. He slept often, and I took short walks to break the monotony and stress. He didn't complain when he was poked, prodded and pricked.

One afternoon, a female dressed in a cotton, partially opened hospital gown wandered into Jim's room while he was sitting on a commode. He swallowed his laughter as she walked around his room. She ignored him. She believed she was in a gift shop and was angry no one would sell her the teddy bear she imagined in the room. A nurse came by to retrieve his visitor.

With his usual sense of humor, he said, "She's off her rocker, I think."

That day, Jim said, "I'm coming back."

And once again, I replied, "I'm sure you are."

Once out of danger, he was transferred to an acute rehabilitation hospital twenty minutes from Shelly's house. I was suffocating and restless from trying to keep Jim entertained. I wanted out—back to the comfort of our home. Twice I drove the six hours home on the excuse of catching up on lawn mowing and paying bills. Mostly, I had to get myself together. After two weeks of rehab, Jim returned home to the usual round of therapists, visiting nurses, and home health aides.

An invitation arrived in August 2009 for the Tupper Lake class reunion. I returned the RSVP immediately. At the end of the month, we headed for the comfort of Mary and Sonny's home. Although I was aware Jim was losing his good looks and ramrod straight carriage, he had changed so gradually that I didn't realize how shocking his appearance would be to others. At the party, I pushed him in his wheelchair towards his former basketball team members.

"I'll be right back. I'm going to the ladies' room."

On my way, a woman Jim had known since second grade stopped me. "Sue, if you hadn't been with Jimmy tonight, I would never have recognized him."

Until then, I was unaware that I had been blocking the enormity of his changed looks from my mind. I turned my head to hide my tears and hurried to the bathroom.

January 2010: Jim was rushed by ambulance to Strong Memorial Hospital. A CAT scan showed he was bleeding internally, and this time the doctors suggested we get our affairs in order. I knew our days together were numbered. I had made up my mind that when he died, I would not grieve. I had been grieving for twenty-two years. What I didn't understand was that grieving was something I couldn't control. It was going to control me. His oncologist continued to hope for a miracle.

"There's a new drug that might help your husband. It's a long shot, but what have we got to lose? Some people with his type of cancer have responded well to the drug."

The drug was ordered at a cost $7,089 a month. In his final year of life, Jim's Parkinson's and cancer drugs cost $70,000. Every day, I thanked God for our health insurance. While I was dealing with day-to-day discussions with doctors and nurses, he was calling friends and planning a Super Bowl party. He made all of the arrangements from his hospital bed. His capacity for celebrating life was unquenchable.

"Hey Dan and Lorna. We're planning a Super Bowl party. Can you come? Great. We'll make it easy and have everyone bring something to pass. Why don't you come over around four o'clock?"

Unfortunately, he was mixed up about details. People arrived for the party at different times—anywhere from four till six p.m. Guests laughed, food was laid out, drinks were consumed, Euchre was played, and Jim was in high spirits.

As his disease progressed, Jim could no longer control his emotions. Saying, "You look pretty today" could bring on a flood of tears. *What happened to my tough Marine?* But, he didn't cry if a doctor told him he was going to die.

One morning, while eating breakfast, his tears began to flow. "What's the matter, Honey?"

"I'm really disappointed in Luke."

"Why?"

"He doesn't call."

"Luke never calls. He never has called. He's not a caller. He's still your friend. When we visit Tupper Lake, he comes to Sonny's to see you. He always invites us for dinner. He comes down to visit sometimes. He just doesn't call. Now eat your breakfast and stop your blubbering."

He sniffled a little and said, "Okay, thanks for being so understanding."

Our laughter eased the tension, and was our best medicine.

After breakfast, he sat in his chair watching the squirrels eating the birdseed. His favorite thing to do when he spotted them was to get out of his chair, make his way with his walker to his shooting window (one with the screen removed), open the window, and let out a war hoop to scare any unsuspecting squirrels. Then, he'd chuckle as they scurried away. That afternoon, instead of squirrels, he spotted two geese landing in our small pond.

"Get my gun," he said and maneuvered his way to his window.

"Okay. I'll get your pellet gun."

"NO. Not that one. That's no good. Get my shotgun," he demanded.

"I'm not getting your shotgun."

"Why not? Geese are in the pond. They'll poop all over the place."

"I don't care if they crap all over our three acres. If you shoot the shotgun, it will kick back, knock you on your butt, and you'll shoot a hole in our ceiling. You are NOT shooting your gun."

Stomp, stomp, and stomp he went towards his chair with his walker. "Why do you continually stop me from doing something I know I can do?" he muttered.

His determination and stubbornness were the character traits that kept Jim an active participant in living, but it sure infuriated me at times.

CHAPTER 16 - CONFLICT AND TURMOIL

I'm in such internal conflict, I can barely get through the day. From the outside looking on, friends and family think we're doing great. If only they could witness the maelstrom in my brain, they would know it's all a façade. The turmoil in my head won't stop.

I weed the garden. I feel my mind spinning out of control. I go for a walk. I can't stop my thoughts. They replay over and over as if in the same scratched groove of a 78 rpm record. I argue with my conscience. The bombarding messages make no sense. My feelings spiral round and round with no end.

I can't live another day like this.
How can he stand it?
What about me?
There are two of us in this marriage.
Didn't I vow For Better or Worse?
I wish the Lord would take him.
Oh, no. I didn't mean that.
If he dies, I can't get him back.
Don't think that way.
All right then, God, make him better.
He'll never be better.
I hate my life.
I hate myself for my thoughts.

What will I do without him?

Stop these thoughts right now.
I can't.
How can I complain?
I'm selfish.
What about him and how he feels?
He never complains.
But he's sick, and I'm not.
Don't I count?
His disease is my disease.
Why did this happen to us?
It's his fault.
What did he do to deserve this?
Nothing.
He's a good man.

Take it away.
No one can.
Pull it together girl.

What will I do without him?

He's dying an inch at a time.
I can't stand to see him like this.
I've given him every ounce of myself.
He wants more.
There is no more to give.
Why do I punish myself?
I've done the best I can.
No other woman I know would do as much as I've done.
It's not enough.
I need to talk to someone.
I haven't got time.
I want my life back the way it was.

What will I do without him?

I have to place him.
How can I place him?
He belongs in his own home.
I can't take care of him.
He will hate it.
I'll feel guilty.
More guilt piled onto what I'm already feeling.
Why doesn't he help me by staying put for two minutes?
He can't help it.
Shit, shit, shit.
What's wrong with me?
Am I going crazy?
If you love someone so much, how can you want him gone?
He is my life.

What will I do without him?

My neck is stiff.
My shoulders ache.
Take more Tylenol.
Are these feelings normal?

He doesn't look like the man I married.
Do I still love him?
I've never loved anyone else.
Stop it. Stop it.
Get control.
Maybe a massage will help.
I'll get an appointment tomorrow.
I can't wait that long.
I need one now.
It won't help.
I still have to face each day.

He's awake.
My routine begins
I tell stories, flirt, exaggerate, make him laugh.

"Hey, Honey. What a beautiful day. Let's get you showered and dressed. How about going out for breakfast this morning?"

What will I do without him?

I push on.

CHAPTER 17 - THE TIME IS RIGHT

He was dead weight. It was becoming more and more challenging to get Jim showered and dressed. My back and arms felt as if they would break when I tried to get him out of his recliner. His medicine barely worked, and his Parkinson's mask was ever present.

We paid privately for assistance, but it was impossible to predict when I needed help. Jim's condition was varied, never the same two days or two hours in a row. At times when aides arrived, he would function well enough to challenge them to a few games of Wii bowling or demonstrate on Wii Fit how to ski down a hill. Then when I was alone, he'd fall, pass out, or be unable to move. Even with friends' assistance and hired help, too much was falling on my shoulders. I felt like a prisoner.

When a long-time friend said the wrong thing, I snapped. "How can you say such a thing? Take your comments and stuff them." I knew when I hung up the phone I was close to a nervous breakdown.

Kerry's words echoed in my head. "How much longer can you do this Mom?" My usual answer echoed in my brain.

I'll know when the time is right. I'll know. I'll know.

February 2010: I left the house at 5:45 a.m. to go out for a cup of coffee. As I glanced at the paper, it hit me. I shuddered at the realization that I could no longer take care of Jim. THE TIME IS RIGHT. I knew it right down to my toenails. The idea of telling him shot dread through my veins. *What will I say? How should I broach the subject? How will he respond?* I turned these thoughts over and over in my head, but no answer came. Still, I knew the heart-wrenching truth. I had to tell him.

When I returned home, I sat next to Jim, held his hand and said, "Hon, I can't do this anymore. I have reached my limit. I'm going to begin the process of placing you in a home. It won't happen immediately. There's a lot of paperwork involved."

The look of betrayal in his scared, blue eyes told me everything I needed to know. He cried deep guttural sobs; tears poured from his closed lids; his chest heaved; his words stuck in his mouth like taffy. I felt like a failure, as if I were abandoning him. It was Wednesday morning—his day to sing with the senior chorus.

Why didn't I wait? Why did I have to break the news on a day when he would have been engaging in his favorite hobby?

I called Sal. "Don't pick Jim up this morning. He won't be singing. We're both too distressed. I just told Jim that I have to place him."

Sal's voice cracked, "I understand, and I know how hard this must be for both of you. I'll call later."

Jim needed to use the bathroom. We raised his lift chair to its full tilt, and I pulled and tugged. His wasted body looked weightless but was the heaviest thing I had ever tried to move. Finally, I got his dead weight upright; his head bent down in rejection; his shaking hands gripped the walker; he shuffled towards the bathroom. His body froze halfway through the doorway. His legs refused to move. His shoulders shook as he sobbed. I stood behind, threaded my arms around his waist, held him upright, and laid my cheek against the hollow of his back for the next five minutes.

"Hon, for the rest of my life I'll feel guilty for every time I lost my temper or nagged you. I'm sorry I wasn't more patient. I'll never forgive myself."

"Please don't do that, Sue. You've been amazing."

I didn't feel amazing. I was giving up on him when he needed me most.

An underlying darkness descended on us, but gradually, the day took on its usual routine of showering, dressing, getting his breakfast and pills.

A week after our discussion, I began the arduous task of applying for Medicaid. Although we had some savings, it wasn't enough to cover the $8,500-$11,000 a month cost of a nursing home. I filled out page after page of an application and mailed it to social services. On days when I hired help, I visited nursing homes, determined to find the right one. He was still social and needed mental stimulation. A few of the facilities were small and friendly, but none of the residents could even speak. No matter what, I knew I couldn't place Jim in such surroundings.

On several occasions, I called Social Services. "This is Sue Savard. I mailed an application to your office several weeks ago. I'm applying for Medicaid for my husband. Have you processed it yet?"

Each time I heard the same reply. "We haven't even entered him into our system yet. We're behind."

I tried to be patient. The country was in a recession. Many people were out of work, losing their homes, and applying for aid. New staff hadn't been added to handle the influx of requests. At last, in mid March, Social Services called to schedule an interview. I was prepared with approximately 500 pages of information: five years of checking and savings account statements, his discharge and insurance papers, copies of our income tax and 401B statements. It wasn't enough. The interviewer gave me a list of a few hundred more pages of information she needed. In the next weeks, I gathered together and mailed the requested documentation.

Our life continued to be a daily struggle, but I tried to remain positive. I relayed funny stories from my morning trip for coffee, talked about the two of us taking in a movie, and discussed national news. Inside, I was drowning.

In late March, I received a temporary number giving us preliminary—not final—approval for Medicaid. I felt as if I were holding a golden passport. Nursing homes admit patients with a temporary number if they have a room available. Wrong. I was no further ahead than I was before. One afternoon, I went away from Jim's hearing and called two different nursing homes.

"This is Sue Savard. You have my application for placement for my husband, Jim. I can't take care of him anymore," I blubbered into the phone. "I have been doing this for years. I have a preliminary number. As I understand the system, this number qualifies my husband for placement."

"I'm sorry," the Admission's Office clerks said. "We don't have any beds, and that number is not enough. You need final approval." They both hung up.

I waited for a few minutes, dried my tears, and tried to get control before I went back into the sunroom.

As the days turned into weeks and Jim was still home, he began to forget about being placed. One afternoon, he said, "Could you drive me to Wal-Mart? I want to buy a new fishing rod."

Once there, I helped him into an electric shopping cart, and he headed for the sporting goods section where he found a long fishing rod, some fishing line, and a few new lures.

"Jim, remember we talked about this before," I said. "I'm getting ready to place you."

"Yeah, I know." He stared at me with a look of despair. "But, the guys will pick me up and take me fishing."

Shut up Sue, and let the man have some hope.

He drove his cart into the checkout and swung the fishing rod to and fro with one hand while struggling to get his wallet with the other. I watched in horror as the clerk ducked, trying to avoid getting hit with the rod.

"Here Jim. Let me hold the rod while you get your wallet out."

"Let me be. I'm not going to hit anyone."

I wasn't certain of that, but said no more.

Once home, I tried to help him put on the new line, but I wasn't doing it correctly.

"Let's wait until Kerry comes over tomorrow. He can help you get the line on."

The next day Kerry and Jim put the line on the rod, and I thought everything was set. Kerry left, and Jim pulled the line off the rod. It wasn't done to his satisfaction. Jim continued to struggle but didn't have the dexterity to do the task.

"Rudy is coming over tonight for a visit. Maybe he can help you," I suggested.

Jim and Rudy strung the line again that evening. When Rudy left, Jim took the line off.

"This isn't right. Damn it all. If I were well, I'd have this line on in two minutes, and I wouldn't need help to do it."

The following day, Jim spent three hours trying to get the line on the rod. I said, "Jim, I hate to see you struggle like this. Dick and Cathy are coming over tonight to play cards. Dick can help you get the line on."

"Will you leave me alone? If I want to work on this for three hours and be frustrated, let me. It's better than being bored out of my mind. Besides, I know more about fishing than Dick could even begin to know."

The rod is still without line.

My Dearest Friend,

Knowing you and loving you has always been in my book, the greatest experience of my life. Happy Birthday, may you have 50 more.

I am, as I ever was and evermore shall be - Yours!

Love Always
Jim

PART V

CHAPTER 18 – THE BIRTHDAY GIFT

March 2010: Dick and Cathy Contant were expected at seven p.m. for an evening of card playing. Jim's legs were swollen and red, and his eyes were creased tight at the corners as he struggled against pain. I was certain he had a blood clot.

"Let's cancel our plans," I suggested

"NO. We're going to play cards."

In spite of Jim's condition, the evening of Euchre, sharing jokes, and laughing was a balm for the doldrums.

How could Jim get through the evening in such high spirits? I knew he was in pain, but he didn't complain. When our guests left at 10:30, I picked up the dishes, helped Jim into a comfortable chair by the TV, gave him his medicine, and placed a snack and drink nearby.

"Don't get up or move," I said. "I'm going to shower, and then I'll get you ready for bed. Please stay put."

"Okay, I promise."

I hurried down the hall, took a fast shower, threw on my robe, and hustled back to the kitchen.

Jim was on the floor.

"I was just taking my dirty dishes to the sink," he said.

I was heartsick and discouraged. My nerves were stretched like a rubber band ready to break at any moment.

The next morning, I called an ambulance to transport my husband to Strong Memorial Hospital. As we waited for the ambulance, Jim said, "I don't mind dying, Sue. I just don't want to leave you."

I held him close to me, nuzzled my head in his neck and said, "I don't want you to leave me either, Honey. We have to hope something can be done."

There was an unspoken understanding that he was never coming home again. The fear and sadness in his eyes only gave me a small clue to his feelings.

Once he was admitted, I called the doctors aside. "I won't take Jim home again. I can't take care of him any longer."

The doctors and staff could see that his needs were far greater than one caregiver could handle.

After several days in the cancer ward, doctors informed us, "Jim's tumor is pressing on his kidneys causing them to shut down. We can do surgery and place tubes into them to drain his urine. If we don't do that, his kidneys will gradually fail, and he will slowly drift off to sleep."

When the doctors left, I asked, "Do you understand what the doctors just said?"

"Yes. I don't want any more surgeries."

He was well aware that he would remain in the hospital and wait for death.

For the next few weeks, our children and grandchildren visited often and buoyed Jim's spirits by entertaining him with songs, stories, and dance routines. I stayed by his side during the day and paced the room. We chatted about everything but his death, avoiding its inevitability. We'd said everything there was to say. I went home for short periods of time to take care of household responsibilities.

One evening, Jim's chorus stopped in for a sing-a-long. Jim took out his pitch pipe.

"Hey guys, how about a few barbershop songs?" It was party time.

Doctors and nurses heard singing coming from Jim's room and came in to listen and take pictures. They may have been surprised by all of the activity, but I wasn't. It was Jim's way of living his life on his own terms. He wasn't going to miss an opportunity to enjoy his friends.

"This is great," the doctors said. "It's the only room on the cancer ward where a party is going on."

A few nights later, two members of his barbershop quartet and their wives visited. They were missing a lead singer and quickly placed a call to a fellow barbershopper.

"Hey, we're at Strong with Savard, and we need a lead. Can you come over?" asked Dave Preston.

"I'll be right there."

When their lead arrived, Jim's face glowed while they all told stories, sang songs, and teased one another.

Dave later told me, "We couldn't believe we'd just spent the night with a dying man and had such fun. We wanted to do that for Jim. He's special to all of us, and he made the evening fun."

The discharge nurse, whose job it was to find a nursing home placement for Jim, and I conferred on several occasions. He was still too sick to move and needed more care than a nursing home could provide. After a week, he was transferred to the Palliative Care unit of Strong. His appetite continued to decline. We brought in milk shakes, Kentucky fried chicken, favorite foods from home, and selected different combinations from the hospital's menu. He'd push the food around with his fork and take a few bites.

"I'm just not hungry. I don't feel like eating."

Each day, he talked less and slept more. Sometimes he brightened when friends came in. When John stopped to visit, they rehashed school stories.

"Do you remember the day when you helped my students cheat on a quiz?" John asked.

Jim lay back on his pillow and closed his eyes. His lip curled into a smile at the memory.

John turned to me and recounted the story, "Jim and I taught social studies back to back, and our classrooms were next to each other. A door with an inset window separated our two rooms. When Jim heard me giving my students a pop quiz, he printed the answers on a large sheet of paper and held it in the window for my students to see. My entire class received 100 on the quiz that day. At first, I thought it couldn't be right because I'd never before had an entire class get 100. Then, I began to think I'd done a really great job on the chapter. At lunchtime, I told everyone about the quiz. Jim couldn't keep a straight face any longer and told me the truth. That was one of my fondest memories of teaching with Jim."

I had heard the story many years before, but hearing it again reminded me once more of the Jim I had loved for so many years.

The owner of the bowling alley stopped by. He patiently spooned chocolate pudding into Jim's mouth, all the while telling him jokes. Jim always rallied when he heard a funny story.

Each day, I brought in ten or twelve letters from our days of courtship. It was all I could think of doing to keep Jim amused. As I read, Jim listened attentively and then said, "Okay. When you're done reading these, burn them."

Again I responded. "I will not. They're my letters."

During his last week, I no longer went home at night but slept on a couch in his room. I wanted to spend every minute with him, and I knew he hated to be alone.

While this drama was playing out in the Palliative unit, Kim was in the same hospital giving birth to Jim's seventh grandchild—a boy. On the second day after Kieran was born, the nurses allowed her to bring the baby into Jim's room.

"Look, Dad, at your new grandson."

"He's cuter than Nolan was when he was born."

Gladys's skill at raw honesty seemed to have reincarnated in Jim.

When Kim, her husband, and their two older children visited Pappy on Tuesday night, they brought him a chocolate milk shake. He sat in a chair and drank the whole shake.

"Watch this Pappy," Talia said and performed all of her dance numbers from her upcoming recital.

Nolan sang, "Oh, you better watch out. You better not cry."

Jim was laughing and talking with everyone.

"Mom. I couldn't believe Dad tonight. He was great," Kim said. "He may be rallying again and coming home."

It was the last night Jim spoke. Every day he got weaker. He was in a semi-conscious state. From time to time, his lips fluttered with a puff of breath as he tried to talk, but nothing came out—just air. He no longer recognized anyone. He couldn't eat. The staff kept him comfortable with shots of morphine. He was slipping away.

While I sat in his room listening to the beeping machines, I thought of all the things I should be whispering in his ear. The nurses said that hearing is the last thing to go. But I no longer knew what to say. If he could hear my movements, maybe he understood I was there by his side.

His brothers, Dick and Don, called and said they wanted to come to visit Jim.

"You're more than welcome to come, but you have to understand that he will not know you and can no longer talk. He's in a deep sleep."

Until that call, neither of them realized that Jim was close to death. They decided to attend his funeral instead.

When a nurse checked his pulse, I said, "My husband is going to die when he's good and ready and not a minute sooner."

"He hasn't finished his agenda yet," she said.

Thursday, April 15, was my birthday. I got up in the morning, went over to Jim and rubbed his shoulder. I said, "Good morning, Honey. I love you."

He replied more clearly than he had spoken in weeks. "I love you, too."

"Are you in pain?"

"No."

These last words from Jim were my birthday gift. His agenda was finished.

At 8:00 Saturday morning, Kerry called to check on his father.

"Well," I said. "he's still with us. He's not ready to go yet. I'll call you if anything happens."

I replaced the phone and noticed Jim's utter stillness. I leaned over him and couldn't hear his soft breathing. He looked serene—the lines on his face from the strain of living were gone.

8:05: I dialed Kerry. "He's gone, Kerry."

"What?"

"He's gone."

CHAPTER 19 – ALONE

A blanket of finality covers my mind. He's at peace. I'm in my robe and pajamas gazing out the window as the April day dawns gray and cold. Traffic is picking up. The pace of life continues. Don't they know he's gone? The halls are eerily quiet, and the lights are dim. The soft chatting of the new shift of nurses echoes in the background as they catch up on the night's events.

I move to Jim's bed and squeeze his hand. He doesn't respond. I brush his wispy hair from his forehead. He doesn't feel. I kiss his cheek and whisper I love you. He doesn't answer. His fight is over. His body is still. No more tremors. He has waged a fight worthy of a gladiator, but the diseases that ravaged his body have won. I feel the presence of his spirit. Soon they will take him away from me. I don't want to let go. I know I must. I feel strangely alone. Nothing is making sense. I'm suspended in time, empty, confused.

I shiver and wonder what will happen next. What should I do? How should I feel? No one ever taught me how to let go of a soul mate? I've never done it before. Is there a right way? Maybe. Is he in heaven? I don't know. Will the people whose lives he touched remember him? I pray yes. I take a deep breath and try to gather myself together.

How could 52 ½ years go by so quickly? It seems like a minute—just a blink. I sit in the quiet room, and I'm flooded with memories. That's all I have now—memories. It's inconceivable that the man who made those memories is gone. People will tell me I'm lucky to have had a good marriage and wonderful memories, but I don't want it to end. I still want to feel his arms around me as we glide across the dance floor. I still want to feel the shelter of his hugs. He was my rock, my safety net. Now I'm alone.

"Mrs. Savard. I'm sorry to disturb you. We've notified the funeral director. He will be here shortly."

I don't want to witness his body leaving me.

Bending down, I brush my lips against Jim's forehead for our final kiss. *Even in death, you are still handsome. When my time comes to join you, I hope I will show the same dignity in accepting death as you have. I love you.*

I gather my clothes, purse and jacket, straighten my shoulders, tighten my lips, and leave the room.

PART VI

*Tegest was a student who escaped from the civil war in Ethiopia and was placed in Jim's eighth grade Social Studies class. At the beginning of the year, she spoke very little English.

> Dear mr savard
> Even though you are my teacher for a short time, I am pleased and I want to thank you for it. Even if I am new for the country, the cultura and the languag but you do a remarkable effort to make things easy and feel at home in the country. I am forced to write this letter as I am unable to speak it out and feel guilty to go with out saying good-by. I hope I will speak my fellings out next year. I want to thank you very very much again for the know-ledge you give me. please thatnk you my class mates for their hospitaly and make things easier in the school and good-by then too. Have a nice summer.
> your student
> Tegest Belete

CHAPTER 20 - LEGACY

Reflection: A vast gaping hole exists in our family's world. He was the grandfather who played King in the Corner with his grandchildren for hours. He was the father who carefully instructed his sons on the jay stroke for canoeing, and who taught his daughters to bake bread. He was the teacher who showed compassion to his struggling students.
Now, these things were but a fond memory.

****

We were preparing for Jim's funeral. Everything was nailed down except the way we would exit church.

Kim said, "We've got to end Dad's mass on a high note."

I remembered that Jim loved the way funerals were conducted in New Orleans—not in a sad way, but by marching, singing, and clapping.

The school's music teacher suggested I contact Johnny Squires, one of her instrumental students. I called him and asked if he would be kind enough to play "The Saints Go Marching In" at the end of Jim's funeral service.

"This is the most wonderful honor for me. You can't know how happy I am to be included. Can I really get into it?" Johnny asked.

I was speechless. I hadn't expected such a response. "Johnny," I said, "let her rip."

Later, I called Johnny's mother. "I'm pleased that your son wanted to do this."

"He wants his playing to be perfect. He's practicing every night. Since you asked him, he seems changed. He's gaining confidence in himself. It was the best thing that could have happened to him."

Wondering why my request was so pivotal to Johnny, I smiled as I hung up the phone.

On the day before the calling hours, I asked Elaine Bolthouse, "Do you think the Monday night quilters might prepare a buffet dinner to serve between the afternoon and evening calling hours? I can't even think straight at this point."

My friends seemed happy to oblige, and I knew everything would be beautifully prepared. The ladies would work as a team in setting up the table, preparing and arranging the food, and cleaning up afterwards. It was one thing off my plate.

There, we're finished planning the service.
Then the mailman delivered two poignant letters.
As I read the letters, I wondered, *did Jim know the results of his work or the lives he touched?*

The first letter came from Renard, who was Jim's student thirty years ago. He was a young African American boy who took the bus daily from the inner city to attend a suburban school. Renard was shy and didn't know many of the other students. Jim formed a uncommon bond with him and understood how insecure he felt in his new surroundings. The letters were such a tribute to Jim, I decided we had to include them in the mass.

For the service, I dressed in red and black—Jim's favorite color combination. A sweeping arrangement of soft greenery surrounded his urn at the front of the church. The flowers, plus the carving of a mountain scene on the front of his wooden urn, were perfect reminders of his love of nature.

The barbershop group Jim organized eight years ago sang, "Shine on Me" as people entered. They had placed Jim's picture on a chair in the middle of the quartet.

As the mass began, members of the congregation closed their eyes and drank in the spectacular voice of a female student from the Eastman School of Music. She lifted all of us to the heavens with her rendition of "How Great Thou Art" and "Amazing Grace."

The senior chorus to which Jim belonged sang "Why We Sing," lending their talents to the occasion. Surely Jim was shining down on everyone that morning.

When the letter from Renard Beaty entitled "He Mattered" was read, friends and family were touched.

> When Mr. Savard told me how a big kid bullied him, his father told him to pick up a brick the next time. He was shocked because that wouldn't make it a fair fight. His father said, "Fair is what you make it." When Mr. Savard made the class debate the pros and cons of slavery, and he told me to take the pros, did he forget that I was black? I could not think of anything and felt failure when I told him. He told me that if you can't understand the other side, you can't argue your side. Because of Mr. Savard, I try to find fairness in all I do versus sitting around feeling sorry about my challenges. Because of Mr. Savard, I now listen and try to understand things I don't like in order to better establish my opinion and position. Heck, I may even find common ground. Yes, he mattered, and I try to live my life

like he mattered. I achieved a master's degree because he mattered. I am a better husband, father, and teacher because he mattered.

The second letter was from Brian Drennen, Jim's student twenty-one years ago. Brian was a bright, talented boy from a good home who was also affected by his time in Jim's class.

While each one of my former teachers shaped my future in some way, there was only one that truly impacted my life. He knew when I didn't apply myself, and he was certain to let me know. But, grades are only what you did yesterday. He made a lasting impression by helping me find the strength within to do better. His impact was equal parts teacher, paternal figure, and genuine motivator. Recently, my wife and I reconnected with Mr. And Mrs. Savard. What was amazing was that Mr. Savard still had his penchant for storytelling, an unwavering love of his wife, and there was still an unspoken bond between student and teacher that developed so many years ago. Thank you for the lifetime of learning!

After the letters had been read, our grandchildren made a few remarks, and then Jim Bolthouse delivered a warm eulogy. "Jim was an inspiration to all of us and has shown us that it is possible to handle the trials that life throws at us."

The entire service seemed a perfect celebration of the man I loved. When Johnny began playing a slow dirge that gradually built up to a rousing song, the congregation clapped, stomped, and sang their way out of the church in true New Orleans's style.

Everyone headed to the Morgan Manning house for a reception. I was pleased when a friend pulled me aside. "Sue, that was the most beautiful service I have ever attended. It was truly a celebration and was all about Jim and what he was like as a person."

Knowing Jim had always loved a party and attention, I patted myself on the back. I had held myself together and pulled it off. I looked up to the heavens and whispered, *Lord, how you loved music, Jim. You received the music you deserved, and I know you heard it.*

We left the reception to join family and friends gathered at our house. I carried Jim's urn with me into the house and glanced around the living room. Shelly and Kim were hurrying to place snacks and sandwich fixings on the tables. Kerry and Tracy were standing in the kitchen sharing a laugh over one of Sonny's stories.

It was a button-busting moment for me. Somehow, we had managed to help all four offspring go to college. They represented one master's degree, two bachelors' degrees and an associate's degree—not terrible considering our low income. They're all different, and their father was proud of each one although he wasn't one to give voice to his feelings. It was his theory that he showed love by working hard to provide for them, by disciplining them when they needed it, by participating with them in a myriad of activities, and by teaching them to love their natural world. Was it necessary that he utter the words? I believe they know how he felt.

    For some reason, as I watched our family interact, my head was full of memories of Jim with his children. A picture of him with Kerry was vivid in my mind. From the time Kerry was about four, he and Jim liked to sit along a stream and cast a line into the water in hopes of catching the really big one. I thought about the time we all went to Churchville Park on a picnic. It was quite early in the season and too chilly for good fishing, but Kerry brought along his Donald Duck rod. He sat patiently waiting for a nibble. Finally, a small fish took the lure, and Kerry reeled it into shore. Jim helped him take the hook from the fish's mouth, and Kerry laid his catch on the dock. He began to stroke the fish and said, "I had to get you out little fishy. It's pleezin in there." After a short time, Jim helped Kerry slip the fish back in the water and convinced him the fish would be happier in his own home. The two continued to enjoy the sport, and when Jim owned a bass boat, they often headed out on Canandaigua Lake for an afternoon of bonding.

    Tracy, on the other hand, never especially enjoyed fishing. For him, too many hours were spent casting a line without getting any action. But, he was chomping at the bit when it came to hunting with his father. He learned early to respect and care for guns. When Tracy was too young to hunt, he took part in our afternoons of target practice. We owned a trap shooter and invited friends to have a go at skeet shooting in preparation for hunting season. Jim let his son feel part of the action by having him sit under the trap and pull the cord to release the clay pigeons. Tracy liked to listen to the hunters' war stories of the monster buck that got away and hear their plans for the day's hunt. He was anxious to be part of the annual pilgrimage. By five a.m. on opening day when Tracy could finally hunt, he arose to join Uncle Bill, Jim Bolthouse, and his father for a hearty breakfast. Jim assigned him to a deer stand right in the corner of our woods. The sun was just beginning to break when an eight-point buck strolled down the path directly towards him. Tracy lifted his gun, sighted in the buck, and shot. He was done hunting by 7:30 a.m. and wondering what's so hard about deer hunting?

    Our girls didn't hunt or fish with their father, but he played an equally big role in their lives, although, Shelly has been eternally grateful that her name isn't Desiree. Like the boys, our girls climbed mountains, camped, learned to canoe, ice skate, and ski. He taught them to bake bread and to enjoy cooking. I could picture how thrilled he was when Shelly was born and, in my mind's eye, I still see him sitting with her and reading <u>The Night Before Christmas</u>. She knew the book by heart and heaven help him if he should skip a page. Then, when he was too ill to hold a book and read, Shelly took over. One afternoon she was staying with Jim while I shopped. When I came home, the site I saw warmed my heart. Shelly was sitting near her dad, reading to him Ted Kennedy's book, <u>True Compass</u>. The tables had turned. When she left, I said, "Someday, you will be happy that you've taken the time to spend with your father. You'll remember these days always, and I'll remember seeing you reading to him always."

Kim had achieved far more already in her young life than we ever would have imagined. At a remarkably young age, she was a partner in a lobbying firm in New York City and dealt with an array of famous people. She loved the excitement of the Big Apple. Jim enjoyed hearing her stories of life in the fast lane, but once she was a mother and 9/11 hit, we both wanted her out of New York. It was no place to raise a child, and we were worried about her safety. She moved to Mendon. Jim enjoyed puttering around her historic home, and he and a friend built a sizeable farm table for her large kitchen. When our 50th anniversary was near, Kim and her siblings planned the most elegant party. Jim was downright flabbergasted by the crowd and the perfection of the day. After that, when we drove by the Senator's Mansion, he never failed to remark, "That was the most beautiful party I've ever had, and I was definitely surprised."

Turning from the commotion and my reverie, I went into our bedroom to place his urn and talk to him. "They're good kids, Jim. We have a right to be proud. We made a lot of mistakes, but we did all right. We improved upon our upbringing, and as I watch how our children are parenting, I'm well aware that they are far better parents than we ever were. Maybe the Savard line will continue to improve with the each generation."

It was time for me to join our guests who were still sharing stories of Jim's escapades. After a few hours, people began to leave, and I settled into an easy chair and asked the grandchildren to join me. "What would you kids like as a remembrance of Pappy?" I asked.

Their choice of items was intriguing. Mackenzie wanted a wooden bowl Jim had made while in college and the *butt* cards. The *butt* cards, as we called them, were playing cards sent to us as a joke. They showed a group of male's bare backsides. At her selection, we all laughed so hard we were crying. Dylan chose Jim's favorite pool stick. Kristin selected her grandfather's gray felt Tyrolean hat with a feather in the brim that Jim purchased when we were in Austria. Jake wanted his grandfather's Marine Corps insignias and medals. Talia was anxious to take home the card shuffler, but it no longer worked. Instead, she took his golfing trophy. Nolan was interested in Jim's engraved ID bracelet. To Kieran, I passed on the watch I had engraved for my husband on our 25th anniversary.

In the following weeks, I straightened out our affairs. Some of the cards I'd received contained checks. Friends wrote, "Just use this in any way you choose."

I decided to add to the donations and give a one-time award to a graduating senior. I knew Jim would be happy to help a deserving student. Upon hearing of the award, a number of his former colleagues sweetened the pot with additional donations.

I hoped to give the gift to a graduate who displayed strength and courage and was from a lower income household. Soon I made an appointment with the school's Dean—a former Brockport high school graduate. After explaining my criteria, I asked for his help in making a selection.

"I think this student meets your criteria," the dean said and handed me Will Noel's scholarship application. "I don't know about the family's finances, and I'm not privy to that information. I'll call Will into my office and assess his situation."

The young man suggested by the Dean personified the type of person for whom I was looking. His family wasn't poor, but they already had a daughter in college, and Will was concerned about how they'd pay for his education.

"He's the perfect choice," I said.

Once the selection was made, the Dean relayed another story.

In eighth grade, I wasn't in Jim's class or on his team. It was a strange set of circumstances that placed me on the Washington trip with Jim. Four or five of us couldn't take part in the trip with our regular team because we had a scheduling conflict. As a solution, we were sent with Jim's team. We were nervous because we knew few of the students and none of the teachers. At one point, we were touring a Gettysburg battlefield, and the bus stopped to let any interested students off to walk around the battlefield. It was a beautiful spot, and Jim was talking to us about how sound ricocheted off the surrounding rocks during a battle. As it turned out, we were also good singers. Jim got out his pitch pipe and began to teach us the various parts of a barbershop song. Soon he had us singing, all the while including the history of the battlefield. I recall that moment so well because it was a gorgeous day, a perfect spot, and a special moment. I've always remembered that event as one of the highlights of my trip. Your husband was in a league of his own.

I had never heard the story before, but it wasn't really a shock. Jim never missed an opportunity to engage someone in his favorite hobby.

The chance encounters with former students continued to happen. Our car needed its annual inspection, and the mechanic's analysis took me by surprise. "Your car won't pass inspection unless I do these brakes."

"Go ahead with the repairs. Could someone give me a ride home?" His wife offered to drive me.

"Was your husband a teacher?" she asked as soon as I got in the car.

"Yes. He taught eighth grade social studies."

"I thought he might be the one who was my eighth grade teacher. I had such a crush on him. He was my favorite teacher that year. I'll never forget him. I wanted to quit school, but he talked me out of it."

"Why did you want to quit? Were you having trouble with your studies?"

"That and a lot of personal problems with my stepfather. Your husband convinced me to try harder and to not quit school. Had it not been for him, I'm certain I wouldn't have graduated."

"Jim was also from an abusive home," I said. "I think he understood when students had problems."

"You know when he talked to me, I could tell—he knew, he knew."

Then she began to cry.

Jim's former students seemed to be everywhere. I was delighted to hear their stories and know he was so fondly remembered.

Our cable repairman was a former student. "He was my favorite teacher. He made such an impression on the whole class and me that year. I learned to love history that year. One day, he showed a film on the Nazi concentration camps, and he got all choked up. He's one teacher I'll never forget."

The owner of a new restaurant in Mt. Morris found out I was Mrs. Savard from Brockport, and commented, "I'll never forget the first day he stood in front of our class. We knew he was a Marine when he walked into the room. He was a handsome man—held himself perfectly straight, had slicked-back hair, and a sharp crease on his trouser legs. He let us know what he expected of us and how he planned to run his class. I kept wondering what kind of class I was in. It wasn't going to be any fun this year. I might have to behave. But we loved him. He was fun, and we always knew exactly where we stood with him. He made the class interesting. Your husband was one teacher I'll never forget."

A neighbor's son was turned on to history when Jim talked to his class about how he and his siblings had to steal coal during the depression. The young man became a history teacher and now reads only history books.

Another former student from the 1980s sent an E-mail and relayed a story of how one of Jim's assignment came in handy when she became a lawyer.

"As an assignment, we could volunteer to recite the first part of the Declaration of Independence. I was excited about the opportunity, but I had a stuttering problem. Your husband pulled me aside and said, 'You don't have to do this. Only do it if you're comfortable.' I was up for the challenge, and on the day of the recitation, I raised my hand to be first. I recited the paragraphs without stuttering, and I was proud of my accomplishment. After I became a lawyer, thanks to Mr. Savard, I was the star for a while with my lawyer friends. I was working for a Federal appellate judge, and she hosted a 4th of July party at her cottage. A group of lawyers, including the judge's two sons who were law professors, began discussing the Declaration of Independence, and none of them could remember the beginning. They could recite part of the Gettysburg address and a few other documents but not the Declaration. I stood up and recited the whole beginning section from memory. The lawyers were very impressed, and I told them of my experience in your husband's eighth grade social studies class.

"I even used my new knowledge to thwart my father. I was so taken with the material I'd memorized that a few months later, when it was winter and my father was chasing squirrels away from the bird feeder, I wrote a declaration of their rights modeled on the Declaration of Independence and making the point that they were no less entitled to the seeds and suet than the birds were."

Bill Visick from England wrote the following words:

"Jim was an example to all. He simply would not give up. His spirit ruled. To share his company and quiet presence was always rewarding. One also soon became aware, with added wisdom, of his insight regarding war. Jim said to me, war is folly and a waste to all that is precious to mankind."

The tributes people shared were a healing balm as I struggled with my loss. They once again validated all that I felt about Jim.

As with most of us, Jim wasn't famous. He never achieved greatness. He didn't change the world. He just quietly went off to work every day doing the best job he could to have an impact on his students and on his family.

Ernie Bank's quote says it best, "The measure of a man is in the lives he's touched."[vii]

is all about. You are both brave, determined and unfaltering with your support of each other. Facing each day, I know, is a challenge. We are all thankful, grateful and continuously amazed that you do! Thank you for giving all of us a shining example of dealing with life head on, never quitting when things get tough and for loving each other no matter what.

Devi, Shelly, Don, Madeline & Dylan

Dear Mom & Dad: 1/09

Thank you for making yet another Christmas special. We had a good time staying with you (minus the hospital visits of course)! Thank you for letting us stay for so long. We know it's not easy to have your routine and house turned upside down for a week! ☺

Most of all, I wanted to thank you for being such a good example of what love

---

experiences that have mostly taken place @ your home —

Easter, Christmas Eve, playing games with dad, singing songs and being free to be themselves.

I'm glad that they truly know you (and dad, too!) and will be able to have that all of their lives. What an exceptional gift!

Love, Kim

P.S. We still sing dad Happy Hour songs to him every night. I know he can see us, too. The kids will always have him in their hearts, even Kieran.

9-1-10

Dear Mom,

Thanks so much for all that you do for me — we are all especially grateful to have your presence at our events — it's all the little things that add up over the course of a life that create the memories, the bigger than life impressions!

Our children will always (and most importantly) remember you just being there. And that's really what it's supposed to be about, anyway.

Of course, we delight in your calls, your handicrafts, your talents. But when we ask the kids what they most appreciate about their relationships with their grandparents — most profoundly, "they recount

Always a Friend...

someone to *laugh* with

and *share* things with,

someone you can count on

to help you out,

back you up,

and *never let you down.*

Thank you for being

a wonderful mother

and the very best kind

of friend.

Happy Mother's Day

Thank you so much Mom for helping me with money and for showing me where I am getting my house ready. I could not be where I am today without much great parents. You and dad are my favorite. I love you more than a gift shop. I'd not buy you another. You are the best. I'll take you and we went shopping. Love Kelsey

---

Thank you for all your help and support for the last few years. Without your help I would have never gone back to school and for that I owe you my life. It was a hard road to take but the lessons learned were invaluable. One of the reasons I did it was to show Kristi and Jake how hard work pays off. I am almost done and I am glad I did it (all by myself) as I have said before, I could only hope to do half the parents you guys are and I'll be OK! You're the best! Love me! saying "thank you" is so fake! Tracy

CHAPTER 21 – HEALING

Pete Seeger's Song expresses what I must ultimately accept.

> To everything, turn, turn, turn
> There is a season, turn, turn, turn
> And a time for every purpose under heaven
> A time to be born and a time to die
> A time to plant and a time to reap
> A time to live and a time to weep
> To everything turn, turn, turn
> There is a season. Turn, turn, turn
> And a time for every purpose under heaven[viii] . . .

It's 10 a.m., eleven days after Jim's death, when I arrive for my appointment with a counselor. I feel like my mind is locked in an elevator with the doors unable to open.

I found counseling helpful when Vicki died, but remembering that event still hurt deep down in the pit of my stomach. Thoughts of how Kerry is rebuilding his life go through my brain. If he can be strong, surely I can.

"Good morning," Mrs. Savard. "Have a seat in the waiting room. Make yourself comfortable. The counselor will be with you in a minute," remarks the cheerful receptionist.

I sit in the waiting room and pick up a *Good Housekeeping* magazine. It sits opened and unread on my lap. I can't focus. *I have known Jim's death was coming for a long time. Why aren't I better prepared?*

"The counselor will see you now."

It's quiet and peaceful in her office. A couch of worn leather, a rocker, and a well-used green upholstered chair looks soft and comforting. I sit on the couch. A candy dish and a large box of Kleenex sit on the coffee table. I mindlessly take a tootsie roll and wait. She enters.

"Hi. I haven't seen you in a while. Tell me what's going on," she begins.

The bottled up emotions give way to a never-ending stream of tears. I wipe my tears away with my palm. My nose runs. I reach over, pull a handful of tissues from the box and blow it. I choke as I try to explain the reason for my visit.

"What can you possibly do for me? I am carrying a hundred-pound bag of guilt on my shoulders."

Her voice is soothing. "Why are you feeling guilty?"

Gradually I begin to talk.

"I'm dealing with such conflict in my mind. How could I love someone so much and pray for his death? Then again, if I truly loved him, why would I want him to continue to suffer? I have terrible remorse that I was impatient at times and then angry that he was sick. I'm lost without him." My breathing becomes labored.

"Take your time, Mrs. Savard. Do you need a drink of water?"

"No. I'll be all right in a minute."

I continue. "In his last few years, he seemed like a shell of the man I married. Since his death, I've come to realize that even as he lay in the hospital dying, the Jim I loved was still there. Only the outside covering had changed. Now, our home is filled with his absence. I want him back so that I can undo every time I lost my temper—make amends. All of these thoughts keep rolling around in my head tormenting me."

The counselor listens and offers reassuring words that my feelings are normal—that everyone has a tolerance limit. The hour slips by.

"Why don't I book you for an appointment next week at the same time?"

I robotically drive home not noticing the passing cars or houses.

Just get me home, where I can curl up into a cocoon of self-pity and blame.

The next days and weeks are a blur. I take his clothing out of the closets and drawers, but I find it impossible to get rid of his things. Gently worn suits, dress shirts, casual trousers, shorts, polo shirts stay piled high on the pool table. It seems too final to part with his belongings—as if I'm denying his existence in my life.

In the long evenings, I try to concentrate on reading or watching television. When I look at his favorite chair, I think of him. *"Why aren't you here? Why did you have to get sick? There is no joy in our home. There's no one to hold me close, kiss me goodnight, dance with me, or croon the verse you used to sing to me, "After all these years, I still love you."*

In the morning, his ashes are still there, and I know it's real. "I miss you, Jim, but your death will not wipe out the memories."

A girlfriend calls one evening. "Would you like to join me this Friday?" she asks. "I'm going to the church play with my girlfriends."

I attend and sit in the audience but I hear nothing. I am lost in my own thoughts—floating above the room, alone, and disconnected from everything around me. I get up and move into the church vestibule. As I walk around, I try to calm my thoughts.

This is how my life will be from now on—evenings with the girls.

The idea of eliminating "We" from my vocabulary is beginning to sink into my brain.

A friend recommends a book that helped her when her husband passed away. I begin to read <u>Seven Choices</u> but can't concentrate.

Friends and neighbors say, "Let me know if there is anything I can do—anything at all."

That comment was repeated over and over at the calling hours, the funeral, and through calls and notes after the funeral. People genuinely want to help and are sincere, but they don't know what I need. I begin to respond by asking for specific things. "Would you mind stopping by and taking the handicapped bars off the walls and filling the holes?" I ask a neighbor. "That would be a terrific help because I need to have the kitchen repainted."

"Could you mow the lawn next week? I'll be away for a few days."

The explicit requests make friends and neighbors feel helpful and my life easier.

Now I take walks out of habit and to think. I take short trips to visit relatives and to reconnect with friends I haven't seen in years. The trips take me away from our empty house and insulate me from facing my new reality.

But, no matter where I go, I see Jim, even though I was never a believer in the hereafter. It's scary at first but then comforting. There he is—everywhere. He's sitting in trees, on rocks, in a chair. I feel I can reach out and touch him. In each case, he is about fifty years old, and wearing a vivid blue v-necked shirt. I see him healthy. He's smiling. Maybe that's Jim's way of letting me know he's okay and happy. I don't know, but I see him as surely as I see anything. In the night's stillness, I feel his presence gliding through a room like a soft whisper.

The children call. When are we going to Tupper Lake to bury Dad's ashes? I keep stalling. Then the answer comes like a broom clearing the cobwebs of my mind.

"We aren't going to bury Dad until I die. He hated to be alone. About three weeks before he died, he said he didn't mind dying, but he didn't want to leave me. There's no reason he has to leave me. I brought him home to stay; he's right next to my bed. When I die, you can bury us together." I feel relieved to make that decision and that my children accept my choice.

At night, I curl into bed and read the letters we wrote each other in 1955 and 56. They remind me of happy, carefree times. Sometimes I laugh out loud at how young and foolish we were. The letters bring me comfort and reinforce who he was before his illnesses. "Thank God I didn't burn these as you wished," I say to Jim's ashes.

I look at pictures of him towards the end of his life. I have trouble believing it's Jim; his facial features collapsed; his body shrunken; his hair sparse. Outside, he's no longer Eagle Eye. But, time and the ravages of his disease did not diminish him. The real Jim was always there. I remember every look, touch, and word that passed between us as if it just happened yesterday. While he was alive, I was alive with anticipation of another adventure. Now, I don't know.

On my second visit to the counselor, I tell her about the day I took Jim to Wal-Mart to buy a fishing rod.

"Oh, my God," she says. "I was there that day and watched the whole episode. I watched you in the checkout. I said to myself, that poor woman."

Then I recount stories about Jim's upbringing like the time his father had him arrested for supposedly stealing the family van or the time Leon stapled his young son to the cutting table. I can't explain why I feel the need to tell these stories, but I rattle on.

"You've got to write these stories down."

"But why? How can I do that? I'm not a writer. I don't think I can write anything that's worthy enough for anyone to read."

"Write them as you're telling me because you weave a story as you tell it."

With that, the odyssey of becoming a memoir writer begins.

Each day, I sit at my computer in our small office and begin writing Jim's story. I draw the shades and turn on a small reading light. The darkness and warm sage color of the room enclose me in safety as I write and write, spilling the contents of my mind onto paper in no specific order. I look at albums and his letters for inspiration. I call his siblings and high school friends. Soon I have pages of typing and shorthand notes strewn everywhere—on the floor, in boxes, in a storage cupboard, and on the daybed. I wonder how I will ever organize everything into a story that makes sense.

Writing serves a lot of purposes along the path of healing. It gives me an opportunity to put on paper feelings I have but can't express to anyone. Writing about Jim makes me feel as if he's still here. Looking at how far he came as an individual makes me admire him even more. Seeing in black and white a history of Jim's illness and frequent crises makes me realize how all consuming his condition had become. Writing about our marriage helps me remember the good years we had—that we were lovers once and young. I had been so focused on caring for Jim that

I had forgotten the joy of our marriage. Sometimes, just the act of writing relieves some of the emptiness I'm feeling. At other times, writing makes me miss the comfort of his presence even more. I begin to worry I'm already losing sight of the way he once was and what we were like as a couple. I'm in a hurry to get it all down.

I struggle with this project, and I question why I'm writing the memoir and what is driving me. Will our children or grandchildren even care to read it? Will they laugh at my attempts or will they applaud my efforts? Do I even have a story to tell that's intriguing to anyone but me? All of these thoughts scramble my brain, and I don't have an answer. That is until I attend mass one Sunday at Holy Name Church in Tupper Lake, the church where we married. I sit in a pew trying hard to pay attention to the homily but think of Jim and the day we wed. I look up towards the altar. There's Jim standing to the right of the altar, dressed in his black tuxedo and patent leather shoes. He's smiling and turned slightly towards the back of the church as if beckoning to me. He's as real to me as the priest on the altar. I have chills all over and can't take my eyes away. He's slowly fading from view. The choir is singing a hymn called "The Summons"—a hymn I'd never heard before. I open the hymnal, and the words speak directly to me.

> Will you come and follow me if I but call your name? Will you go where you don't know and never be the same? Will you let my love be shown? Will you let my name be known? Will you let my life be grown in you and you in me?[ix]

Those words answer my questions. I'm writing to celebrate Jim and to tell the truth of our family life as I remember it, and so that his descendants will know his name.

After mass, I feel renewed energy to continue Jim's story, but I need help. *Maybe writing classes will help me improve. I'll get some suggestions from other writers. I'll meet new people.*

It's March of 2011, a year after Jim's death, when I hear about RIT Osher (a program of classes for seniors) and call for a catalog. Two interesting writing classes in the spring semester offer promise.

I sit at our yellow enamel kitchen table sipping my morning coffee. The spring sun streams through the windows warming the room as I fill out the membership application. For the first time in my life, I check the widow's box. I burst into tears. Widow is a word I can't accept—one I don't want to accept. I can't imagine not being married to Jim; missing the rhythm and predictability of our lives together. This first step into my new world is frightening.

On my first day of class, the participants are welcoming and inspiring, but I quickly realize I have a long way to go in the world of writing.

A few days later, I read a flyer on the counter of the local bookstore listing a writer's group that meets on Tuesday evenings. I arrive early. A woman enters and greets me. "We really haven't been doing much writing lately. We've become friends, and we usually end up chatting."

"I'm hoping to get help with my writing," I say. "Maybe we can get started, and a few others will show up."

Tuesday's group becomes a working session with everyone sharing their current writing attempts. When I read a page of my work, the four members are encouraging and inspire me to continue my efforts.

One evening, I read a few paragraphs, and a member comments. "Wait a minute. You can't leave that there. I want to know more. I want to visualize that scene. It's a powerful scene, but you're not taking enough time with it." He continues to push me to describe situations that I am glossing over. My writing begins to improve.

I ask my friend Margi Lewis, "Would you mind reading some of my writing? Let me know if something doesn't make sense or if it's out of order."

"I'd love to do that. I feel honored that you would trust me," she responds.

When she reads excerpts from our letters, she asks, "Why did you keep the letters you wrote each other?"

"I don't really know. I just always thought that someday, when I was old and had the time, I might want to read them again. Thank God I kept them. They bring me pleasure."

For a while, I go to counseling weekly. Then I pull back to every other week and finally once a month. At the same time that I am struggling with Jim's death, the counselor is dealing with a sister who is severely ill with an unidentified condition. One day at the end of our session, the counselor says, "If I may, I'd like to take just a minute of your time to say something personal to you."

"Certainly."

"I believe that everything in life happens for a reason. Somehow, God put you in my office at the right time. You have helped me so much."

"How can that be?"

"After listening to what you went through with your husband's multiple problems and how you dealt with them, I realized I could step up to the plate and be an advocate for my sister. You gave me the strength to do that, and I want to thank you."

I honestly can't believe my ears. In my quest for healing, I had inadvertently helped someone else. I thank her for sharing that with me.

The guilt begins to unload from my shoulders as I continue counseling. Sometimes I cry, wishing I had been more patient with Jim. I question why I left him in a respite facility while I took a break. Maybe I should have spent every waking moment with him. Sometimes I grumble to the counselor that I feel weak and selfish for feeling trapped while Jim, ensnared in his body, never complained. Other times, I express anger that he was sick. On a few occasions, I read parts of the memoir to the counselor. Slowly, I am beginning to accept my limitations as a caregiver and appreciate my strengths. Picking up the pieces after Jim's death involves reinventing myself. The vision that I had of how our lives would evolve is shattered. I soon realize that it's a couple's world. Many of the activities in which we participated involved two people. Friends and family are thoughtful and caring, but they can't fill the vacuum I am experiencing. I keep Jim close to my thoughts as I go through each day. I talk to him during the day and wonder if he hears me. His presence is all around me whether in the golf ball I find in the flowerbed or a favorite song that plays on the radio.

But, sadness strikes me when I least expect it. I open a box of old negatives that had been languishing on a shelf in our cellar untouched for years. In the box is Jim's social security card. How did it get there? He'd been looking for the card for months. I believe that Jim is just letting me know he's still around.

One evening, I read "The Birthday Gift" chapter at one of the writer's groups I attend each month. As I was packing up to leave for home, a new member stopped me.

"May I speak with you a minute?" she asks. "Do you believe in spirits?"

"If you had asked me that question two years ago, I would have said absolutely not. Since my husband passed away, I see him, and I feel his presence near me. Now I'm not sure."

"When you were reading that chapter, I looked over and saw a spirit brushing your hair." I don't question her but accept the fact that Jim is with me once again listening to the story of the day he died.

In July of 2010, the phone rings. "Hello."

"This is Social Services calling with regard to your husband's application for Medicaid."

"We won't need that now. My husband passed away in April. Just out of curiosity, how close were you to granting approval."

"Oh, we've just started looking at his file."

"Are you aware that I applied in February?"

"Yes, I am. But we're swamped, and we have to handle these requests in the order in which they come. Besides, you had your preliminary number."

"Yes, I did have that," I say. "But, nursing homes won't accept those."

"They have to."

"I'm telling you they won't. I called two homes crying and begging for them to take my husband. They refused and said I needed a final number."

"They can't do that. I'll be speaking with my supervisor about this today."

I hang up the phone. I wonder whether or not she'll follow through, but it's no longer my problem.

I am a work in progress as I figure out the new reality of my life. I don't always like it, but I have no other choice. My day-to-day routine has changed drastically. I no longer have to worry about working to make money so that we can buy a new piece of furniture or a new car. I don't have to save money for our children's education. I don't have to give Jim medicine every three hours or help him shower and dress. All that used to be part of my life is now gone. In its place, I am trying new activities and expanding my interests. Writing is consuming hours of my free time and giving me a new goal. I am surrounding myself with people who lift me up and make me laugh. I am accepting the fact that healing is an ongoing process.

As counseling continues, I don't see Jim as often, and I'm finding it harder to see his face exactly as it was. I still long for him and for his hugs and quick wit. When he appears, I tell him, "Don't fade from me. I still want to see you. I'm not ready to let you go."

Like pealing the layers of an onion, my feelings of guilt are gradually falling away. I'm beginning to accept the fact that I did my best. Maybe it wasn't perfect, but as human beings, we aren't perfect. We all have limitations, and that's all right. Sometimes, the guilt raises its ugly head again. The onion still has many layers so I'll continue to write, to reinvent myself, and peal away at the layers. I also accept I have to grieve—there is no way around it. I still have many dreadful days and some good ones. And, that's okay—just let it happen—as my counselor says.

The one thing above all others that Jim's disease and death has taught me is that life is fragile and limited. I have to do as he did. He

ninute of the time he had left on earth escape him. He
day and gave me and our family unconditional love
g with Jim's death, I see my mortality looming closer, and
Will I accept my passing with the same dignity as Jim? I
na. Shelly my wishes in terms of funeral arrangements.

"When your father got older, he often signed his notes to me with a quote from John Adam's letter to Abigail on February 16, 1780. Put your father's ashes in the casket with me and make sure that quote is on our tombstone."

I am, as I ever was and ever shall be,
Yours, yours, yours.

John Adams.

ADDENDUM

CHAPTER 22 – THE INVERVIEWS

"As part of my healing process, I am writing a story about Jim and our family. I need more information about his upbringing. What do you remember about growing up in the Savard household that you would like to share?"

A floodgate opened. They finally had permission to unload their stories. I have left the interviews unaltered and used the information to create this book.

<u>Marie</u> "We had to be survivors. Otherwise, given the parents we had, we would have been vegetables."

Marie, the oldest child, was born in 1927.
"I had to grow up too soon because Mom and the other kids depended on me so much. I never felt as if I had a childhood. It seemed to me as if I were the mother. Our parents never hugged us. Now I remember things that happened as bad, but at the time, I didn't realize how damaging. At eighty-five, I still feel I can't sit around. I have trouble doing things for pleasure. It's almost as if I have to earn the right to enjoy myself.
"Our grandparents helped by giving us home-canned produce. Sonny and I were about eight and ten, and we took a sled with a box tied on top to their house. My grandmother, Agnes, filled the box with jars of canned vegetables. She told us to be careful not to break any of the jars, and we took her advice. At the time, I thought my grandmother was just being nice. I didn't understand that our family was starving.
"Just before it was time for me to come home from school each day, I developed a terrible migraine because I never knew what type of mood Dad would be in. I feel guilty talking about my parents this way. I don't want my children to know all of this stuff. I've never shared any of these stories with them."
Marie protected her siblings and was tough. She held her own with the neighborhood ruffians who soon learned not to ruffle her feathers.
"Mom would tell Dad everything we did wrong, and then after he beat us, she would be on our side. But we stuck together. Whenever Mom and Dad were out, we laughed so much our stomachs hurt. The other kids listened to me and treated me like their mother.

"We lived on Webb Row when my father lost his leg. After that, he stopped running around, but he was angrier than ever and took it out on all of us.

"We used rags for everything. Mom used them for diapers, and I used them for sanitary napkins. I had to wash the rags and my one pair of underwear out at night.

"There was never enough food to eat. Sometimes, when we were eating, Mom would yell about the cost of food. It made me feel guilty for eating. Whoever rose first in the morning, got a slice of bread or potato slices toasted on top of a wood stove. Often, there was no breakfast. One time, my elementary school teacher was discussing the food groups. We were asked to write down what we ate for breakfast that morning. I didn't have breakfast, but I was too embarrassed to let my teacher know. I wrote down everything I would have enjoyed such as bacon, eggs, juice, and toast with jam.

"Dad didn't go to the welfare office to get our food. He sent us. We went to Mikall's store in The Junction. Sometimes, they placed a little bag of candy in with our groceries and didn't charge us.

"I knew my family was poor, but one day I visited a friend's home, and that home had a dirt floor. I thought to myself that we're not as poor as my friend because we don't have a dirt floor."

Soap, warm water, and privacy were at a premium for the Savard family of ten. "We had a hot water tank, but it never seemed to work. I used the last period of the school day to get excused to the gym to shower. Everything in our house was always gray and dirty looking.

"One day, my Aunt Grace noticed my arms were chapped all the way to my elbows. When Grace asked what was wrong, I told her that we didn't have clean, dry towels so when I leave the house in the cold, my arms are still wet, and they get chapped.

"When I was sick and home from school one time, Dad bought me a pair of blue pajamas. I think that was his way of offering a small apology to me for his nasty behavior.

"Mom and Dad went out grocery shopping on Saturday nights, and I stayed home to start cooking Sunday dinner. Mom never owned a cookbook, and one time, I wanted to make a cake. When they got home, I asked her how to make a cake. She guessed at the portions of flour and so on. Our oven didn't have a working temperature gauge, so Mom put her hand in the oven, and she said it was hot enough.

"I remember Mom making creamed hamburger over potatoes and creamed boiled eggs over potatoes.

"One of her ditties was, 'Our father who art in a two-wheeled car and hallowed be that driver.'

"I don't even know what that means.

"I was in study hall when the principal announced over the PA system that the teachers should take Sonny Savard's name off their registers because he was leaving school. I sat in my seat and cried. I knew my brother didn't want to quit, but our father was insisting. Sonny was too afraid to defy Dad.

"It was hard to do homework at home because of the constant noise, the close quarters, the lack of privacy and school supplies. Dad slept downstairs because it was hard for him to go up the stairs with his peg leg. The only place to do homework was the dining room table, but Dad had to have the light out. He used to urinate in a jug, and we kids had to empty it. I was always thrilled whenever Dr. Bury hired me to baby-sit for an evening. It meant that I could earn some money and still have quiet time to do my homework after the children went to bed. One afternoon I told Dad that I had accepted a baby-sitting job for Dr. Bury. Dad was furious and said I had to call and cancel. When I called, Dr. Burry's wife said, 'Let me talk to your father.' Dad became syrupy sweet.

'Why, of course, Marie can baby sit tonight,' he said in that sugary voice he used with anyone of prominence.

"I was seventeen years old when my parents took a trip to Canada leaving me responsible for my six siblings.

"I straightened up the dresser drawers and folded the clothes. When Mom came home, she threw things in drawers without caring how anything looked. I told her that I had just straightened out the drawers.

"She replied, 'It's my house and I'll do what I want.' She never even thanked us for all we had done.

"When Mom and Dad went to Canada, I took my siblings to Coney Beach for a swim. A man my father knew (an X-Ray technician) was there and said, 'Be good, and if you can't be good, be careful.' I didn't know what he was talking about. When my parents returned home, Dad accused me of having sex with someone while they were away and took me to the technician to be examined. Dad went in first, and then I was called in. I was so embarrassed because I had on an old pair of underpants held tight with a pin. When I came out, I said, 'Well, you didn't find out anything, did you?' I didn't know what that was all about."

During the summer, Gladys's half brothers sent some of their children to Tupper Lake to stay for a month. Marie, Sonny, and Dick developed a relationship with their half cousins that lasted throughout their lives. Although Jim was young, he remembered when these exchanges took place. Later in life, he renewed their acquaintance while on a trip to Gaspé.

"For two summers, I worked at the American Legion Camp as a waitress where I met my future husband, Robert Kraft. He was hired as a dishwasher. Bob was out of the Navy and studying electrical engineering at RPI.

"Bob came to the house one night for dinner. In the middle of dinner, Dad told Bob that my mother had given birth to an illegitimate baby before he married her. I was so embarrassed. He was always doing things like that to put Mom down.

"During our second summer of working at the Legion, we fell in love. I became pregnant with our first child, Jerry. We were married in August 1947. I was twenty and Bob was twenty-four."

For the wedding, Gladys wore a large hat and high heels making her appear larger than ever. In a picture taken at the wedding, Gladys stood with her hand resting on Leon's shoulder appearing to press him into the ground.

"After my marriage, Dad often called and told me to get home because my mother needed my help. One day, Bob answered the phone and said, 'She's married now, and I need her here.' That put an end to most of Dad's calls.

"At the end of summer, Bob and I moved to Troy where he began a new semester, and we awaited the arrival of our first baby. Dad was ashamed that Jerry arrived six months after our marriage. When Jerry was three months old, Dad called his brother, Buck, and announced that he was a grandfather. Buck was already aware of the situation but knew my father wanted to save face.

"Bob was struggling to complete his education and take care of us. When our second son was born, we named him John. Sonny and Dick came to visit us, and found out we hadn't had any meat to eat in a month. My two brothers pooled their limited money and bought meat for dinner.

"One time, Bob and I were visiting Tupper Lake with another couple, and we stopped to visit Mom. We stood in the kitchen and Mom poured us a glass of lemonade. The glasses were old peanut butter jars, and my mother had neglected to soak off the label. 'Which is yours? The crunchy or creamy?' Bob said to our friends.

"My mother started a lot of the problems. When she noticed my grandmother had bruises on her body, she had me accuse the nuns of abusing my grandmother. Mom stood back and didn't say a word. She didn't realize that older people bruise easily. I was embarrassed."

Bob finished his electrical engineering degree in 1950. During his working years, he and Marie lived in various locations around the country and raised six children. They were married for 62 years. For a number of years before Bob passed away, he and Marie resided in Florida.

Sonny

Leon and Gladys's second child, Sonny, was born on June 14, 1929. He was named Leon after his father but called Sonny all of his life.

When Sonny was four, he was living with his mother, father, and sister at his grandmother Savard's home. "One night, I wet the bed. For punishment, Dad held my head under the kitchen faucet until I thought I would drown. Mom kept yelling, 'Leon. Leon. Stop.' My grandmother, Rose, thought the punishment was appropriate.

"Sometimes we stayed on Silver Street with my grandparents, Randolph and Agnes. I don't remember the reason, but it might have been when Mom gave birth to Jim and Evelyn. I remember that we had to sleep on the floor or couch. Marie, Dick, and I went to the Holy Ghost Academy and often went to my grandparents for lunch. I was about ten and almost finished third grade when we moved to Water Street in The Junction. I told the nun, and she got mad and said, 'I think you're going to fail.' When I got to the public school, Ethel Girard was my teacher. I told her what the nun said. Ms. Girard said, 'You sit down in class, and eventually I'll tell you how you're doing.' After a while, she told me that I was doing fine.

"There were two schools in The Junction. Fourth, fifth, and sixth graders went to the brick schoolhouse, and the lower grades attended the wooden schoolhouse. Every classroom had quite a few students.

"I was always afraid of my grandfather, Randolph. He was so tall, had huge hands, and always looked angry. He held my hand when we walked to church, and I had to run to keep up with his big steps.

"When I was young, Aunt Rose promised to buy me a cowboy suit. Each time she came to visit, I looked for the cowboy suit. It never materialized. Now that I'm 80, I still say, 'That Rose, she promised me a cowboy suit. She never brought it.' I didn't like her after that.

"When Mom's brother, Wilbert, married Theresa in about 1938 or 39, they moved in with my grandparents and continued to live in that house after my grandparents died.

"We moved to Webb Row in the early 1940s. The street was named Webb Row after Seward H. Webb, who extended the railroad line into the Adirondacks to Montreal. The railroad company maintained a railroad shack at the end of Webb Row for their workers who slept there overnight and got free meals. People who were on hard times went there to get a meal. I used to sneak in from time to time to get warm."

The train engineer had a soft spot for local children. When the workers changed shifts, neighborhood children went out to greet the train because they knew the engineer saved them a treat from his lunch—a little bit of fruit, a cookie. That was a real treat for the Webb Row kids who rarely saw such foods on their dinner table.

"I always felt guilty about stealing coal. Years later, I was giving an estimate to the wife of the train engineer. I told her my father made us steal coal, and I still feel bad. The engineer's wife said, 'Don't worry, Sonny. How do you think we heated our house? The Savards weren't the only poor family in Tupper Lake.'

"When Dad sent us to pick up welfare food, the woman in charge made us feel guilty. She'd yell, 'Those Savards are here again.' Later on, I heard she'd been hoarding some of the food in her hunting camp.

"We managed to have fun with very little money and a lot of cunning. There was a movie house around the corner from our house, and my friends and I found a way to get in free. Whoever had a dime, paid for a ticket, and entered the theater. Then, he'd go upstairs, walk past the projection booth, and unlock a door leading to the roof. The rest of the group shimmied up a drainpipe, crossed the roof, and sneaked into the balcony to watch the movie.

"I often wondered what the ticket seller thought about one child buying a ticket to the show and twelve leaving after the movie.

"Dick and I earned fifty cents an hour one time by helping Uncle Howard. He and Aunt Lorraine bought an old three-story house in Saranac Lake, and we helped him tear it down board by board—even straightening the nails. He moved all the lumber and supplies to Tupper Lake and built a home.

"When Jim was in high school, Coach Perry made arrangements for Jim and Beaver Charland to go to Tuscaloosa and work out with the college team. Len saw something special in Jim and Beaver, and he wanted them to have an opportunity to spend a few days practicing with a top-notch team. After a while, Jim and Beaver realized they were way out of their league and didn't belong there. They hitchhiked home.

"The first time I went into the Gull Pond camp with my father, I was twelve. I told him I had to go to church in the morning. After dark, he handed me an old flashlight and told me to head home. The woods were pitch black, the flashlight was dim, and my imagination ran wild. I managed to find my way home and decided there was really nothing to be afraid of in the woods.

"Mom and Dad used to take all of us to Massawepie to pick blueberries, and we usually filled two pack baskets. Dad used a crutch to get around. Uncle Buck came with us to Gull Pond to pick blackberries and raspberries, and then sometimes we stayed in camp."

When the Korean War was in progress, Sonny was exempt because he was helping to support his mother, father, and siblings. He often went without a paycheck himself in order to pay off his father's old bills. Yet, Leon still accused Sonny of stealing money. Leon couldn't understand why he couldn't take whatever money he wanted from the till and spend it however he wanted. That's how he had lived his life before Sonny was involved in the shop.

"Dad used to say, 'We took in $400 this week. Where is it?'

"Try as I might to explain that bills had to be paid before any money was divvied up, my father was always suspicious that he was being cheated out of what was rightfully his. Sometimes village people stopped me on the street and asked me for payment on old bills. I was so embarrassed, I quit the shop."

In 1951 when Sonny was twenty-two, Bill Bennett's father loaned him $300. Sonny moved to Syracuse and got a job working for Bill's brother-in-law. For $3.50 an hour and a couch to sleep on at Jim Brown's house, Sonny dug ditches for water and sewer lines, did carpentry work, delivered lumber, and cleared wood lots.

After a while, he moved into one room at a boarding house on James Street in Syracuse. He found a job at an upholstery shop during the day and tended bar at night. He was drafted for the Korean War when the draft board learned he was no longer helping support his family.

Before he left for service in July, Sonny stopped in Oneida, a small village near Syracuse, to visit Mary LaPlante. They had previously dated. In August on a trip to Tupper Lake, Mary visited Gladys and asked for Sonny's address.

Mary said, "I never wrote the address down but remembered it until I got home, and I immediately started writing letters to Sonny. I had decided that he was the one for me—even though he didn't know it yet."

Correspondence between the two was soon flying across the ocean. After Sonny was issued uniforms, he mailed a pair of pants and a shirt to Oneida for use when he came home. He left his other clothing items in Tupper Lake, and Dick and Jim wore the clothes.

After his discharge in April 1953, Sonny found work at the Dye Molding Company in Canastota, a few miles from Oneida. He didn't own a car, so he hitchhiked to Oneida to see Mary. She worked in the sales office at Oneida Silverware in Kenmore, NY. By June, Gladys was begging him to come home. Leon was in debt, not paying for his fabric or supplies, and wasting his money.

Sonny returned to Tupper Lake in 1953.

"I told my father that the only way I'd take over was with the understanding that I'd be the boss, control the money, and pay off debts.

And get Mom out of here. She hates the work, and she isn't doing a good job sewing."

Leon was afraid of having another heart attack and turned the driving over to Sonny.

Suppliers would only do business with Savard's Upholstery Shop if they could send supplies COD. "I finally convinced the companies to tack on an extra $10 to any order over $50 and apply that extra payment to Dad's outstanding bills."

After Gladys was struck by the car and received a $2,000 settlement, she wanted to buy a red coat. She was so tall and obese that Leon and Sonny were horrified at the prospect of Gladys in a red coat.

Mary said, "Leave her alone. If she wants a red coat, let her have it." Gladys bought the coat.

After the war, it was difficult to get a new car because manufacturers were having trouble keeping up with the demand. A salesman at the Chevy Garage said he'd help Leon get a van as long as Sonny took his daughter to the prom. The salesman paid all the expenses and loaned Sonny a good car for the evening.

When Leon wanted to build a furniture store addition, he borrowed $10,000 on his mortgage. The bank refused to lend him an additional $2,000 to buy inventory. Because of his poor health, the insurance company would not risk insuring him. Mary and Sonny borrowed $2,000 on their mortgage with which to buy the showroom furniture.

Soon after Sonny took over the business, he realized his father had never paid into social security. Sonny insisted that Leon pay Social Security taxes, including back paying for the previous three-years.

On the night of Leon's heart attack, Gladys notified Sonny that his father was in the hospital. He said, "I was especially exhausted that night and decided to get a decent night's sleep and visit him in the morning. This wasn't our first scare, and he always pulled through. By four a.m., I still hadn't been able to sleep. I went to the hospital, but I arrived after Dad had died."

After the funeral, there was enough life insurance money left to repay Mary and Sonny the $2,000.

Leon never collected Social Security, but because of Sonny's persistence, his father had the required ten years in the system. Upon Leon's death, Gladys was able to collect support money for Don for four months. At seventeen, Don enlisted in the Navy, and Gladys no longer had an income. She babysat for a few people to earn spending money. When Gladys was 62, she received $50 a month. After the law changed in 1978, Gladys received $300 a month—the full amount of Leon's Social Security.

Other than that, Sonny paid all the bills for Gladys and Ed until they both passed away.

Sonny remained in the upholstery business until he was 69. He and Mary continued to live in Tupper Lake and raised four children.

Dick

Dick, child number three, was born in 1931 and was often the object of his father's wrath. When Leon was in a black mood, he took it out on everyone in his path. Dick said, "A day never went by without receiving a beating from my father.

"I slept with my mother when I was a small child. One night, my father was out with a girlfriend. A rat got under the covers and bit me. My mother got everyone together, and we walked to her parent's home to sleep.

"When I was just a little boy, my father told me Mom had a baby before he married her. That upset me. Why did he talk such trash to me about my mother?"

Dick was falling behind in school, and he was fifteen when Leon convinced school personnel that Dick would be better off going into a trade. He pulled his son from school and made him work in the shop. The authorities looked the other way. It was many years before Dick realized he had trouble learning to read because he had dyslexia. There were no special programs at that time to help a student.

"I defied my father and took a lot of risks. I used to jump out the window and go ice-skating instead of working in the shop. I knew I'd get in trouble, but the fun I had was worth the beating."

If a mistake were made in the shop, Sonny took the blame to spare Dick a beating. Sonny tried hard to please Leon, and his father was kinder to Sonny because he needed his help. Leon could no longer manage the business by himself.

One day, Dick, Sonny, and some male and female friends used the shop van to drive to Middle Saranac Lake to go swimming. One of the girls changed into her bathing suit and put her clothes in the glove compartment of the van. After swimming, the girl put her dress over her bathing suit and left with another boy. Unfortunately, she forgot her underpants in the glove compartment. When Leon discovered the underpants, he accused his sons of having sex with the girl.

Dick said, "We couldn't convince Dad that he was wrong. I think he was always jealous of us and didn't want us to have any fun."

The Savard boys finally had wheels when Dick purchased a used Buick Limousine that had been owned by one of the summer residents in Long Lake.

"I was eighteen, and I couldn't stand the constant fighting between my parents. I got Dad in a head hold and threatened to take him down if he ever to hit Mom or me again, but their arguing didn't stop. I decided to leave. When I came out of the bedroom with my suitcase packed, our neighbor, Roy Brown, was there. He gave me $50 and the keys to his car."

Roy said, "Get out of here. Get a job and then bring back my car."

"After a few weeks, I got a job with Zig Kryevsky, the man who had trained my father to upholster. I brought Roy's car back and took a bus out of town. I stayed with Zig for a while and eventually rented a room with two men who worked at GE. A year later, Dad had another heart attack, and I came back to help. The situation soon deteriorated again. I left for the final time."

By 1960, Dick was married, working construction on the St. Lawrence Seaway project, and saving his money. When he had enough saved, he bought a new Chevrolet. He drove to the shop to show his car to his father and Sonny.

Leon said, "You just came here to show off and make the rest of us feel bad. Get out of here."

Dick was employed as an ironworker at the missile base in Plattsburgh when Leon had his heart attack. "The boss located me, and I was brought up in a cage from a deep tunnel. After talking to Theresa, I told my boss I was leaving to go home. When I got home, I slept for a while. At three a.m., Mom called to tell me Dad was in the hospital and was dying. He was dead by the time I got there. I never had a chance to make things right with Dad."

When Dick was 79, I asked, "Are there other stories you'd like to share with me?"

He tried to fight back the tears. "There was a lot more that went on, but I can't talk about it."

Dick became an ironworker and often drove long distances to job sites. Later, he and his family moved to Orlando, Florida, where he worked on the construction of Disney World. He and Theresa raised three children.

Evelyn

Evelyn, the fifth child, was born in 1937. She was six when a man who hung around the neighborhood raped her. During the incident, her yellow dress was torn. She fretted she'd be in trouble because of the dress more than the fact she was raped. Neither her children nor siblings know the name of the perpetrator.

From a young age, Evelyn suffered from migraine headaches so severe she vomited. To relieve her daughter's headaches, Gladys opened the bedroom window and rubbed Evelyn's forehead with a cold cloth wrapped around sliced potatoes. By age 13, she was so sickly and skinny that her ribs and collarbones protruded.

One time on a visit to Mary's home, Sonny brought his sister with him. She was sick to her stomach from Tupper Lake to Oneida. Evelyn continued to vomit after arriving in Oneida, so Sonny left immediately and took her home.

Evelyn loved to get off the school bus at Aunt Grace's house to play with Grace's daughters. The house was neat, the girls had toys, and there was food for snacks. On most days, Leon called Grace's and told his daughter to hurry home.

Larry Willett was two years ahead of Evelyn in school. He was a foster child from a troubled home. Larry often skipped school and even missed the day his yearbook picture was to be taken. Jim's yearbook contained a blank square with Larry's name below it.

The two began dating shortly after he graduated from high school. She was crazy about him, but Leon hated Larry. One afternoon, Leon chased Larry around the shop with a large upholstery needle and called him a liar and a cheat. Evelyn moved out and lived most of the winter with Dick and Theresa until she married.

Leon said, "If you marry Larry, I won't walk you down the aisle."

But, she understood her father's soft spot. She said, "Don't worry. Uncle Buck will gladly walk me down the aisle." Leon never mentioned the subject again and walked her down the aisle.

Evelyn and Larry returned from their honeymoon early, as she was so violently ill with vomiting and stomach pains that she was placed in the hospital.

By 1968, Evelyn and Larry had four young children. Larry was working in Utica as a bookkeeper. The youngest children were one and two years old. Evelyn attempted suicide and was placed in Marcy Mental Hospital for her own protection.

At the time, I was six months pregnant for Tracy. We took Evelyn's two younger children to live with us for a month until she recuperated. After a while she stabilized, and her family reunited.

Evelyn was a good housekeeper and cook, but every day was a struggle. She couldn't face the day and rarely got out of bed before eleven a.m. After she awakened, she did her housework, cooked supper, and then stayed up late reading and smoking and repeated the same pattern the next day.

Odd things bothered her. She didn't like that Jim buttered his toast to the edges of his bread. She didn't like to grocery shop in Tupper Lake because someone might say hello to her. Larry also had unusual hang ups. He told Mary he didn't like to walk on the street in Tupper Lake because someone might see him.

Evelyn spent her lifetime depressed, attempting suicide, and in and out of mental hospitals trying to get herself emotionally strong. None of the counseling or drugs helped. She seemed to feel safe in an institution and didn't have to make any decisions or be responsible for anything. During the day, she participated in craft activities and social events.

When her brother, Don, was in the hospital for removal of a brain tumor, she called him and said, "I have $5,000 in the bank. If you need it, it's yours."

Two years before she died, Evelyn spent a year and a half in Ogdensburg, New York's mental hospital. At the same time, Gladys was extremely ill.

"I'm glad I'm here," Evelyn remarked. "Then I don't have to help with Mom."

It wasn't until after her death in 2001 that we learned how often Evelyn was in mental hospitals. Besides Marcy, she spent time in institutions in Bangor, Maine, Warren, Pennsylvania, Bluefield, West Virginia and Ogdensburg, New York.

Larry worked as an accountant. They often moved to new areas because of his job, but eventually returned to Tupper Lake to live. He and Evelyn raised four children.

Ed

Child number six, Ed, was born in 1939 with a number of problems. He had a nonfunctioning extra finger on each hand that was surgically removed. Ed was limited mentally. He never learned to read.

He had buckteeth and screwed up his face when he squinted at the sun. The neighborhood children called him "Crazy Ed." They didn't understand why he looked and acted the way he did. Leon was ashamed of Ed and never introduced him when he introduced his other sons. One day, Leon ran into the yard and started beating Ed for looking stupid. Don and Gladys were too afraid of Leon to stop him.

When Ed reached age sixteen, the school called Leon suggesting he pull his son from school because the other children were picking on him.

Ed tried several jobs. Mrs. Fortune hired him to work at her trailer park, and when she went to check on him, he was sitting on a porch watching traffic. Another time, he was hired by the American Legion to work in the kitchen. After a day, they asked him to leave.

Sonny kept Ed employed in the shop. One day, he was angry with Sonny and said he was going to quit and get a job painting houses in Saranac Lake. Ed couldn't drive, so someone drove him to and from work every day. After a few days, the contractor called Sonny and said,

"Come get your brother." It seems Ed was fond of climbing the ladders and peaking in the windows of partially clad females.

For the remainder of Ed's life, he worked with Sonny who gave him a job, a home, food, health insurance, IRA's, telephone, cable, and a salary. In exchange, Ed worked slowly and reluctantly and always felt he was underpaid. He told local people that Sonny didn't pay him what he was worth, and they actually believed him.

One day, I was driving Ed to a bus station and he boasted, "I shouldn't have stayed at the shop. I should have gotten a job in industry and moved up the corporate ladder." I think he truly believed he could accomplish that.

Ed was good natured and kind. One time, he had saved his money for months in order to buy a snowmobile coat. He was wearing his new coat and riding with his brother, Don, when he saw someone on the street without a coat. Ed told Don, "Stop the car." He got out of the car and gave a complete stranger his snowmobile coat.

"Why did you do that?" Don asked.

"He needs it more than I do, and when I die, God will take care of me."

Ed loved being a member of the Moose Club. During special dinners at the Club, he boasted, "I cooked spaghetti dinner for 100 people last night." We all realized that he probably hadn't done all the work.

Ed lived with Gladys for his entire life. As an adult, he liked to go out at night, but Gladys wanted him to stay home.

One morning she said, "What would you do if you came home and found me dead?"

"I'd call Richer's funeral home," he said.

I guess Ed wasn't so slow after all.

Gladys was quite angry with his reply, but Sonny said, "Well, that's what he would have to do, Mom."

From time to time Ed had girlfriends, but they didn't last long. Mary and Sonny worried that he would get married or father a child. He dated one woman for a few years, babysat for her, and bought her a TV. When he found out she was dating other men, he was broken hearted and asked his nephew, Dana, to help him take back the items he had purchased for her.

One summer, Ed fell in love with a black Go-Go dancer. Gladys didn't like African Americans, but not wanting to be too obvious, she said, "She's not very dark is she?"

Ed replied, "Well, her hair is a little curly."

Gladys responded, "Well for heaven sakes, don't take her out where anyone can see you."

So, Ed being Ed, took her to the local beach for a picnic on a busy Sunday.

He was always singing, whistling, and doing a little dance step as he walked. He loved to party and had moves on the dance floor no one else could master.

Ed visited us for a week one summer. We took him to his first stage play, fishing, to dinner, and the mall. He even drove Jim's John Deere tractor. Life was good for Ed that week.

Sonny planned on working until Ed could collect Social Security.

In May of 1994, a few months after Gladys died, Mary and Sonny noticed Ed wasn't as chipper as usual. When Mary asked him to sign his income tax papers, his signature went downward. His daily routine changed. He stopped walking uptown after work and was more content to be home. In May, Ed had an infection on the calf of one leg, but he said it had healed after taking an antibiotic. On June 7, Mary noticed Ed was limping. When she asked what was wrong, he said, "I still have an infection on my leg, and I can't lift my left arm either."

Mary scheduled Ed immediately for an evaluation. After X-rays at the Saranac Lake hospital, doctors determined he had a cancerous brain tumor. Radiation was tried. It was to no avail. Ed suffered in pain for five months while being taken care of at home by family members until he passed away on October 23, 1994 at age 55.

Some weeks later, we realized just how much natural mechanical ability he possessed. Jim had a new watch that could be set to ring like an alarm clock. Jim, with instructions and a Master's degree, and Sonny, with instructions and mechanical ability, couldn't figure out how to set the watch. Ed, with no instructions and unable to read, had punched a few keys and programmed the watch. After Ed's death, the watch continued to ring at the time he had set. Since no one could figure out how to change the watch, Jim bought a new one.

Roy

Roy was born in 1941 and was more Marie's child than Gladys's. At age 14, Marie took complete care of Roy. She slept with him, fed him at night, and toilet trained him, even though she had homework to do and had to get up early for school.

At 17, Roy disappointed Sonny and quit high school to enlist in the Navy.

Marie said to Roy, "Sue is writing a book about Jim and our family. What do you remember about your upbringing?"

Roy replied, "I hated my father, the old bastard, and I don't want to talk about him. Sonny was more of a father to me."

Roy became an ironworker. He married a Tupper Lake girl named Mary. They remained in Tupper Lake and raised five children.

Don

Don, child number eight, was born in April 27, 1944.

"Dad loved newborn babies and showed me off to his friends. When I was seven or eight everything changed, and he started beating on me as much as on the other children.

"On the morning after Dad had tacked me to the cutting table, he got me up and then he started hitting me again. That was his way of proving to me there was no reason to be afraid of the dark. At that point, I wished my father were dead.

"Dad thought that playing sports was foolish, and no one needed it. He often tried to get Jim to quit school, but Jim refused. He never went to watch Jim's games until the team was doing well, and he could look good.

"When I was getting older, Dad was trying to save on food, so he sent Roy and me out to fish. He let me use his filleting knife to cut up the fish. When I got home and told Dad I had forgotten the filleting knife in the woods, he was livid and sent me back up the tracks alone after dark to get the knife."

Later, Don and his older brothers went into the Gull Pond camp. The brothers asked Don to get a bucket of water from the stream. It was dark out, and his brothers threatened to tell their father that Don was afraid of the dark. That was enough to make Don hurry out and get the water.

"Mom cuddled and kissed us often. Any tenderness we received was from Mom.

"I remember one night when Roy and I were giggling after we went to bed. Dad got mad because we wouldn't settle down and go to sleep. He came in the room and started beating us with a piece of 2 x 4. He hit Roy so hard that Roy got water on the elbows and knees, but Roy refused to cry. That made Dad even angrier."

Sometimes Leon, Gladys and Don went to Gladys's sister's house to watch wrestling matches, and Leon would joke around and be a lot of fun.

"If Dad were in a good mood, he was like a different person."

As a teenager, Don hitchhiked to Saranac Lake to earn money by caddying for golfers. By the end of the day, if he caddied for four golfers at a time at $8 per bag, he came home with $32 in his pocket. Some caddies got hired for two 36-rounds of golf.

"When Dad found out about the other caddies, he kicked me and yelled at me, accusing me of being lazy. He wouldn't listen when I tried to explain that it all depended on whether there were golfers out who needed a caddy. Whenever I got home from Saranac, Dad took my money and said it was time I started paying room and board and carrying my load."

At 16, Leon made Don lay a new floor in the boy's bedroom. Leon was especially harsh and mean that day and shoved Don around. "I was so angry, I told my mother that I wished my father would die. Mom said, 'Don't say those things.'

"That night I dreamed I was stabbing my father. I got up from the cot in the living room and was sleep walking. I walked through the living room, into the kitchen, past the knives, and into my parent's bedroom. I leaned over my father and jammed my finger into his stomach as hard as I could. The next thing I knew, Dad was punching me in the gut, and I woke up. To this day, I don't really know what my intentions were that night. I could have just as easily grabbed a knife to kill my father, but instead, I poked him with my finger."

Don was a daydreamer, uninterested in school, often truant, and failing. He told Sonny he wanted to quit school.

Sonny cautioned, "If you stay home, you have to work and pay room and board."

At 17, Don joined the Navy to get away from school, Tupper Lake, and his family. Six months later he called home begging Sonny to say he was needed to help support the family.

Sonny told him, "You are not going to quit, and I don't need your help. For once, you have to stick with something."

Don wouldn't talk to Sonny for five or six years after that.

While stationed in Norfolk, Don fell in love with a woman named Sandy who hung around the naval base and had an illegitimate child. He was under 21 and needed Gladys's signature to get married. Sonny convinced Gladys that Don could wait a few months until he turned 21. Then the decision would be his alone.

He married Sandy and fathered two children by her. Sandy was an alcoholic and a poor mother and wife. Before long, Don realized he had made a terrible mistake. They soon divorced. Sandy gained custody and brought up their two children in Elmira.

Don later married Pat, and he worked as a long-haul UPS driver. He became stepfather to her two children. They were happily married until she passed away in October of 2012.

Robert

In October 1948, Gladys gave birth to her ninth child, Robert Randolph Savard. His legs and hips were deformed, possibly because in her eighth month of pregnancy, Gladys fell down a flight of stairs. Don remembers sitting on the kitchen counter while his mother changed

Robert's diapers. When the baby died in February 1949, he was laid out in a room of their home.

Mary, daughter-in-law

"One time, Gladys asked me what was wrong with Evelyn. I said I didn't know. I always thought Gladys wanted to turn Evelyn's problems over to someone else so she wouldn't have deal with it.

"If Leon wanted something, he was very aggressive. When the phone in the shop wasn't working, he called the telephone company, and Pete Ferrill came to do the repairs and drove his truck over the back lawn leaving ruts. Leon called the company and said, 'I want my lawn fixed.' The phone company offered to pay Leon for the damage. Leon said, 'I don't want payment. I want the same man who damaged the lawn to come back and fix it.' Pete repaired the ruts and never forgot that story.

"Gladys started a lot of the problems. After Roy decided to move to Florida to find a job, he stayed with Dick and Theresa. Gladys wrote Dick and said she didn't want Roy to leave, and Sonny was to blame. Dick and Theresa believed Gladys and were angry with Sonny and wrote him a letter. Once they got the true story, the problem was straightened out."

At one point, Mary took the Literacy Volunteers course and attempted to teach Ed to read. Ed was enthusiastic for a few weeks and then became disinterested.

"For many years, Gladys hung her laundry on clotheslines in the back yard. Finally, I suggested we buy her a dryer for a Christmas present. I thought she was too old to hang clothes outside in the wintertime.

"One Christmas, I only had $25 to spend on Sonny, our children, Mom and Dad, and Gladys. I made Gladys a cotton robe for a gift. She opened the gift and then showed me the pretty slip Marie had sent her and said, 'Marie doesn't give me junk.'

"Gladys ran Leon down to the kids all the time. The kids grew to hate him."

After Leon died, Mary set up an appointment with the state rehabilitation center to have Ed evaluated. The tests indicated his comprehension was low, and his mechanical ability was high. Social Services refused to give Gladys SSI for Ed, claiming he could work in a factory stacking boxes but would need constant supervision.

CHAPTER 23- PARENT'S BACKGROUND

Gladys

Little is known about Gladys's early life except that she was born in 1904 in Tupper Lake, New York, to Randolph and Agnes Boucher. Gladys was tall and big boned like her father, Randolph.

Her mother was a petite, delicate, Irish woman named Agnes Henley. She was cousin to Randolph's first wife who had died in childbirth. Agnes's mother and father were both deceased by the time she was ten, so she was brought up in a convent in Montreal. As a result, she was very religious.

Some time after his first wife died, Randolph visited Agnes at the convent. She left the convent at age 22 and lived with a sister in Tupper Lake. Randolph came back to Tupper Lake in search of work. He and Agnes courted and eventually married in Saranac Lake in 1903.

Randolph and Agnes moved back to Barachois, Canada when Gladys was two, and he worked in lumber camps. While there, Agnes gave birth to five more children. Gladys's sister, Evelyn, was twelve when she died of rheumatic fever. Before her death, she asked Randolph to become a Catholic. He was not religious and had not been baptized Catholic because his mother detested Catholics. He followed through on Evelyn's request. At 71, Randolph was baptized Catholic.

While living in Barachois, fishing was one of Gladys's favorite pastimes. There was a large barn behind her family home. The barn spanned a small creek, with part of the foundation on one side of the creek and part on the other. There was a trap door in the floor. Gladys would open the trap door, lower a line into the creek, and catch salmon. But, times were harsh and work was scarce, so in 1921, when Gladys was 17, Randolph and Agnes moved back to Tupper Lake in search of work.

Randolph was tough as nails. One time, while working in the woods, he missed his mark with the hatchet and cut his foot between his toes. He wouldn't go to the doctor. The next day, he put a piece of salt bacon between his toes, put on his socks and boots, and went to work in the woods. At age 87, he climbed a ladder and worked on the roof of Lorraine's home. He died the following year of throat cancer.

Marie said, "Once in a while Mom would read a newspaper or magazine when she could get her hands on them. She learned about the world around her by watching television."

In her younger years, Gladys claimed she weighed 130 pounds. She was 5'8" tall, and for most of her life, weighed around 230 pounds. She had large hands for a woman—even larger than her grown boys. Her hair was dark brown until she was sixty years old.

Although Gladys had many faults, she had a wonderful sense of humor and often made the entire family chuckle. When frustrated she said, "Jesus, Mary and Joseph." If referring to a color, she'd say, "His eyes were blue, blue. Or her dress was red, red." If someone made noise when they ate, she admonished, "Stop pee-acking." One time Jim tried to find out if there was such a word but he was unsuccessful. He decided it was just a "Gladysism."

A few neighborhood children lived in the same type of abusive home as the Savards. When things got rough at home because their fathers were drunk and beating them, the children packed their clothing in a paper bag and showed up at Gladys's door. She allowed them to sleep on the floor and stay until their fathers calmed down. She never sent them away because she didn't have food or an extra bed.

During the depression, bums often roamed from village to village. One knocked on Gladys's door and asked her for food. Although her own family was starving, she cooked the man some sliced potatoes. When he sat down to eat, he complained about the food. Leon overheard him. "Get out of here, you ungrateful bum," he said and made the man leave.

As a widow, Gladys liked to go out to the Moose Club on Saturday evenings to dance. She would fuss for days over what to wear. She hated black or dark navy blue clothing, and she loved to wear bright colors, strong perfume, and heavy makeup. When her hair turned grey, she dyed it with a semi-permanent dye that gradually turned a reddish color.

In her later years, Gladys sat out her days in her small living quarters in Tupper Lake and rarely left the house. She complained about sore knees and joints and rubbed her legs with Ben Gay. The smell of Ben Gay in her apartment was overpowering

She never wore slacks or shorts until she was old and feeble, and then she only wore comfortable sweat suits.

When Gladys died in 1994 at the age of 90 after a long illness, she was again 130 pounds.

Leon

Leon was born in 1905 in Brandon, NY, to Rose and Edmund Savard. He was baptized at the Church of the Wilderness on Easy Street across from Lake Clear. When the lumbering industry in Brandon began to fail, the Savards had their entire house shipped by train to Tupper Lake at a cost of $25. It still exists in 2012 on Maple Street.

It's been reported that his parents didn't get along because Rose was jealous and mean tempered while Edmund was soft spoken and gentle. One day Rose got so angry with Edmund because he had his picture taken standing next to one of his female co-workers, that she pushed him through a kitchen window.

Leon's parents supported themselves by working as cooks in lumber camps. In those days, lumber camps were rough and cold. Working hours were long and difficult. At one time, they had thirteen children, but within a short span of time, pneumonia and other ailments took the lives of all but three children. Leon, Frederick (Buck), and Mildred were the only three who survived to adulthood. Leon's mother explained, "When a child came down with a cold, they soon died." Jeanette lived until age sixteen and died from peritonitis after an operation.

No one knows for certain how long Leon attended school.

Before they married, Leon asked Gladys about rumors that she had given birth to an out-of-wedlock baby. She said she had, but the baby died. That was a lie. A baby boy was born to Gladys and given up for adoption at an orphanage in Lackawanna. Leon and Gladys married on February 26, 1926 against his parents' objections. She was 22, and he was 21.

For a time Leon ran a gas station in Tupper Lake. His brother, Buck worked for him for a while and was promised $10 a week, but he never got it. Buck would take $10 out of the till whenever he could grab it. As soon as there was money in the till, Leon took the money, closed the station, and went out drinking. The company turned the station over to Buck, who made it into a thriving business that comfortably supported his family.

The Savard family existed on welfare until 1940. Leon filled out the original application, but sent Sonny and Marie to collect the food, consisting of molasses, honey, butter, cheese, and canned greasy meat that the family called "Bully Beef."

Leon cheated on Gladys for years after they were married. One day, Marie saw her father drive by with one of his girlfriends, nicknamed "The Black Diamond." Later on, Marie was working at the American Legion, and saw "The Black Diamond" come in with her husband.

Gladys had Leon arrested for chasing women, not working, and not supporting his family. A trooper named LaFavre put Leon in jail for a while. On another occasion, Trooper LaFavre heard Leon bragging about something to Sonny. The trooper listened for a while and then said, "Don't believe all of your father's bullshit. I arrested him one time for non-support." Leon didn't like hearing that.

Jim's father had his first heart attack at 26 and was 32 when he lost his leg. At the time, Gladys was pregnant for Ed. Leon was working for the town of Altamont on a road crew when a chunk of ice fell on his foot and damaged his big toe. His toe became infected and the doctors advised amputating it, but Leon refused. Gangrene set in and traveled up his leg. The doctors kept taking more off his leg until it was amputated below the knee. He was fitted with a peg leg and walked for the remainder of his life with a limp. He was more mean and angry after he lost his leg, but he did stop running around with other women. One day, he forgot that he wasn't wearing his peg leg when he got up from a chair, and he fell onto a furnace grate on the floor, further damaging his stump and making it necessary to amputate more of his leg.

After he lost part of his leg, Leon convinced the state to send him to Albany to learn to be an upholsterer so that he could support his large family.

Before his health failed, Leon was 5' 9" tall and weighed around 160 pounds. He had sleepy-looking hazel eyes and thick, dark hair. As he aged and became more ill, he began to shrink in stature and weight, and his nose became more prominent. By the time he died he was barely 5' 6" tall, weighed 130 pounds, was almost bald, and had big bags under his eyes.

In 1960, they expanded the building at 54 Pine Street. Jim was 26 and in college when he went home for several weeks during the summer to help Leon, Sonny, and a few hired contractors with the addition. On December 4, 1960, at age 55 and six months after completing the addition, Leon died. Leon's will left the building to Gladys and the business to Sonny who added Ed as a partner. In 1974, Gladys turned the building over to Sonny (since he had already paid off the mortgage once) and Ed.

After Leon's funeral, Marie asked Gladys how she felt. Gladys said, "Peaceful." She never mentioned missing him.

ENDNOTES

[i] www.historyorb.com (all Historical facts are taken from this web site).
[ii] www.brainyquotes.com
[iii] http://www.brainyquote.com/quotes/quotes/a/abrahamlin109276.html
[iv] http://www.jfklibrary.org/Asset-Viewer/sUVmCh-sB0moLfrBcaHaSg.aspx
[v] http://www.washingtonpost.com/wp-dyn/content/article/2006/10/24/AR2006102400691.html
[vi] http://www.lyricsmode.com/lyrics/c/charlie_landsborough/after_all_these_years.html
[vii] http://www.brainyquote.com/quotes/authors/e/ernie_banks.html
[viii] http://www.allthelyrics.com/lyrics/pete_seeger/turn_turn_turn-lyrics-223571.html
[ix] http://www.hymns.me.uk/the-summons-hymn.htm

Made in the USA
Lexington, KY
26 March 2013